ENGLAND VERSUS NEW ZEALAND

England versus New Zealand

A History of the Tests and Other Matches

Gerry Cotter

The Crowood Press

First published in 1990 by
The Crowood Press
Ramsbury, Marlborough,
Wiltshire SN8 2HE

British Library Cataloguing in Publication Data

Cotter, Gerry
England versus New Zealand: a history of the tests and
other matches.
1. Cricket. Test matches to 1988
I. Title 796.35′865

ISBN 1 85223 348 6

**For Jean, who likes to go to cricket
but would prefer to go to New Zealand**

Typeset by Inforum Typesetting, Portsmouth
Printed in Great Britain at
The Bath Press

Contents

Acknowledgements

Men in White by Don Neely, Richard King and Francis Payne is *the* history of New Zealand international cricket and I am happy to acknowledge my great indebtedness to it. Other reference books which have been of invaluable help are:

Bill Frindall, *The Wisden Book of Test Cricket* (Queen Anne Press);
Bill Frindall, *The Wisden Book of Cricket Records* (Queen Anne Press);
Christopher Martin-Jenkins, *The Complete Who's Who of Test Cricketers* (Orbis);
E.W. Swanton (ed.), *Barclays World of Cricket* (Collins).

My thanks to Don Mosey for his help, and to Stephen Green and June Bayliss of the Lord's Library and John Tuck of the John Rylands University Library of Manchester.

I am especially grateful to Ken Kelly for his work in collecting together the photographs, particularly as some of the older ones proved very difficult to track down.

Forewords

I am delighted to pen a few thoughts on England's battles with New Zealand, especially as my thoughts go out automatically to one of my best mates from the world of cricket – Geoff Howarth. Right from our early days together playing for Surrey at the Oval we have been firm friends. For a time he even lived with my family at Guildford and we invariably shared drinking money from our pitiful salary bestowed on us by Surrey CCC. In later years my trips to New Zealand were distinguished by several rewarding visits to the Howarth family home. Here their expertise at fish-farming was greatly appreciated by a certain English fast bowler who craved for snapper and oysters. Indeed one of my happiest times in New Zealand came right at the start of our 1978 trip, just after the interesting experience of a long tour of Pakistan. I spent an afternoon sampling the wares of the Howarth fishermen, washed down by some cool white wine; what with numerous anecdotes from Geoff and his brother Hedley it was the perfect day. My pleasure on this trip was even more complete when I helped to bowl out New Zealand cheaply!

It seemed appropriate that when we were humbled at Wellington in 1978, giving New Zealand their first win over England, I should be the last man out – caught at slip by Geoff Howarth off the bowling of Richard Hadlee. I never thought that Richard gave Geoff as much as he might have done – he seemed rather keen on rationing his stamina – but by that year he was beginning to show his prowess as a bowler. A decade later, he was still a great technician, a superb tactical bowler with a great memory and a wonderful, economical action. He was definitely New Zealand's man of the 1980s, possibly of their Test history. By the time we met up again, in 1983, Hadlee could certainly be classed as an all-rounder because he could hit a ball disconcertingly far – as well as bowl sides out with metronomic accuracy. That 1983 series in England was a very happy one; by common consent among the players the last where genuine good fellowship existed between both sides, where verbal attacks on the field were scarce and the presence of so many spinners helped the over-rate. I like to think that Geoff Howarth and I as the rival captains had something to do with that happy atmosphere. The Test that I remember most of all those I played against New Zealand came in this series, when at Headingley I managed to reach 300 Test wickets, bagging a brace of Crowes, Martin and Jeff, for the 299th and 300th – but it was a pity we lost the match! It was a disappointing result for us, although New Zealand deserved to win and I was very pleased for Geoff that he led them so well to their first Test victory in England. Many other outstanding memories come flooding back from that series: Hadlee's blistering hitting; Ian Botham's wonderful hundred at Trent Bridge; the haul of wickets by Nick Cook – and the beautiful weather. Happy days.

The same could not apply to my memories of my last trip to New Zealand as a player in 1984. It was agreeable to pass Fred Trueman's England record of 307 wickets at Wellington but we were bowled out at Christchurch for 93 in a lamentable display of batting and bowling. Full marks again to Hadlee – and who can blame the Kiwis for then preparing a flat wicket at Auckland to clinch the series? Their pleasure at finally taking a series off England was sincere and tangible – and they played the better cricket. Certainly, if any side is to take a series off us I should always wish it to be the Kiwis. Perhaps that is because we are fairly similar in our attitudes to cricket and how it should be played – hard but fairly. The New Zealanders do not like being mistaken for Australians and I can see why. There is no doubt that the Aussies are more ruthless in their approach to cricket, and when they are on top they are hardly reticent about it. I like the way the Kiwis handle both triumph and defeat in the same rational manner – it is only a sport, after all. So it is no hardship to wish this book Godspeed; in reading it I have been reminded of many happy times in friendly combat with the Kiwis. Even the times when their umpires never heard the snicks off my bowling!

Bob Willis
1989

It is particularly pleasing to share the foreword for this book with my old mate Bob Willis. Bob was not only cricket's leading expert on Bob Dylan, not only a great fast bowler and a loyal, generous friend but I also think that his contribution as England captain has been underrated. I cannot remember a happier Test series than the one in England in 1983 when we captained our respective sides. For once the sun shone continually and the cricket was uniformly entertaining and positive. England triumphed 3–1 but not before we had our own moment of glory at Leeds, when we beat them for the first time in England. It was a fine team effort that also gave me great personal satisfaction, being the first captain of a victorious New Zealand team in England and, not surprisingly, it will always be the outstanding memory of my games against England. Our delight was best summed up by Jeremy Coney, who hit the winning run: 'The main feeling was thinking of all the New Zealand players who have been coming here for fifty-two years – better players than myself – and making sure that their sweat and effort had not been in vain.' He spoke for myself and all the players concerned – but what a struggle we had had before that winning run was hit. We did not need much to win, around a hundred, but Bob bowled heroically to take the first five wickets and frighten the life out of us. That was typical Willis; he led by example, always insisting on the highest professional standards. It was not his fault that the ban on players going to South Africa had robbed England of some fine cricketers during that period, but he never moaned; he just got on with his job. When England bowled dreadfully at Christchurch in 1984 (and Richard Hadlee scored 99), Bob was the only one of them who looked like an England player, but he never took notice of his personal performances.

Above all Bob would never forget the sportsman's ethics; he would always help others in trouble with their game and to this day I am convinced that he helped save my Test career. In the 1978 series in New Zealand I had four low scores on the trot and was feeling pretty dispirited. At a party Bob got hold of me and gave me a right sorting out regarding my technique and my attitude to failure. I went straight from there to get a hundred in each innings in the Auckland Test and did not look back. Within a few months I had scored another hundred against England at Lords and at the Oval missed out on another by just six runs when I smashed a full toss from Ian Botham to Phil Edmonds who took a superb catch. Botham often got wickets that way; there is no doubt that he is a great player.

I was present at the start of his memorable days as a Test all-rounder when he roared through us early in 1978 after his frustrations in Pakistan. It was obvious he was a star in the making; a few months later, in the return series in England, he was even more dynamic and productive. Botham's duels with Richard Hadlee, over the years, have been marvellous value – not least because they are hardly great friends and yet still have great respect for each other. I consider myself very lucky to have played so many Tests in the company of two such great all-rounders.

There is another great debt that we owe English cricket. Many of us have undoubtedly become better players because we have had the privilege of playing county cricket in England. It has toughened us up mentally, helped tighten our techniques and made us understand what is involved in the sheer grind of competing in top-class cricket day after day. Richard Hadlee, John Wright, Martin Crowe and myself would never have developed into Test players without the influence of the English game. It is no fluke that we have won our last two series against England because we have become battle-hardened. It was not until some of us had played consistently in England that we managed to record our first Test victory over our old friends, 'friends' being the right word for our English counterparts. When we play them there is none of the bitterness that often comes to the surface when, for example, Australia are the opposition; nobody appears to have a chip on their shoulder about something irrelevant. Long may our friendly rivalry continue and if England manage to get one over us, rest assured that they will never beat us at Rugby!

Geoff Howarth
1989

1

Against Odds

In the beginning was the Treaty of Waitangi, under which, on 6 February 1840, New Zealand was bound to the British Crown. Only that wasn't the beginning; Captain Cook had taken possession of the country in the name of George III in 1769, British missionaries had been there since 1814, and the earliest reference to any form of cricket being played had come on 23 December 1835 when Charles Darwin recorded seeing a game taking place in the Bay of Islands between a number of freed Maori slaves, with the son of one of the missionaries joining in. How long the game had been played before that we don't know. Now the Treaty of Waitangi is a matter for the historians; but surely to the cricket fanatic it is altogether more pleasing to think that the real beginning, the day from which New Zealand was bound to Britain in spirit if not in law, came at the moment that the first ball was bowled on one island or the other, whenever that was.

The first match of which there is a proper record, Reds v Blues, took place on 28 December 1842 in Wellington. The Reds began with 64 notches to which the Blues replied with 67; in the second innings the Reds made 60, leaving the Blues to make 58 to win. They made 59, but their margin of victory is not recorded. It sounds distinctly exciting, although one suspects that for some of the players at least the 'true Christmas dinner of roast beef and plum pudding' which followed it may have been more to the point. The sport steadily grew in the major townships and a landmark was reached in 1860 when the first interprovincial match was played. Auckland challenged Wellington to a game and the challenge was accepted, but no details were arranged. The Auckland team therefore just turned up out of the blue in Wellington and because there was no time for the Wellingtonians to assemble their team — as the visitors may well have realised — they fielded a scratch side. Despite this they took a first innings lead of 28, but then collapsed for 39 in their second innings, allowing the Aucklanders to polish off the runs and go home well pleased with themselves.

That game took place on an unprepared wicket on the parade ground of Mt Cook Barracks as Wellington lacked a large flat area suitable for use as a sports ground. With timing so good that it almost smacks of divine intervention an earthquake came to the rescue in January 1855. It lifted up most of the harbour perimeter, leaving a tidal platform of about eight acres that was quite level. A group of people requested that it should be made into a sports ground; this was agreed and it was subsequently drained by prison labour. It was first used for cricket in 1868, when it was reported that 'stones and thistles prevailed on the ground' and the ball looked as though it were suffering from smallpox, but after much hard work the Basin Reserve was properly fit for cricket by 1873.

New Year's Day in 1862 saw the beginning of the first match played by an English cricket team in Australia; against XVIII of Victoria England won by an innings. That tour, led by H.H. Stephenson of Surrey, proved a great success and precisely two years later the first match of the second tour began. The English party were led this time by George Parr, the Nottinghamshire batsman who had become captain of the All-England XI on the death of their founder, William Clarke, in 1856. His prowess with the bat earned him the nickname 'Lion of the North', for like Jessop after him his crouching stance was no hindrance to dispatching the ball vast distances – indeed the tree near the Trent Bridge Inn became known as 'Parr's tree' because of the frequency with which, as it were, he left his autograph on it. Reputed to be the inventor of the sweep shot, he was one of the leading cricketing figures of the middle of the century, playing the first-class game from 1844 to 1871. Parr was a strong, handsome character who organised and led his team well, although in those days the intricacies of tactics and the business of motivation caused the captain much less furrowing of the brow than they were to do later.

Touring was not a pastime for the faint-hearted in those days. Before Parr's team left England several of them were begged by relatives not to go as they believed that their loved ones would be attacked and eaten by aborigines. The travelling itself, of course, could be mind-bogglingly slow and difficult, and for anyone who was a poor sailor it must have been nightmarish. (At one point during this tour, sailing from Sydney to Melbourne, their ship was in a collision and the boat they hit sank almost immediately.) Once on land the roads were generally poor, railways were in their infancy, and the horse was a very important creature. When Parr's team were invited to New Zealand they found conditions even more wild. To travel any distance in those days you had, quite simply, to be tough.

The man who had invited them to New Zealand was a hotelier and theatrical agent from Dunedin with the fine Victorian name of Shadrach Jones. Dunedin was currently enjoying the fruits of the Otago gold rush, and as the game was growing in popularity all the time Jones decided to stage a cricket tournament there with teams from Canterbury, Otago and Southland. He asked Parr and his men to come and join in the fun, at his expense, and they agreed. It took them six days just to get across the Tasman Sea. When they arrived at Port Chalmers they were presented to the local Maori chief, and to Parr's consternation this gentleman took a liking to him and followed him, we are told, everywhere. They were taken to Dunedin in a coach with six white horses, part of a procession of players and officials in carriages and on horseback; their driver was a famous coachman who also rejoiced in a fine Victorian name, 'Cabbage Tree Ned'. A name like that is a licence for a writer to create an exotically colourful character — perhaps he had just one eye and always wore a red and black kerchief at his throat and so forth — but we will content ourselves with the cricket.

An English cricket team first took the field against a New Zealand team on 2 February 1864 at Dunedin; the opponents were XXII of Otago, the weather was blowing a gale, and it had been agreed that George 'Tear 'em' Tarrant should not be allowed to bowl really fast because the wicket was so poor. It is difficult to imagine now what it must have been like to play against a team of twenty-two but in those days it was common for the top teams to do so; the difference in class usually meant that the junior team would lose, as the opposing batsmen could only rarely make much of their bowlers. Over the years many players who were supposedly in the team for their batting turned in some good performances with the ball, for against weak opposition the captain would be happy to let them show their skills — on the understanding that they didn't get carried away by their success and expect to continue bowling in first-class matches. One aspect of such games is that the bowling figures can sometimes look positively ludicrous to us now, as indeed they do for this match. Otago's first innings made 71, with Tom Hayward's return being 15 for 34 — not bad for someone described by *Wisden* as 'in the 60's by common consent the leading professional batsman in England'; he was, needless to say, an all-rounder and the uncle of the Tom Hayward who achieved great deeds for Surrey and England around the turn of the century. In reply Parr's XI made 99, with E.M. Grace, the only amateur in the party, and Lockyer joint top scorers with 24. Otago improved in their second innings and reached 83, Hayward merely taking 9 for 36 this time, leaving the visitors to score 56 to win. This they accomplished for the loss of just one wicket, Grace remaining unbeaten on 26. The English began as they clearly intended to continue.

The second match, against XXII of Canterbury and Otago, took place immediately afterwards, also at Dunedin. This time the home team scored 91, with the bowling honours going to Robert 'Spider' Tinley with 13 for

49. Tinley was one of the great lob bowlers of cricketing history and the New Zealanders evidently had little idea of how to deal with him, for after Parr's team had scored 73 (of which 42 came from Grace) Tinley took another 13 wickets in their second innings of 66. There was no more time, though, and the match was left as a draw.

During one of the games at Dunedin George Parr had an experience that must have made him feel a long way from Trent Bridge: 'The Queen of the Maoris was at the match and she sent for the captain of the England team and his players. It was explained to me that the Queen wished to kiss me. Now I did not like the job as she was a very tattooed lady. So I turned to John Jackson, our great fast bowler, and said "Here Jack, you kiss her, you're a gypsy." Our fast bowler was nervous so I said that if there was any dirty work to do it always fell to me, and I went up and kissed her. She gave me a greenstone and said that as long as I kept it in my pocket it would act as a charm and that I should never have to work. I have carried the greenstone ever since. I have not had to work, so that I am glad I kissed the Queen of the Maoris.'

Then it was on to Christchurch, where they arrived late at night by ship, all the boats in the harbour sending up rockets to greet them. The ship had been delayed, however, and the local officials, finding the waiting rather tedious, had amused themselves by opening the bottles of champagne that had been intended for the Englishmen and drinking the contents. The game was against XXII of the locals, who once more could make nothing of Tinley. In their first innings he had figures of 13 wickets for just 18 runs as they disintegrated for 30, whereupon Parr's team rattled up 137, with 23 each from Carpenter and Lockyer and 6 for 55 from the local bowler Wills. Maybe the Englishmen then got a little complacent, or maybe some of the batsmen worked out how to play Tinley; whatever the reason, his figures took a nosedive as a mere 12 wickets cost all of 68 runs. A fighting home total of 105, 28 of them from A.E. Tennant, was a creditable effort, but still not enough to make the tourists bat again and the winning margin was an innings and 2 runs. The match inspired Samuel Butler, then rearing sheep in the Rangitata district, to send in an account of it to the local *Press*:

Claud: Which side went in first?
Hor: We did;
        And scored a paltry thirty runs in all.
        The lissom Lockyer gambolled round the stumps
        With many a crafty curvet: you had thought
        An Indian rubber were endued

With wicket keeping instincts: teazing Tinley
Issued his treacherous notices to quit
Ruthlessly truthful to his fame, and who
Shall speak of Jackson? Oh, 'twas sad indeed
To watch the downcast faces of our men
Returning from the wickets; one by one
Like patients at the gratis consultation
Of some skilled leech, they took their turn at physic,
And each came sadly homeward with a face
Awry through inward anguish; they were pale
As ghosts of some dead but deep mourned love
Grim with a great despair, but forced to smile.
Claud: Poor souls! Th'unkindest heart had bled for them.
  But what came after?
Hor: Fortune turned her wheel
  And Grace disgraced for the nonce was bowled
  First ball, and all the welkin roared applause.
  As for the rest they scored a goodly score
  And showed some splendid cricket, but their deeds
  Were not colossal, and our own brave Tennant
  Proved himself all as good a man as they.

Later the same day an exhibition match was staged. Parr and George Anderson each picked a team – shades of schoolboy games in the play-ground – made up of tourists and locals, Parr's XI scoring 64 and 89 to beat Anderson's XI's 71 and 75 by 7 runs in what sounds as though it was one of the most exciting games of the tour. Then it was back to Otago for another exhibition piece, Grace and Tarrant taking on XI of Otago; they scored 8 in their first innings, Tarrant bowled the locals out for 7, the Englishmen scored another 16 and then, just as it was getting exciting, they called it off, the home team not playing a second innings. While it was obviously just a spot of harmless fun, it is difficult to escape the feeling that at bottom it was desperately patronising; to continue the schoolboy analogy, like two fifth-formers challenging a bunch of first-formers. What a pity they didn't get the come-uppance such arrogance deserves.

The last game in New Zealand was played at Dunedin against XXII of Otago and was, unfortunately, rather one-sided. The locals made 98, Jackson taking 10 for 21, and Parr's XI then exceeded that by exactly 100, with 43 from Caffyn and 40 from Hayward. Tinley then took another eleven wickets to help shoot the home team out for 49, leaving the

Englishmen victorious by an innings and 51 runs. After that it was back to Australia.

It is estimated that to stage the tournament that he did — there were a number of other matches played between local teams – cost Shadrach Jones the best part of £3,000. The games, especially those with the tourists, attracted large crowds, but opinions vary as to whether or not he actually made a profit. At Christchurch it was said that 'the hill facing the Grand Stand was much patronised by a class of people who could have well afforded the admission money to the ground', which seems to suggest that he lost out, but the authors of *Men in White* believe that overall he came out in credit. It was obviously a brave and far-seeing venture, and one hopes very much that it paid off.

*

In October 1875 New Zealand's first cricket association was formed in Wellington, to be followed the next year by one in Otago, in 1877 by Canterbury and in 1883 by Auckland. A clear indication that the New Zealanders were beginning to take their cricket seriously was also given when in September 1876 it was arranged that James Lillywhite's team which was about to set off for Australia should visit New Zealand as well.

With the Notts professionals Alfred Shaw and Arthur Shrewsbury, Lillywhite was to organise a number of tours to Australia over the years, making a profit until 1887–8 when another tour by a separate party meant that they came a financial cropper. He was a canny entrepreneur — he also published his *Cricketers' Companion* and *James Lillywhite's Cricketers' Annual* – who saw the opportunity to make some money, and he organised his tours well; the New Zealanders were asked for guarantees of £60 a match as well as the takings at the gate. One of a well-known family of cricketers, he didn't miss a single game for Sussex between 1862 and 1881, bowling left-arm medium-slow with great accuracy; but his chief claim to fame is that he captained the England team in the two matches at Melbourne that later came to be recognised as the first two Tests.

Eight matches were to be played in New Zealand, all of them against odds. In Australia they had lost three games to teams of fifteen players and this provided the impetus that led the Australians to challenge them on equal terms; Billy Caffyn had stayed behind after Parr's visit and, along with the old Surrey player Charles Lawrence, brought about a great improvement in playing standards. New Zealand, however, had shown no such enterprise in persuading anyone to coach them and their progress had accordingly been minimal. This was demonstrated straightaway, when in

James Lillywhite, standing on the right of the picture, led the second tour to New Zealand early in 1877, immediately before playing the first two Tests against Australia. Also shown are, from left to right: back – George Griffith, Tom Humphrey, Frank Silcock; front – Henry Jupp, Richard Humphrey. Southerton and Jupp played in the first two Tests.

the first match against XXII of Auckland the Englishmen scored 225 and put the opposition out for 109 and 94 to win by an innings and 22 runs.

The people of Wellington took the visit very seriously, and set about improving the Basin Reserve ground. The local paper asked all members of their team to dress alike 'as nothing looks so bad as a motley group', and also, rather revealingly, asked the team to 'forget their quarrels, pull together well and support each other throughout the match so that Wellington may make as good a show as other towns in New Zealand.' All to no avail; their XXII were skittled out for 31 (Shaw had the crazy figures of 13 for 11) and 38 (Lillywhite 13 for 22), with the tourists scoring 190 in between times. The local press must have felt pretty despondent at losing by an innings and 121 runs after their pleas.

On what must have been a humdinger of a pitch at New Plymouth against XXII of Taranaki, the Englishmen scored 80 and won by an innings and one run, the locals making 32 and 47. At Nelson, the local XXII went under by an innings and 163 runs, making 56 and 39 against Lillywhite's 258 – Shaw had match figures of 26 for 43 – while at Greymouth, XXII of Westland got away with a draw when the weather intervened, the English team scoring 119 and 99 for 4 to the home team's 50.

The perils of travelling were then brought home to them very forcibly. On the way to Christchurch their coach became stuck in the flooded Otira Gorge in pitch-darkness and they got thoroughly soaked in getting it out. With no dry clothes to change into they spent the night on the floor of a wooden hostel. Next day they found their road blocked by a landslide and so returned to the hostel, but there was no food available. Eventually, having had precious little sleep in three days, they got to Christchurch just half an hour or so before the next match was due to begin. If anything comparable were to happen to a present-day touring team one suspects that the hardship payment they would receive would pay the bills back home for some time to come. Lillywhite and his chums seem to have taken it all in their stride; at least, it didn't stop them doing the business over XVIII of Canterbury, a match played before some 15,000 spectators. Their first innings made 70, although at one stage they were 39 for 9, with the local bowler Charlie Frith taking 6 for 23 and, it was claimed, sending a bail a distance of thirty-four yards. The home team replied with 65, after which the Englishmen ran up 102; Canterbury were then bowled out for 84, Hill's figures being 12 for 17, leaving Lillywhite victorious by 23 runs. This was the nearest anyone came to beating the tourists, and the Cantabrians, choosing to put the hardships they had suffered before the game to the back of their minds, were duly proud of their performance.

There was no respite in the travelling, for now it was on to Dunedin to play XVIII of Otago. This produced the most exciting finish of all the games in New Zealand; Otago batted first and made 76, to which the Englishmen replied with 163. On the last afternoon word went round the town that the locals were putting up a good battle to avoid defeat and the crowd streamed in – four thousand or so in all. There was, we are told, 'extensive betting on a one innings defeat'. Needing 87 to make the visitors bat again, the sixteenth wicket, the penultimate, fell at 86. David Kynaston, in his book *Archie's Last Stand*, quotes from a local paper of the time as to what happened next: 'Several gentlemen then surrounded Collinson, who, on account of a bad leg, had not intended to go in, and persuaded him to take his stand at the wickets with the hopes of Nicholls being able to make the necessary run. This he did in his ordinary dress, without pads or gloves, and got through the rest of Lillywhite's over successfully.' There was, one imagines, a breathless hush in the close that night. As it happened that last wicket put on 20, Collinson making 2 not out, and when eventually Nicholls fell there were only five minutes left; the game had been saved and Dunedin had two new heroes.

Witnessing these heroics were some members of the police force who had come there with a mission – namely to arrest the English wicket-keeper, Edward Pooley. Back in Christchurch Pooley had tried an old trick on one of the locals, saying that he could forecast the score of each member of the home team. Versions differ as to the amount of the bet, but the odds were such that in saying each batsman would score nought there was no way Pooley could fail to make a good profit, since the team would inevitably contain a number of rabbits. When he tried to claim his dues the aggrieved gentleman claimed that it was an unfair bet and refused to pay, whereupon a scuffle broke out; hence the presence of the constabulary and their request to 'come along with us, sir'. Pooley and the team's baggage man, Alf Bramall, were charged with assault and with damaging property, but after a delay of six weeks or so the case was dismissed as there was no real evidence against them. The people of Christchurch, believing them to have been hard done by, raised a subscription of £50 and gave Pooley a gold watch, but it meant that they missed the rest of the tour. Indeed this had further repercussions for Pooley since by missing the two representative games in Australia he did not become a Test player. For Lillywhite it also meant that he was without his wicket-keeper, and with the reserve keeper suffering from an eye injury he was in some trouble. In the event, the man who did keep wicket in the two Tests, Selby, didn't distinguish himself, so Pooley's little adventure had quite serious implications.

After the excitement on and off the field at the end of the last game the final match in New Zealand was a distinct anticlimax. At Invercargill XXII of Southland were beaten by an innings and 65 runs; the tourists made 158 with 66 from Greenwood and put out the home team for 47 and 46. At least this would have meant that they weren't too exhausted before they began the return trip to Australia; after several days of being buffeted by the Tasman, though, they were feeling very sorry for themselves. The problem was that the day after they arrived they had to begin the grand match that was to go down in history as one of the most important ever played.

There had been some large crowds in New Zealand, but because the arrangements had for the most part been poorly prepared the visit was not a financial success. The home teams hadn't given as good an account of themselves as might have been hoped, and the time when there might be a representative New Zealand XI was clearly still some way off; but some of the better players had undoubtedly benefited from meeting professionals and further tours were obviously essential in helping the game to develop. All in all, Lillywhite and his men, like Parr and his, had played their small part in helping New Zealand's cricket move steadily, if slowly, forward.

*

The following year, 1878, the Australian team that was about to tour England came to New Zealand for some practice matches. Canterbury, having lost only narrowly to Lillywhite, wanted to play on even terms; the Australians felt the game would be more realistic if their opposition fielded twenty-two. A compromise of fifteen was reached — and the locals duly won by six wickets. This prompted Canterbury to feel sufficiently confident of their prowess to undertake a tour to Victoria and Tasmania, the first overseas tour by a domestic cricket association from any country. They did in fact win three of their seven games and so were able to feel reasonably pleased with themselves. However, since the visit coincided with the Australian team playing several more games as well as an English team under Lord Harris making an extensive tour, the poor Cantabrian country cousins provoked very little interest; so little indeed that money had to be sent from Christchurch to allow them to pay their fare home. Not long afterwards, at the second annual meeting of the Canterbury Cricket Association, a curious motion was passed which perhaps had its roots in this unfortunate little episode: 'That this association does not hold itself responsible for any criticism on matches or matters connected with cricket which appear in the local papers, unless authorised by the association.' It sounds altogether sad; or perhaps pathetic.

As it happened Lord Harris's team had enjoyed mixed fortunes in Australia, coming a distinct cropper in the one Test played and losing two other games as well. His team was also involved in a fracas in Sydney concerning the competence of an umpire in which the noble body of his Lordship was actually smitten with a stick wielded by some despicable larrikin. This did nothing to improve Anglo-Australian relations. After leaving Australia the Englishmen stopped off at Christchurch for a match against Canterbury, which resulted in a draw, before going home via America.

In 1881–2 Lillywhite was again in Australia with his co-adventurers Shaw and Shrewsbury, Shaw being team captain. Alfred Shaw was one of the greatest defensive medium-pace bowlers in cricket history, so accurate that he never once delivered a wide, and who could boast that he conceded fewer runs than he bowled overs – which, even if many of them were of only four balls, is no mean claim to fame. The previous season he and Shrewsbury had organised a strike at Nottinghamshire over contracts but this did not stop the club appointing him captain the following season. He was vastly experienced, having been with them for nearly twenty years, and was to lead them to five successive championships. In Australia he was to lose two and draw two of the Tests played, making an excursion to New Zealand between the first two Tests.

The story of that excursion is altogether similar to that of the previous tour, the matches again all being played against odds. At Dunedin XVIII of Otago were beaten by ten wickets, England's 156 and 4 for 0 being rather better than the home team's 84 and 74. At Oamaru the margin against XXII of Oamaru was an innings and 29 runs, the score being 146 to England and 60 and 57 to the locals. In a one-day match at Timaru, XXII of Timaru made 111 but still went down by six wickets. In a two-day match at Christchurch, XVIII of Canterbury managed to salvage a draw because of the weather, although scores of 100 and 15 for 6, when compared to 230 from England, could hardly have sent the fans home bubbling with euphoria. This was, incidentally, the first representative match played at Lancaster Park; previous matches had been played at Hagley Park but because this was a government reserve no charge could be made at the gate and the club had to make do with whatever they could get from a collection inside the ground. Needless to say, they hadn't found this a particularly satisfactory arrangement.

On they went. Another draw in similar circumstances against XXII of Wellington; the home team managed 80 and 54 for 10 against England's 222. In a one-day match against XXII of Waikato, the New Zealanders

Alfred Shaw, bowler of the first ball in Test cricket, took a team to New Zealand in 1881–2. On the previous tour under Lillywhite he had bowling figures in one innings of 13 wickets for 11 runs.

Arthur Shrewsbury, England captain on the tours of Australia in 1884–5 and 1886–7. Early in 1888 his team made the fourth tour of New Zealand by an English party.

scored 44 and England 84 to win the game, although then, to entertain the spectators, the locals had a second innings and made 53. The last match was against XXII of Auckland, and was as anticlimactic as the last game of the previous tour. Auckland made 122 and England 214, whereupon Auckland's 94 meant that the tourists needed just three runs to win, which didn't cause many problems. This fixture had been expected to provide a decent financial return, and was indeed well attended; unfortunately, someone had arranged it on the Domain ground, which the public could enter without paying.

In those seven games Billy Midwinter took seventy-eight wickets at 3.18 and Edmund Peate fifty-two at 5.00. Clearly the pitches must have been pretty grim, yet several of the English batsmen managed some good scores and the fact that Shrewsbury and Bates could average over thirty must have left the home players quite impressed. Some good things came out of the tour, such as the advice that Shaw was able to give about pitch preparation and tending, but it was clear that what was badly needed were some good coaches. It was several years before they came.

*

The next visit, in March 1888, was again organised by Lillywhite, Shaw and Shrewsbury, but it coincided with another tour of Australia and so failed financially. Just three matches were played in New Zealand, the final ones of the tour, the Englishmen being led by C.A. Smith (who later achieved much renown as a Hollywood actor and was knighted for furthering Anglo-American friendship). He was principally a slow-medium bowler, known as 'Round-the-Corner' Smith because of the curve at which he approached the wicket; in later years he was to call his home in Beverly Hills – from which he organised countless cricket matches – 'The Round Corner'. He played for Sussex for sixteen years, captaining them in two seasons. The year after this trip he captained England in what was later recognised as the very first Test against South Africa; as he missed the return game because of fever this proved to be his only Test and he remains the only player to captain England in his only appearance in Test cricket.

England played the three matches under the banner of A. Shrewsbury's XI against teams of eighteen. In the first, against Wellington, played over two days, the home team seemed to be heading for defeat after being dismissed for 86 and seeing the visitors knock up 207. A good second innings, though, took them to 222 and saved the game, for there was time only for the Englishmen to reach 21 for 0 before stumps were drawn. Two matches were then played at Christchurch, the first one extending over four

C.A. Smith, captain on Shrewsbury's tour of 1887–8 to New
Zealand. In later years familiarity with the camera would mean
that the poses were rather less studied.

days because of bad weather. Canterbury made 145 and then to great excitement put Shrewsbury's team out for 78; 80 in the second home innings left the tourists to score 148 to win, which may well have embarrassed them, but with the score at 31 for 0 the match was left drawn. In the return match starting the next day the Englishmen made sure there would be no further embarrassment. They made 140 and then put out Canterbury for 64, following this with 100 which left the locals with a steep hill to climb. This again was only a two-day game, however, and when they had reached 37 for 9 the time ran out. It wasn't a particularly successful little visit, mainly because the weather was bad and the matches were poorly attended.

This was the last proper English visit to New Zealand for over fourteen years. There were, though, some important developments in New Zealand from the 1880s onward. The spread of the railways made travelling easier and so encouraged more competition among the various associations, which meant that cricket became established as the principal summer sport; Canterbury, Otago and Wellington were the leading teams, Auckland suffering from the fact that it was still rather isolated as the main trunk railway did not reach there till 1908. Club matches were not usually completed in one day but were played over two successive Saturday afternoons, an unsatisfactory arrangement that must have caused many problems and which can't have done much to help the sport develop. From about 1890 professional coaches were at last brought in – one of them was Charles Bannerman, the hero of the first Test match who coached at Christ's College – and they were soon able to help the promising players make progress. Nonetheless in 1900 Dan Reese, one of the outstanding players of the period, was able to say that he believed there had been little development in New Zealand cricket over the past twenty years.

One major problem, inevitably, was lack of money – a problem that was to be the principal bugbear for the country's cricket administrators for decade after decade. Another was the lack of population from which to draw their cricketers; at the beginning of the 1880s there were under half a million Europeans in New Zealand – the Maoris never showed any real interest in the game – and even by the time of the First World War this had risen only to about a million. In the early years some of their best cricketers had been those who had come out to New Zealand from the English public schools, but as time went by this source dried up and they had to rely on home-grown players – many of the best of these also coming from the leading schools and colleges.

It was Rugby that was proving the more popular sport and it took both potential players and spectators away from cricket; admittedly they were played at different seasons, but for some people it must have been a question of choosing between the two. This was especially the case after the All Blacks toured England in 1905 and met with only one defeat. Suddenly the sport became a national obsession, something of which a small country could be mightily proud; it was the duty of everyone, player and fan alike, to keep their name at the top, and since the cricket team could not begin to compete at this level the sport inevitably lost out in the public consciousness. They also lacked the leisured class that existed in England, the gentleman who could devote his time, and occasionally his money, to playing and promoting the game. In short it was all very amateur and was to remain that way for a very long time; the New Zealanders were, with some justification, proud of their amateur status, but it meant that they took many years to catch up with the rest of the cricketing world. It was not only the English teams that were playing against odds.

— **2** —

Fit to Disport on
the Playing Field

The first team to represent New Zealand officially did so against New South Wales in a match at Christchurch beginning on 15 February 1894. They lost by 160 runs when, surprise surprise, their second innings collapsed — a problem that was to become depressingly familiar. This match did in fact predate the formation of the New Zealand Cricket Council which took place, also in Christchurch, on 27 December of the same year. The Council's influence seems immediately to have been for the good; the following year another team from New South Wales were beaten at Christchurch, and the year after that a team from Queensland were beaten at Wellington. The results against Victoria and New South Wales during their first tour of Australia may conveniently be overlooked.

In England, however, the last thirty or so years of the century had seen the game advance enormously. Principally this was because of the influence of W.G. Grace, whose all-round skills were so far above anything previously known that the game was simply transformed. Batting, in particular, became a multi-faceted skill as he developed both back-foot and front-foot play; in the past, batsmen had generally played off either one or the other, and had lacked the ability to combine the two until Grace showed how it could be done. It is true that Fuller Pilch* had preceded Grace in this, but the doctor's charisma and high public profile ensured that his example would be copied whereas Pilch's had not been. His cricketing deeds so far transcended those of any previous player that he became a hero in a way we perhaps can no longer quite comprehend; Rowland Bowen, in his history of the game, suggested that as the monarchy was withdrawing into privacy at the same time as Grace was rising, he became the figurehead that the nation needed. Cricket was already a popular sport, but Grace turned it into a national institution.

---

* *Men in White* is an admirable work but it contains one delightfully appropriate misprint: Fuller Pilch is referred to as 'Fuller *Pitch*!

The operation of the snowball effect did the rest. The professionals could earn reasonably good money, at least during the season, while in another social stratum the public schools were refining the art of batsmanship to a degree hitherto unknown, helped by the important fact that pitches had improved considerably as the century neared its close. In 1890 the County Championship was officially constituted, marking the beginning of the Golden Age which lasted until 1914. Now the Golden Age has been the subject of endless romantic outpourings, and it is popularly seen as the time when the sun always shone and majestic batsmen such as Ranji, Fry, Jackson and their chums – none of whom had to taint themselves by worrying about money – stroked the ball with effortless grace to all corners of the ground. The spectators turned up in their thousands to savour this rich feast and everyone, players and fans alike, had a thoroughly enjoyable time. Perhaps in practice it wasn't always *quite* like that, but the crucial point for our present purpose is that English cricket had a head start on New Zealand cricket, enabling it to call the tune until more than three-quarters of the twentieth century had elapsed.

It was almost forty years after George Parr's visit that a cricket team finally left England with New Zealand as their prime destination. Over the years Lord Hawke, the captain of Yorkshire whose cricketing zeal and longevity were matched only by Grace, had led teams to all corners of the globe, ever prepared to spread the gospel of the noble game to anywhere that he thought needed civilising. In 1902 he was invited by the NZCC to tour New Zealand and he duly organised a team; but shortly before the departure his mother was taken ill and he was unable to travel with them, although they still played under the name of Lord Hawke's team. The captaincy was taken over by P.F. Warner of Middlesex.

'Plum' Warner was to become one of cricket's great servants, being associated with MCC in various capacities for most of his life. A neat, balanced batsman good enough to score 29,000 runs with sixty centuries, he was to become one of the best captains of his time; he led England in Australia in 1903–4 and came back with the Ashes, and captained Middlesex from 1908 to 1920, winning the Championship in his last season. He also led England on the 1911–12 tour, but was taken ill early on; the captaincy passed to Johnny Douglas and the series was won convincingly, but Douglas was very ready to acknowledge the part Warner had played from his sick-bed. By the time of this 1902–3 tour he had been playing for some eight years and had two Tests against South Africa to his name; there was no doubt that he and the players he led were altogether more experienced than the New Zealanders. The party included just two professionals,

Lord Hawke, captain of Yorkshire and England. He organised a
tour to New Zealand but was then unable to travel on it.

P.F. Warner, captain on Lord Hawke's tour of 1902–3. There were too many Salt Bush Bills for his liking.

George Thompson of Northamptonshire and Sam Hargreave of Warwickshire, and was no more than reasonable county standard.

They travelled via America, playing one game in San Francisco on a ground where the umpires carried brooms and swept the wicket after each over. In New Zealand they played eleven games against odds of up to twenty-two, winning all of them, and five first-class games which they also won. None of the games had really been close; there had been eight victories by an innings, and the closest any team got was either five wickets or 124 runs. Warner wrote afterwards in his book about the tour that the programme had been badly arranged, with too many odds matches 'against cricketers of the rustic and Salt Bush Bill type'. They had enjoyed seeing plenty of the country but there had been too much tiring travelling; more than once they travelled all night, arrived at ten or eleven in the morning and began the game by half past eleven. On one occasion, he said, they rose at three in the morning, coached all day till nine at night, slept at a hotel for a few hours, were woken early, took a three-hour train journey and rushed on to the ground for an 11.30 start. He certainly manages to make it sound pretty grim.

The tour was rounded off with two representative games at Christchurch and Wellington, the first time an English team had played an official New Zealand team. The home team was captained by Charles Richardson, an Australian who had played for New South Wales before moving to New Zealand in 1897. He was a sound, determined batsman who in 1900 had become the first player to score a century for New Zealand; this was at Christchurch when he made 114 not out against the touring Melbourne team, but the match was not given first-class status. His team still lost by an innings, but he was carried off on the shoulders of his team-mates. He was an experienced player who was a good choice as captain, but he failed to produce the goods with the bat in the two matches. His problem was that his players were simply not up to the standard of Warner's men.

He was also unlucky with the weather. Having won the toss, it began to rain after just two overs – and when play began again an hour later conditions were distinctly difficult. Dan Reese, the opener, made 32 and Ken Tucker 50, but Thompson in particular found the damp pitch to his liking and the wickets fell steadily. Wicket-keeper Boxshall provided a breezy little 21, but with Thompson taking 6 for 38 and Dowson 4 for 27 the New Zealanders were all out for 164. Warner went early on, but on the second day Frederick Fane, accompanied first by Burnup and then by Tom Taylor, passed the home total for the loss of two wickets. Burnup made 30 and Taylor 54, but Fane went on to 124, although Warner said he was lucky

*Frederick Fane – the
first Englishman to score
a century in a
representative game in
New Zealand.*

not to be given out caught behind in the 70s. He was an Irishman who was
to gain fourteen caps for England and captain them five times, a steady if
unspectacular batsman who played for Essex on and off for nearly thirty
years. In an age of golden batsmen he tended to be overshadowed, but as he
proved here he was a more than capable performer.

From 172 for 2 the score subsided to 186 for 6, but Fane and Stanning put
on 71 for the seventh wicket to put the initiative firmly back with the
Englishmen, and the final total was 304 for a lead of 140 – which Warner
thought should have been a great deal less since Fane should have been
given out. Richardson tried a radical reorganisation of his batting order for
the second innings, deciding that he would open the innings with Reese, but
as before it was Tucker and Reese who got the bulk of the runs. Tucker
made 67 and Reese another 32, and from being 129 for 2 the wickets fell
steadily as five batsmen reached the teens and then departed. Before this
tour New Zealand batsmen knew nothing of Bosanquet's new-fangled
'googly', and not surprisingly they were still at something of a loss against
him, as figures of 4 for 44 showed. Downes managed 26, but once again
Thompson was among the wickets with 4 for 74; the total of 214 showed an
improvement, but left the Englishmen needing just 75 for victory. This was

managed for the loss of three wickets with an hour to spare, Warner and Burnup each passing thirty before falling lbw to McCarthy in quick succession.

Before a large crowd at Wellington Richardson again won the toss and batted, and before long was back in the pavilion with just 5 to his name. Fortunately, Dan Reese was enjoying a good day; for four hours he stood firm as the wickets fell at the other end, only Tucker and Mahoney getting past twenty, and with a fine piece of sensible attacking batting and a bit of good fortune he scored 148 to help his team to the respectable total of 274. Thompson was having a good day too, despite bowling into a strong wind – 44.3 overs yielded him 8 for 124. For the first two days of the match the weather was good, enabling Hawke's team to make a substantial reply. One of the openers, Randall Johnson of Somerset, was a New Zealander who had returned to his native land in the ranks of the enemy, and he now performed unkind deeds against his compatriots, as he was also to do on the next tour. His 88 saw the innings off to a very sound start, helped by Stanning, Burnup and Fane who all got to the twenties. And then Warner came along to play a fine captain's innings, making 125 in his own neat, unshowy way and delighting the crowd with some beautiful stroke-making. The wicket-keeper, Arnold Williams, had an unhappy time and conceded 30 byes, making extras the third-top score in a total of 380; come the next tour, though, and he would have his revenge.

Faced with a deficit of 106 the New Zealanders also found themselves faced with a pitch that was beginning to break up and a strengthening wind that made batting difficult. They were in trouble almost immediately; 21 for 2 became 49 for 2 and then 49 for 4; 74 for 4 became 84 all out before lunch. Mahoney's 24 was the best effort as Thompson took 3 for 29 to finish the match with eleven wickets, and Burnup went through the lower order to take 5 for 8 from 4.5 overs. Warner's remark that he had not anticipated such an easy victory 'after the colonials had put on such a respectable score in their first innings' sounds a touch patronising, but perhaps like good umpires we may give him the benefit of the doubt.

Because of shortage of funds the tourists had stayed in private houses rather than hotels, which meant that there was less chance for the local players to talk to and learn from their experienced visitors. In that respect the tour was not as satisfactory as it might have been, but in most other ways it was. They proved to have good drawing power and the matches were usually well attended; the arrangement was that the amateurs were paid their travelling and boarding expenses less their wine and washing bills, and the professionals, as well as being given 'a liberal sum', had everything except their wine bills paid, while the New Zealanders took all of the gate money. This meant that the NZCC's treasurer was able to breathe a sigh of relief when it was over; they were some £600 better off.

The fact that all eighteen games had been lost by some margin showed clearly that New Zealand's cricketers had a long way to go before they could hope regularly to put up a good account of themselves against the mother country. Warner rated the best New Zealand team about equal to the poorest of the first-class counties, praising the bowling and fielding but being less enthusiastic about the batting. He was also critical of the standard of umpiring, not because it was biased but because it was incompetent. The only good umpire they had encountered all tour, apparently, was Charles Bannerman, the man who had made the first Test century for Australia in 1877 and who had officiated in the first 'Test'. After leaving New Zealand, the Englishmen played three matches in Australia; even allowing that they were tired and travel-worn the fact that they lost twice and drew once does show clearly the difference in standard between New Zealand and the two senior countries.

*

Three years or so later, in the summer of 1906, there was talk that MCC would be sending a team to Australia that winter. The problem was that the Australian authorities were having their own internal arguments and by the time these had been resolved the MCC felt it was too late to raise a team. The visit was therefore put off till the following year – when it proved singularly unsuccessful, as the Test series was lost 4–1 – and instead an invitation from the NZCC was accepted. The team that the MCC sent – it was the first tour to New Zealand under the MCC banner – was all-amateur and a weak one in English first-class terms; in the season just finished only five of them had played regular county cricket, with another four of them having played for universities. The problem with this was that although it meant that the New Zealanders would not be swamped by a vastly better team, it also meant that the tourists would not have the drawing power that more famous players would have had – and so finances might suffer. This indeed proved to be the case, and the NZCC lost quite a bit of money that it simply could not afford.

The appointed MCC captain was Major E.G. Wynyard, the Hampshire batsman who had played three times for England without conspicuous success, but whose partnership with Major R.M. Poore of 411 against Somerset in 1899 is still the English sixth-wicket record. In the second match he was to break a tendon in his right leg, a serious injury that

Charles de Trafford, who took over as captain of the first MCC tour of New Zealand when Major Wynyard was injured.

necessitated his return home; Percy May, one of the amateurs in the party who wrote an account of the tour, insisted that he wasn't just wheeling out some hollow eulogy when he said that everyone was very upset at this and that 'we are like an army that has lost its general'. Yet Wynyard had a reputation as something of an irascible character. There is a story that he once had an argument with Ranjitsinhji because, of all things, the young prince had inadvertently eaten some of his grapes, which hardly suggests that his relations with his fellow-men were all that a cricket captain's really ought to be. A year later, aged 46, he was offered the captaincy to Australia, but he had to decline it. There is, incidentally, a team photograph in May's book which is different from the usual; all of them are standing in a line, with Wynyard in the middle, and all of them have their arms linked to their neighbour's – except Wynyard.

His duties were taken over by his vice-captain, The Honourable Charles de Trafford, who had been captain of Leicestershire since 1890. He had been born at Trafford Park, Manchester, the Old Trafford ground actually belonging to his father at the time, but he had stayed with Lancashire for just one match. He could be a useful middle-order batsman, but although he totalled nearly 10,000 runs he was too inconsistent to be more than a good county player. *Wisden* said that 'his fierce batting was perhaps the chief attraction of the county's cricket', and it was largely because of him that the county attained first-class status in 1895. As it happened he had a wretched time with the bat throughout this tour, his highest score in nine first-class matches being 28 not out – although some of the pitches left a lot to be desired.

There were five games played against odds, of which four were won and one drawn, and eleven first-class matches, of which the last two were representative games. After drawing the first two first-class games the third one, against Canterbury, was lost by seven wickets, although there was some excuse for this. There had been three important injuries in the second match, and the game in Christchurch began only three hours after they had endured an appalling sea crossing in a very crowded ship; no berths had been booked for them and everyone suffered from seasickness. From the tones in which he describes it, the journey clearly made a deep impression on May. Thereafter they got their act together much better and came up with a string of victories, thanks in particular to Johnny Douglas.

Douglas – 'Towser' to his chums – was an all-rounder who had made his début for Essex in 1901 and had improved steadily with each passing season. He had turned in some outstanding performances including one occasion at Leyton when he took five Yorkshire wickets for no runs in eight

*Frank Foster, Johnny Douglas and Plum Warner soon after their
arrival in Australia in 1911–12. Five years earlier the New
Zealanders had found Douglas a distinct handful.*

balls. He was a fine all-round sportsman, in fact, who over the years was to
play amateur football for England and win the Olympic middleweight
boxing gold medal in 1908. As a batsman he was not the most glorious
player to watch for, although he was good enough to score 24,500 runs
with 26 centuries, he was not a natural stroke-maker and could at times be
quite exasperating as he blocked remorselessly; on his first visit to Australia
with the England team he found himself with the nickname, based on his
initials and bestowed on him by a gentleman in the crowd, of Johnny Won't
Hit Today.

As a fast-medium bowler, though, he was outstanding. An endless supply
of stamina – he was always superbly fit and was said to have muscles like
iron – enabled him to keep going for hours without losing speed or accuracy
and he finished his career with almost 1,900 wickets at 23 each. He was to
go on to lead England, winning the Ashes handsomely in 1911–12 after
taking over the captaincy when Warner fell ill – and then not at first being
able to find a place in the team when Australia came to England a few
months later! After the War he was to learn about the other side of the coin,

losing disastrously to Warwick Armstrong's splendid team and finding himself with probably the most curious record of any Test captain in history: four successive victories followed by eight successive defeats. For now, in New Zealand, he was to head both the batting and bowling averages in the first-class matches, and was clearly head and shoulders above any other cricketer in the country.

By the time of the two 'Test' matches – like Warner before him, May refers to the representative games as Tests without putting the word in inverted commas – the tourists had won five, drawn three and lost one. There had been a good deal of travelling, some of it exciting and fascinating and some distinctly uncomfortable. The spectacular scenery of the Otira Gorge was rather lost on them, for instance, when the rain began to fall in torrents; they then had to spend two hours on a train to Greymouth in soaking wet clothes and were not in the best of spirits when they arrived. One hazard of travelling that would never cross the mind of the modern motorist befell George Branston; sitting at the back of the coach he was hit in the eye by a flick from the driver's whip, and spent the day in great pain. When he cursed the driver he was told, 'What yer grumbling at. You ain't the only one I've 'it.'

In the first 'Test', played at Christchurch, New Zealand were led by a local man, Dan Reese, who had recently returned home after four years in England, during which time he had played a few games for W.G. Grace's London County team and also for Essex; Grace had in fact wanted him to stay in England but he had been intent on getting his marine engineer's certificate. He was a good attacking left-handed batsman able to play the ball late – not a common attribute in New Zealand at the time – and a slow-medium bowler, said to be the only New Zealander of his time who would get into an Australian team and described by *Wisden* as 'probably the best left-handed batsman produced by New Zealand' at the point when his career ended in 1921. He was a very popular man, something of a public hero, who had played for Canterbury since 1895–6, had made a fine century against Lord Hawke's team, and was now leading his country for the first time. He was to do so eight times in all up to 1914, and was captain of Canterbury for fourteen years as well. In all he scored over 2,000 runs and took over 200 wickets for Canterbury, impressive figures for the period. After he retired he served as a member of the Management Committee and as President of the NZCC.

The first day of the match was declared a public holiday by the mayor of Christchurch and two thousand people turned up. New Zealand batted first and soon after the start light rain began to fall; it persisted until tea-time but no playing time was lost. Reese went in the first over to Douglas but his partner, James Lawrence, who had been a member of the first official New Zealand team thirteen years earlier, combined with Alf Haddon to put on 52 for the second wicket. Percy May's speed – to say nothing of his suspect action – then accounted for three quick wickets before Mahoney and Tucker put on another fifty partnership. Thereafter only the last two got into double figures as May and Douglas finished with five wickets each. The hero, however, was undoubtedly Mahoney; when they were all out for 207 on the second morning he was undefeated on 71. The MCC team did in fact contain two New Zealanders who had been playing in England, Randall Johnson, who had toured four years earlier, and the wicket-keeper Ronald Fox. They opened the innings and very unpatriotically put on 151 for the first wicket before Johnson fell to Reese on 99; as it happened, the next MCC team to visit, in 1922–3, also contained a New Zealander who took the big stick to his compatriots, Tom Lowry scoring 130 in one of the 'Tests'. After this fine start, though, the innings fell away; Burns made 27 and Douglas 40, but from 151 for 0 to 257 all out is pretty poor stuff. The best bowling figures came from Alec Downes with 4 for 83 from his spinners. For long years New Zealand's catching and fielding was often to let them down, but today they performed well.

For the second innings Reese dropped himself down the order and promoted the newcomer Ned Sale to open with the veteran Lawrence – and it worked. The partnership realised 112 before Sale went for 66, Lawrence later going for 51. The only problem was that everyone else let them down, and Reese's 17 was the next best knock. Douglas took four more wickets for match figures of 9 for 107, and if the MCC innings had crumbled badly New Zealand's completely disintegrated. All ten wickets fell for just 75 for an all out total of 187, leaving MCC with 138 to win in over a day. Only Fox's wicket was lost in getting there, the cruel Johnson making 76 not out and Burns 39 not out as the nine-wicket win was recorded. At least the New Zealanders were to get their own back on Johnson in the next match.

Reese lost both the captaincy and his place in the team for the second game and the leadership went to Arnold Williams. He was a Welshman who had moved to New Zealand as a child, was a noted rifle shot and billiards player, and was a fine wicket-keeper who was also a good attacking batsman with a cool temperament; playing for Wellington earlier in the tour he had scored a century to help earn his team an honourable draw. He was to justify his selection with a vital innings, and the other three changes the selectors made, bringing in Hemus, Fisher and Upham, all proved to be inspired moves. Considering this was an international match the pitch was remarkable; not only had it been over-watered, but the night before the game vandals had dug a hole near one end of it. A repair of sorts was made with a piece of turf and it was considered far enough away from the wicket not to affect a good-length delivery; but balls that hit the spot behaved quite unpredictably, often rising to head height, and there were plenty of bruises sustained before the game was over. In Dick Brittenden's words, the arrangements for the preparation of the pitch and its subsequent care had been 'positively naive'.

Williams won the toss and chose to bat. Lawrence and Sale put on 30 before Douglas struck; bowling with great fire and accuracy he induced three slip chances, all of which were pouched by Branston, and the first four wickets went down for 63. Hemus and Tucker then began to put together a stand, only for a ball from Douglas to rear up and hit Tucker on the head; as he fell backwards he knocked over the stumps, but in Edwardian days sporting chaps didn't claim wickets for accidents like this and he wasn't given out. He retired, though, and was replaced by the captain, Williams, and with Hemus making some good attacking strokes they took the total to 120 before they were separated. The rest of the wickets fell steadily; Tucker came back and took his score to 23, but Hemus's 38 was the best effort in a total of 165, Douglas finishing with 7 for 49 after an excellent display of aggressive bowling. On this pitch that wasn't as bad a score as it sounds, and both of the MCC openers, the New Zealanders Johnson and Fox, had gone with 21 on the board.

Quite a thick mist had by now descended on the ground and obviously conditions were difficult – one can perhaps imagine the reaction of Mr H.D. Bird and his colleagues were that to happen in a match in which they were standing – but the cricket went on and MCC wickets continued to fall. Burns, Harrison and Douglas all got in and got out, the first four wickets falling to medium-fast local bowler Ernest Upham. He was one of those players who favoured wearing his cap back to front whilst bowling, took a run of about ten paces and could often produce a ball that broke back viciously. He had already played six times for New Zealand – this was only their eleventh official match – and had been selected for the first game but wasn't available. On this evidence he might have made a considerable difference, for having reduced them to 79 for 5 at stumps he struck twice more next morning. Page and Branston had taken the score to 127 before he did so, but all the rest of the innings could produce was 18 from de Trafford in four minutes; with Fisher taking 4 for 25 to go with Upham's 6 for 84, MCC were all out for 160.

At least the sun was shining, even if the pitch was crumbling. Sale, the

New Zealand opener, twice had his bat knocked from his hands by Douglas, and the first three wickets went down for 33. The fight back began with Haddon and Hemus. Alf 'Bull' Haddon was an Australian, a powerful forcing batsman with plenty of strokes and he began to demonstrate them as soon as he arrived at the crease. With dark close-cropped hair he looked very much the tough Aussie, and he now proceeded to hook and pull and cut and drive his adopted country out of trouble. The more punishment he meted out the faster Douglas tried to bowl, and of course his accuracy suffered as a result; sixteen came from one over. With Hemus he put on 48 before he was joined by his captain. The ball was flying all over the place by now; Williams was struck twice on the elbow and Haddon took so much punishment to his hands that he wasn't able to field next day. Yet they put on 107 for the fifth wicket in one of the best pieces of batting that New Zealand cricket had thus far known; May described Haddon's innings as 'the finest recorded against us during the whole tour'. When he was out for 71 Fisher helped his captain put on 38 for the seventh wicket and the innings eventually closed on the third morning for 249, with Williams undefeated for a fine and courageous 72. Maybe George Simpson-Hayward, the lob bowler who had caused the home teams plenty of problems, would have made a difference had he not missed the game with an injured finger. Or maybe not.

Clearly MCC were going to have trouble getting the 255 they needed to win and word went round Wellington that exciting things were happening. Hundreds of people began climbing over the fence to get in, much to the wrath of the officials who were worried that this might mean no more big matches at the ground. Those who made it into the ground must have been overjoyed simply to see what was unfolding before them – as overjoyed as the NZCC member who bet £5 to £1 on a home victory. Both the openers went with only 4 on the board, and then Burns, who had made a confident start, fell to an astonishing one-handed running catch by Sale; 18 for 3. Knowing they could win, the New Zealanders fielded splendidly. The fourth wicket went at 44, but then Douglas and Page made 50 together before departing in quick succession. Fisher, left-arm fast medium, was having a memorable day, swinging the ball around, taking wickets with his slower delivery, and eventually finishing with 5 for 61. At the fall of the ninth wicket only 157 were on the board and the crowd must have been almost delirious; and then the last pair came up with a partnership that made the earlier batting look pathetic. On this very difficult pitch, without taking any apparent risk, Curwen and May scored at the rate of two a minute, running beautifully together and thoroughly rattling the fielders.

They had added 41 before Fisher took a return catch off May, leaving MCC all out for 198 and New Zealand the winners by 56 runs. It was the first ever victory over an English team, and even if there were disgruntled English writers who had to point out that MCC were very tired at the end of an arduous tour, it was still an admirable, as well as historic, triumph.

According to Percy May, it was not just the travelling and playing that were arduous; he freely concedes that the 'strenuous pleasure-seeking' may sometimes have affected their play. Socially, it was clear, the tour was a total success. An Auckland newspaper wrote that 'those who were brought in contact with the Marylebone players on and off the field had no hesitation in expressing the opinion that they were a jolly fine lot of players, whom it was a pleasure to meet. We have of late years been inclined to dub the English amateur cricketer a "snob" . . . It is, therefore, particularly refreshing to find that the present team put on no airs or side, but treat their opponents as persons fit to disport with them on the playing field.' We may smile, secure in the worldly-wisdom of the late twentieth century, or we may turn purple at the thought that there must have been many so-called sportsmen, and especially cricketers, who did *not* treat their opponents as persons fit to disport with them on the playing field; but our reaction is irrelevant, and all that matters is that many thousands were entertained by good cricket, the home players learned from the tourists – and maybe the tourists not only enjoyed themselves but learned a thing or two as well. Unfortunately the tour had made a loss of around £950, but on the credit side Randall Johnson believed the standard of New Zealand cricket had improved by about twenty-five per cent in the past four years.

There was one important development in New Zealand cricket at this time. In September 1906 a lawyer from Auckland, E.C. Beale, wrote to the Governor-General, Lord Plunket, suggesting that as the new interprovincial rugby competition had been so successful he might consider presenting a 'Plunket Shield' for competition among the leading cricket associations. The idea was duly taken up and it was won for the first time by Canterbury. It was to undergo various changes over the years, and was eventually replaced by the Shell Cup and Shell Trophy in 1975–6. The fact that in England the County Championship had been officially constituted since 1890, in Australia the Sheffield Shield had begun in 1892–3, in South Africa the Currie Cup had begun in 1889–90, and in the West Indies there had been an intercolonial tournament since 1892–3, indicates how far behind the New Zealanders were. At least they were now under way.

*

New Zealanders v MCC
Basin Reserve, Wellington 8, 9, 11 March 1907
Toss: New Zealanders

New Zealanders

J.D. Lawrence	c Branston b Douglas	13	b Douglas	18
E.V. Sale	run out	19	b Douglas	6
J.J. Mahoney	c Branston b Douglas	17	c Burns b Douglas	1
A. Haddon	c Branston b Douglas	5	c Johnson b May	71
L.G. Hemus	b Douglas	38	c Page b Branston	28
K.H. Tucker	b Douglas	23	(7) b May	1
A.B. Williams*†	b Douglas	19	(6) not out	72
A.H. Fisher	lbw b Branston	10	c & b Douglas	19
A.D. Downes	run out	0	st Fox b Branston	1
J.H. Bennett	b Douglas	5	c Douglas b Branston	3
E.F. Upham	not out	2	c Johnson b Douglas	4
Extras	(b8, lb5, nb1)	14	(b17, lb6, nb2)	25
Total		165		249

Fall of wickets: 30, 50, 50, 63, 120,
127, 152, 152, 158, 165

20, 26, 33, 81, 188, 190,
228, 231, 242, 249

	O	M	R	W	O	M	R	W
Douglas	24.4	9	49	7	19.4	3	75	5
Torrens	18	4	40	0	18	5	47	0
Branston	11	2	38	1	14	3	37	3
May	4	1	24	0	11	1	57	2
Curwen					2	0	8	0

MCC

P.R. Johnson	b Upham	4	b Fisher	4
R.H. Fox†	b Upham	13	run out	0
W.B. Burns	lbw b Upham	24	c Sale b Upham	14
W.P. Harrison	c Downes b Upham	17	c Mahoney b Fisher	5
J.W.H.T. Douglas	c Mahoney b Fisher	18	lbw b Bennett	37
C.C. Page	c Downes b Upham	27	c Hemus b Fisher	27
G.T. Branston	c Williams b Upham	28	b Downes	20
C.E. de Trafford*	b Fisher	18	c Tucker b Fisher	10
W.J.H. Curwen	b Fisher	0	not out	30
A.A. Torrens	b Fisher	4	b Downes	9
P.R. May	not out	0	c & b Fisher	19
Extras	(b5, lb2)	7	(b21, lb2)	23
Total		160		198

Fall of wickets: 12, 21, 50, 75, 79,
127, 152, 154, 158, 160

3, 4, 18, 44, 94, 97,
114, 141, 157, 198

	O	M	R	W	O	M	R	W
Upham	31	7	84	6	22	5	51	1
Downes	11	4	27	0	9	1	27	2
Bennett	9	3	17	0	14	4	36	1
Fisher	13.3	5	25	4	22.2	6	61	5

The New Zealanders won by 56 runs

As the world returned to normal after the First World War, thoughts turned once more to the important things of peace-time life, such as cricket tours. There was a suggestion that MCC might send a team to New Zealand in 1920–1 under Lionel Troughton of Kent, but it didn't materialise; instead an Australian team went there, so at least they were not deprived of competition. The following year MCC assembled an amateur team to make the trip, only to be told by the NZCC that the players selected were not considered good enough to attract the crowds and so make it a financially profitable enterprise; could more big names not be found? Apparently they couldn't and so the NZCC withdrew its invitation, leading to a spot of temporary unpleasantness. Agreement was reached the following year, however, that a team under A.C. MacLaren would be taken out in 1922–3, playing four games in Australia, moving on to New Zealand and then playing four games on the way back. The Australians generously agreed that if the NZCC paid all travel and hotel bills they could take three-quarters of the net profits of the games in Australia and MCC also agreed to meet half of any loss the tour might make overall. Since MacLaren – who had proposed back in September 1921 that he take a team to New Zealand – was very popular in Australia it was hoped that his presence would be sufficiently attractive to bring in the crowds in New Zealand as well.

Archie MacLaren was one of the most interesting characters of an era in which interesting characters were ten a penny. The son of a Manchester businessman, he loved to convey the idea that he should really have been a peer of the realm; he had a patrician bearing and aristocratic mien that sat very readily with batting that was often majestic. For Neville Cardus, a fellow Mancunian who had idolised him as a boy, he was 'the noblest Roman', the man about whom Cardus would wax more lyrical than any other. The lyricism was on account of his batting, which was as powerful, dominating and dismissive of the ball as anyone's in this age of golden batsmen; he was the Ted Dexter of his age and until Graeme Hick repeated the feat in 1988 he was the only man ever to score four hundred in one innings in England, his 424 at Taunton in 1895 coming at a time when he had just missed several games because of a teaching commitment. What Cardus's lyricism would not have referred to, however, was his character, for he was a mass of contradictions; he could be warm and charming one moment, happily telling some story with all the flair of the born raconteur, and bloody-minded, tactless and petty the next. For an intelligent man he could be remarkably haughty and abrasive, was often humourless and intolerant, and frequently sponged money from his professionals – yet when he did have money he would be generous to a fault.

*Imperious to the last, Archie MacLaren ended his first-class career
with 200 not out at Wellington in 1922–3.*

What he didn't know about cricket tactics could be written on a postage stamp – but what he did know about man management could be carved on a pinhead. As a captain he was an excellent judge of a player and of the way a game was going as well as being a master of field-placings. His grasp of tactics was such that C.B. Fry said that he played the game as a kind of athletic chess, and that when playing Lancashire you felt as though you were playing against a brain. Yet he seemed to have very little idea that his players might actually need encouragement, and his imperious nature and authoritarian manner would sometimes produce feelings of inferiority and resentment in his own team as well as in the opposition. He was criticised for being pessimistic and prone to depression; some of his players denied this, but there was no doubt that his aristocratic airs could lead to a feeling of hostility about some matches, and for Fry he was 'an iron and joyless captain'. Because of his tactical awareness he was for years regarded as the best captain in England, and although Lancashire won the Championship only once under his leadership they were rarely far from the top; yet his record as the England captain is a very disappointing one, even if he did have some wretched luck at times. He led his country twenty-two times, the record for an Englishman against Australia, but he won only four and lost no fewer than eleven – and, most important of all, he never won the Ashes.

His abrasive nature meant that he upset many people over the years and so there was never a shortage of critics ready to sharpen their knives; but his differences of opinion with the MCC and the selectors, and his forceful way of expressing himself, made him very popular with the Australians as they saw in him a spirit akin to themselves. As some of his finest performances had come in Australia, especially at Sydney, they had also been able to admire his batting at its best – hence the belief that his presence on this 1922–3 trip would draw the crowds in big numbers. As he would be 51 soon after the tour began, it was very much his swansong.

The team which MacLaren took to New Zealand was composed mostly of young amateurs, with 'Tich' Freeman and Harry Tyldesley flying the professional flag. Few of those amateur names will be familiar to the modern fan apart from Percy Chapman and Freddie Calthorpe, both of whom became England captain, but there were some good players among them. MacLaren had not been able to have the final word in the composition of the squad, but most of them were of his choosing and he seems to have had a belief in the gifted young Oxbridge type. In 1921 he had, after all, pulled off perhaps his greatest triumph when he beat Armstrong's all-conquering Australians at Eastbourne with a team of young amateurs, none of whom had been selected for that summer's Tests and he evidently saw no reason to change his policy. It was some way from being a full-strength England side as there was an official tour of South Africa taking place at the same time – the fact that New Zealand were getting very much second best may have prodded MCC into their offer to make up half of any shortfall in takings – but it would give the New Zealanders some of the experience that they badly needed. MacLaren told the New Zealanders when he arrived that they could expect more problems from his bowlers than his batsmen, although both were generally to prove too good for the home players. One interesting inclusion in the party was the New Zealander Tom Lowry, who was currently playing in England; he will feature very prominently in these pages before too long.

Three of the initial four games in Australia ended in defeat for the Englishmen, with the other drawn. Their opening first-class game in New Zealand – this was, incidentally, the first tour by an English team in which there were no games against odds – was a rain-affected draw, which was followed by two convincing victories, the second being briefly interrupted by an earthquake which set buildings moving but did no damage. Next on the agenda was the first unofficial 'Test', to be played at Wellington.

New Zealand were captained in the first two 'Tests' by Nesbit, or 'Nessie', Snedden, an all-rounder who had been playing for Auckland since 1909. A solicitor by profession, he was a sound batsman with a career average over 30 and a useful medium-pace bowler, one of the many New Zealanders who benefited in his young days from the coaching of the former Sussex and England all-rounder Albert Relf, who had settled there. In all he represented New Zealand nine times just before and after the war, including a tour of Australia in 1913–14. He was considered to be a fine captain with a sound knowledge of the game, but there were some objections to his appointment, principally from Wellington where they were put out that one of their men – either Brice or Collins, they weren't fussy which – had not been given the honour. He was appointed one of the selectors for this series, a job he was to do many times in the next fifteen years. In the event his captaincy, at least in the first game, received plenty of criticism; he was accused of operating his bowlers poorly, not setting his fields properly, and generally failing to provide inspirational leadership. Perhaps he just had a bad day.

Certainly he was hampered by the loss through injury of his first-choice wicket-keeper, Rowntree, for the replacement, Condliffe, although not doing too badly overall, made mistakes that were to cost his team dearly. MacLaren won the toss in the first game and batted, but New Zealand made a good start by sending back the first three batsmen for 61. Immediately before lunch the fourth wicket went down for 108, with Condliffe having missed a chance to stump Calthorpe. MacLaren was given a fine reception; but then came very close to being run out before he had even scored. He played a ball to fine leg and set off for a run, only to change his mind and scramble back to the crease. Reports differ on what actually happened: one says that the fielder took it cleanly and only a fumble by the wicket-keeper allowed him to get back in time, while another says that the throw was 'execrable' and the keeper could be excused for not taking it. Whatever happened, it was a very significant miss. Calthorpe soon departed for 63, but then Lowry joined his captain. Up to this point the bowling and fielding had been good, but as these two fine batsmen tore into them they went to pieces. In an hour and three minutes 128 runs were scored, one flat-batted hook for six from MacLaren making a deep impact on both the fielding side and the spectators for its sheer power. Lowry fell for 54 but, with Brand now supporting him, MacLaren pressed on, reaching his century in 130 minutes with a boundary, although he had been nearly run out again in the nineties. When Brand went for 33 the score was 342 for 7, whereupon MacLean came in and immediately set about the bowling. By the close the score was 432 for 7, MacLaren 162 and MacLean 55. Next morning they took the score to 499 before MacLean was out, his 84 having come in almost even time. MacLaren had had two or three fortunate moments but was now on 194; a single, a four and a single and he had his double century, scored in just under four and a half hours. Not bad for someone aged 51.

With the board showing 505 for 8 he declared; and then took a slip catch to dismiss Hiddleston, New Zealand's best batsman – their first to score a century before lunch in a first-class match – for just 5 runs. By lunch the innings was in tatters at 29 for 4, and though Shepherd made an effort to stem the tide with 33, the wickets kept falling. Only Garrard (47) and Allcott (38), with a stand of 70 for the eighth wicket, pushed the total up near the 200 mark, and the last man went at 222. That last man, Brice, had been dropped first ball by MacLaren, but he made amends when Brice had 16 to his name. The bowling honours went principally to Freeman, whose 40 overs brought him 5 for 114. Before the end of the second day New Zealand were following on – and losing a wicket immediately. Hiddleston and Blunt saw them to 49 for 1 overnight, but when they both went early next morning they were followed by their team-mates in depressingly rapid succession. Five players failed to trouble the scorers as MacLaren took three more catches for a match total of five and Freeman and Gibson took five wickets each, for 72 and 42 respectively, leaving Freeman with match figures of 10 for 186. An all out total of 127 and defeat by an innings and

156 runs naturally earned the wrath of the press, but the main problem was that the home batsmen simply had had too little experience of high-class spin bowling.

MacLaren's innings, while not chanceless, was a splendid achievement for a man of his age and he received many telegrams of congratulation. During the match, though, an old knee injury had flared up and on the doctor's advice he didn't play again on the tour. When he returned home he made an attempt to get back to fitness again, but in the end he gave up the struggle and officially retired. Perhaps at heart he wasn't really sorry; 200 not out in one's last first-class innings is an exit in the grand manner that would appeal to most people. To someone as proud and imperious as MacLaren the injury must have seemed almost heaven-sent.

The man who took over the captaincy was Lieutenant-Colonel 'Jock' Hartley who, at the age of 47, was rather the odd one out of the rest of the team. He had served in both the Boer War and the Great War, had four times been mentioned in dispatches and had a number of decorations, but his military commitments precluded him from playing much cricket. His big cricketing moment had come way back in the University match of 1896, when his slow-medium leg-breaks took eleven wickets to set up an Oxford win; the year before that he had gone on an all-amateur tour to North America without distinguishing himself, and he was later to play occasion-ally for Sussex. In 1905–6 he found himself in the MCC party touring South Africa and he played in two Tests; but 15 runs at 3.75 and 1 wicket for 115 didn't exactly cement his place in the team. Since he had achieved nothing of note for so long one might justifiably wonder what he was doing there at all; David Kynaston, in his book on the tour, *Archie's Last Stand*, suggests that he was 'presumably drafted in by the MCC to act as an "establishment" antidote to MacLaren's vagaries'. In the event his captaincy on the field seems to have been capable if uninspired and the local press didn't miss out on the opportunity to criticise him for lack of imagination in the second 'Test'. Off the field, as we shall see, he failed to charm.

New Zealand made four changes to their team for the Christchurch match and the newcomers, Dacre, Bernau, McGirr and Lambert, all justified their inclusion. Snedden won the toss, chose to bat, and Collins promptly cut the first ball for four. Only Snedden himself and Garrard of the main batsmen failed; Collins went on to a fine 102 in just 133 minutes, Shepherd made 66, Blunt 33, while of the new men Dacre scored a rapid 45, McGirr 40 not out and Lambert 33. A first innings total of 375 made in good time meant that a large crowd turned up next day. They saw their heroes take the first two wickets for 43, but they also saw four catches go down, one of which enabled Chapman to score 50 more than he should have done. With Wilkinson he put on 129 for the third wicket, but then there was something of a collapse; Lowry's 61 shored things up, but the seventh wicket went down at 272. Hartley, however, did his captain's stuff – one can imagine him reflecting that the Colonel mustn't let down his troops – and produced an undefeated 60; Brand, Gibson and Freeman all gave him some support, and on the third morning the innings closed at 384, a lead of nine. Despite the dropped catches the fielding was generally good, and the two new bowlers, McGirr and Bernau, took four wickets apiece. At least one local paper felt that Hartley should have instructed his batsmen to push the score along faster, but since the 384 was made in 349 minutes it is a trifle difficult to take the criticism too seriously.

When three New Zealand wickets then went down for 54 the home fans must have feared a collapse, but Snedden and Dacre each scored 58 to halt the slide. Admittedly 164 for 3 soon became 182 for 7, but then Lambert and Bernau made 88 for the eighth wicket and by tea the score was 270 for 8, Snedden enjoying the rare treat of a declaration. A total of 262 was needed in the last session for victory and not even MacLaren would have attempted that. Hartley certainly didn't, but New Zealand bowled well enough to take five wickets for 145 and suggest that with a bit more time they might have caused real embarrassment.

Before the third game, which like the first was at Wellington, the New Zealand selectors managed to get into a tangle over their team. A telegram to Snedden from one of the other selectors was not properly addressed and went astray, and he, believing he had not been consulted about the composition of the team, took umbrage. He wanted Brice to play as he had just taken 10 for 97 for Wellington, and when he was omitted Snedden resigned from both the selection committee and the team – upon which the other selectors did the simple thing and replaced him with Brice. The captaincy was given to David Collins, so presumably the Wellingtonians who had complained when Snedden was appointed were at least satisfied.

Collins had rowed in the boat race for Cambridge as well as winning his cricketing Blue, performing well in a side that was soundly beaten in both his years. Known as a good forcing batsman and an excellent captain, he had recently been lured back into first-class cricket and was now captain of Wellington, but he was also short on regular practice. He was a neat batsman, attractive to watch, and superstitious in that he always wore his Cambridge cap whilst batting. David Kynaston recounts a story that once in Dunedin he discovered it was missing from his bag, announced that he would not get any runs, and went for nought in both innings.

*Stan Brice, who played against MCC in 1922–3. He had captained
New Zealand at home to Australia two years earlier.*

David Collins, New Zealand captain in the last game of
the 1922–3 tour. The story that he always wore a
Cambridge cap when batting is clearly not true.

Collins won the toss and was promptly out for a single to the first ball of the second over. Unfortunately it seemed to act as a signal to his team; the second wicket fell at 5, the third at 19 and so on. It was a fast wicket and most of the batsmen made the mistake of playing too much from the back foot. Shepherd made 41, but without the 61 from Bernau at number eight it would have been a very sorry tale; both the English quicker bowlers, Gibson and Calthorpe, bowled very well, Calthorpe reaping most of the rewards with 6 for 53. The total of 166 was passed by 36 by the end of the first day; Chapman was on his way to 71 in the style that had gained him countless friends and admirers as the tour had unfolded and Lowry was heading for a century against his compatriots. Driving beautifully, he went on next morning to 130, and with a sprightly half-century from MacLean the total eventually reached 401.

Bernau's good knock gained him promotion to open with his captain in the second innings, only to encounter the spin of Freeman and fall for 3. Shepherd and Dacre also fell to Freeman, before Collins and Blunt combined for a stand of 104 in 90 minutes. On the face of it this sounds altogether praiseworthy, especially as Collins had been hit on the leg early on and played on in some pain, but the crowd and the press were still critical. What could they have wanted? Once they had been separated that was that; on the third morning, in windy conditions that made batting difficult, Gibson's 4 wickets for 3 runs from 11 overs (5 for 65 in all) saw them all out for 215, the deficit being an innings and 20 runs.

In some ways it was a successful tour and in others it was not. The results on the field were satisfactory enough for the tourists, but there were a number of criticisms of them. Some of them remained aloof and patronising towards the locals, it was claimed, and were unnecessarily extravagant in the expenses they were claiming from the NZCC. The way the two professionals and Ferguson the scorer were treated as second-class citizens and bundled into inferior hotels enraged the democratic New Zealanders. There were complaints that, although one of the primary reasons for the tour had been educational, few of the tourists were able to teach the home players much and were more concerned with just having a good time. The press claimed that Hartley would not accept criticism of his team, and felt that since the NZCC stood to lose financially if the tourists did not attract the crowds then the MCC's attitude should be less selfish and pompous. Others defended the tourists and praised their efforts to play entertaining cricket, but it is difficult to escape the feeling that this was just a diplomatic attempt to smooth things down, and that fundamentally there was widespread disappointment with the whole tour. Perhaps the New Zealanders' prime disappointment lay with their own inability to produce a team capable of giving a good account of themselves, and their frustrations spilled over into grumbles about the tourists – grumbles that were undoubtedly justified.

MacLaren left New Zealand before the rest of the team, and just before he did so he gave an interview in which he said that what New Zealand needed was proper coaching and regular play with other teams, and that a properly selected New Zealand team would provide a good match with any of the English counties. It may have been a touch patronising but it was friendly enough and was well received. As soon as he reached Australia, however, he began to criticise the New Zealanders quite severely: there had been too many provincial matches which produced poor gates and were not worth the time or effort; their bowlers were very poor and didn't know what to do when things were going wrong; their fielding was very weak; the match reports were not worth reading as they were written by people who didn't know what they were about, and so on. The New Zealanders were understandably incensed; why could he not have said all this to their faces?

Hartley's idea of diplomacy was to say that he was unconcerned, that he didn't believe the interview and never read interviews – which no doubt firmly convinced the New Zealanders that their opinion of him was fully justified. For a man who was clearly very brave when confronted by enemy gunfire, Hartley seems to have been very reluctant to face the demands of the press and emerges as singularly inept at the diplomatic side of leading a cricket tour. As for MacLaren's outburst, it was, unfortunately, very much in character; the only people who could have been surprised were those who did not know him. One thing that would have upset him and may have partly accounted for his irritation was that not long before he left New Zealand word had come through that Bill Ponsford had beaten his record for the highest individual score in first-class cricket, with 429 for Victoria against Tasmania. Since it was to be some fifty-five years before Tasmania were admitted to the Sheffield Shield one can imagine that their team was not a strong one, and since Ponsford was playing for a Victorian 'second XI' there was a query about its first-class status. MacLaren was so put out at losing his record that he actually tried to have the match reduced to second-class status, taking issue with the editor of *Wisden* the following year when he gave it the official seal of approval. He lost the battle, and then five years later Ponsford took the record even further when he scored 437 against Queensland, a feat with which not even MacLaren could quibble.

The tour finished with four games in Australia, all of which were drawn. Financially, there was an overall loss of £1,929, of which the MCC duly bore half as agreed; the Saturday crowds had been reasonably good, but the mid-week games had been poorly attended. There were some successes, in particular the batting and fielding of Chapman – who charmed everyone, as he invariably did until things began to turn sour on him in later years – and the bowling of Gibson, but whatever the financial loss on the tour the real problem was that most of the tourists were unable to mix with the New Zealanders on an equal social footing; put simply, they appeared to regard themselves as superior to a bunch of colonials. 'Fergie' Ferguson, the Australian who accompanied them as scorer, blamed MacLaren, saying that he set out to enjoy *himself* on the trip and as a result the whole tour suffered. MacLaren, one suspects, didn't quite see it that way.

1902–3	Christchurch	NZ 164, 214;	Hawke 304, 75–3	Hawke 7 wkts
	Wellington	NZ 274, 84;	Hawke 380	Hawke inns 22 runs
1906–7	Christchurch	NZ 207, 187;	MCC 257, 140–1	MCC 9 wkts
	Wellington	NZ 165, 249;	MCC 160, 198	NZ 56 runs
1922–3	Wellington	MCC 505-8d;	NZ 222, 127	MCC inns 156 runs
	Christchurch	NZ 375, 270-8d;	MCC 384, 145–5	Drawn
	Wellington	NZ 166, 215;	MCC 401	MCC inns 20 runs

1902–3

Lord Hawke's Team
Best batting: P.F. Warner 125   F.L. Fane 124   P.R. Johnson 88   T.L. Taylor 54
Best bowling: G.J. Thompson 6–38, 4–74; 8–128, 3–29   C.J. Burnup 5–8
                E.M. Dowson 4–27   B.J.T. Bosanquet 4–44

New Zealand
Best batting: D. Reese 148   K.H. Tucker 50, 67
Best bowling: S.T. Callaway 3–84; 4–80   A.D. Downes 3–64   E.F. Upham 3–79

Wicket-keepers: C. Boxshall (NZ) 2 dismissals   A.B. Williams (NZ) 1 dismissal
                  A.D. Whatman (Lord Hawke's Team) 3 dismissals

1906–7

MCC
Best batting: P.R. Johnson 99, 76*   R.H. Fox 47   J.W.H.T. Douglas 40
Best bowling: J.W.H.T. Douglas 5–56, 4–51; 7–49, 5–75   P.R. May 5–42

New Zealand
Best batting: A.B. Williams 72*   J.J. Mahoney 71*   A. Haddon 71   E.V. Sale 66
                J.D. Lawrence 51
Best bowling: E.F. Upham 6–84   A.H. Fisher 4–25, 5–61   A.D. Downes 4–83

Wicket-keepers: C. Boxshall (NZ) 1 dismissal   A.B. Williams (NZ) 1 dismissal
                  R.H. Fox (MCC) 1 dismissal

1922–3

MCC

Batting	Innings	NO	HS	Runs	Average
A.C. MacLaren	1	1	200*	200	—
J.C. Hartley	2	1	60*	76	76.00
T.C. Lowry	4	0	130	258	64.50
J.F. MacLean	4	1	84	152	50.66
W.A.C. Wilkinson	4	1	59	144	48.00

Bowling	Overs	M	Runs	W	Average
F.S.G. Calthorpe	80.4	23	225	14	16.07
A.P. Freeman	161.3	48	413	18	22.94
C.H. Gibson	161	47	426	18	23.66
D.F. Brand	42	8	187	6	31.16

New Zealand

Batting	Innings	NO	HS	Runs	Average
H.N. Lambert	4	1	47*	114	38.00
D.C. Collins	6	0	102	198	33.00
C.C.R. Dacre	4	0	58	124	31.00
C.F.W. Allcott	3	1	38*	54	27.00
J.S.F. Shepherd	6	0	66	159	26.50

Bowling	Overs	M	Runs	W	Average
E.L.H. Bernau	59	11	187	7	26.71
D.J. McBeath	27	6	81	3	27.00
J.S.F. Shepherd	20	1	84	3	28.00
A.N.C. Snedden	25.3	3	86	3	28.66
H.M. McGirr	62.5	8	192	5	38.40

Wicket-keepers: J.W. Condliffe (NZ) 4 dismissals   W. Cate (NZ) 0 dismissals
J.F. MacLean (MCC) 7 dismissals

— 3 —

Schoolboys in Long Trousers

Sixty-three years, almost a whole lifetime, after George Parr's visit New Zealand were invited to tour England. Probably that invitation owed more than anything to the keenness of the New Zealand officials in promoting their country's cricket; they may have had just the one success twenty years earlier in representative matches against England, but it was obvious that unless the players were given the opportunity to develop then progress would be difficult and slow. The problem for the New Zealand Cricket Council, of course, was that tours cost money, considerably more than it had in the bank. However, a lovely solution was found to this, one that was at the same time business-like and patriotic. A limited liability company was formed called New Zealand Cricket Ltd, and a total of 11,407 shares valued at £1 each were sold throughout the country. None of the subscribers was able to retire on the profits from his investment, but since Test status was granted largely as a result of the performances on this tour there can't have been many who were dissatisfied with their outlay.

For the tour to be a success the choice of captain was clearly of vital importance. Come the hour, come the man. By one of those happy chances, exactly the right leader was available.

Tom Lowry came from one of those sporting families which New Zealand seems to produce so easily. His father owned racehorses, his brothers were notable rugby and tennis players, one of his sisters married R.H.B. Bettington – who in 1923 became the first Australian to captain Oxford and whose 11 wickets for 85, gained with the help of a thunderstorm, played a major part in giving Oxford the biggest ever win in the University match – and another sister married Percy Chapman, one of England's most successful of all captains. Chapman and Lowry, both big, strong young men who enjoyed a sociable evening together, gained themselves something of a reputation for living life to the full, as the euphemism has it; but their skylarks were invariably in a good spirit and never led them into trouble. Lowry followed Chapman into the Cambridge team in 1923

Tom Lowry, New Zealand's first Test captain and one of their best.

and the following year captained them to a nine-wicket win in the University match that must have been especially sweet after the hammering of the previous game. During his undergraduate days he also turned out a number of times for Somerset, his qualification being, so the story of the time had it, that he had been born in Wellington; the fact that Wellington, Somerset and Wellington, New Zealand lack a common identity was conveniently disregarded by everyone – as was the fact that he was actually born in Napier. If this is true it shows that English cricket's administrators were perhaps not as inhuman as they have sometimes been painted; but it is curious that at exactly this time Lord Harris was managing to have Walter Hammond barred from playing for Gloucestershire for the best part of a season on the grounds that, as he had been born in Kent, he had not completed the necessary qualifying period of residence in his new county. The fact that Kent was Harris's county was, of course, quite irrelevant to the issue.

Lowry was an attacking batsman, not renowned for elegance but very powerful and determined and often the man for a crisis, with eighteen first-class centuries to his name. For part of his career he was also a wicket-keeper, so that when he wasn't behind the stumps he was a fine slip fielder – and he was also an occasional slow bowler who deceived his victims by giving the ball plenty of air. However, he is today remembered principally for his captaincy; not simply that he was New Zealand's first Test captain but that he was one of her very best leaders. He combined an astute cricketing brain with the ability to inspire his men and a firm personality that would brook no misdemeanours, especially lateness; yet the iron rod was never too rigid, for like his brother-in-law he believed that the game was primarily about enjoyment. He was also an excellent diplomat and his teams left a fine impression on the English press and public of their friendliness and sportsmanship; this was in the days when friendliness and sportsmanship were widely regarded as important. Never one for half measures, he would set out to win by playing positive and entertaining cricket; fine sentiments, of course, to which many a captain would sub-scribe, and Lowry was lucky to have under him a team of like-minded souls who, despite their inexperience, were good enough cricketers to put up several creditable performances against supposedly more powerful opposi-tion. It is quite possible that had they had a lesser captain on this tour New Zealand would have had to wait for several more years before entering the Test arena. For Robertson-Glasgow he was 'strong, versatile, courageous, original, and a leader in a thousand. His comments on the run of play, had they reached the spectators, would alone have justified the Entertainment Tax. . . He was a man first and a cricketer second, but it was a close finish.'

Modesty was the keynote of the tour. To those few members of the press who bothered to record their arrival Lowry said that his players felt like schoolboys wearing long trousers for the first time and, continuing the theme, insisted that the tour was primarily an educational one. Because the NZCC had instructed the selectors to pick players with at least ten years cricket ahead of them they were a fairly inexperienced squad, but hoped, Lowry said, to put up something of a show against the less strong counties. Probably this was genuinely meant, but one can't help wondering whether, at least in part, it was a deliberate ploy to lull the opposition.

If so, it may have succeeded quite well. The first fixture was a two-day non-first-class match against H.M. Martineau's XI in which the tourists scored 586 for 9 declared and then came close to dismissing the opposition twice. The second fixture was against MCC at Lord's, very much a baptism of fire; it was hardly the first-choice England team, but it contained five past

Left to right: Matthew Henderson, Tom Lowry, Stewie Dempster, Bert McGirr. They all played for Wellington, all toured England in 1927 and all played in the first Test series.

or future Test players, including three Test captains, and was a pretty useful amateur squad. On a cold and overcast day, in front of a very poor crowd, MCC batted first and were soon profiting from the fact that New Zealand were clearly nervous. New Zealand have produced few outstanding slip fielders over the years and have often lost matches through poor catching; this was a definite minus mark on the 1927 tour and they were to pay dearly for one catch that went down early on.

Charles Titchmarsh, the Hertfordshire player who had toured New Zealand with MacLaren in 1922-3 and who was now 46, was dropped in the slips very early on – and went on to make 171 at considerable speed, cutting and driving with great relish. He was supported by Allen and Douglas in particular, the latter in one of his dour Johnny Won't Hit Today moods, and all of the bowlers came in for punishment. As a pointer to the future the pick of the bowlers was the 18-year-old Bill Merritt, playing in only his third first-class game and sending down leg-breaks and googlies that caused the batsmen plenty of problems. Calthorpe and Haig made useful contributions lower down the order, and forty minutes before the close MCC were all out for 392. Thus far it had not been a greatly distinguished New Zealand performance, but in the half hour that was left Blunt and Mills put on no fewer than 51 – an excellent demonstration of the way in which approaches to cricket have changed over the years, for presumably no one had told them that in such circumstances the first priority is to survive until morning.

Next day the sun was shining, but before long New Zealand had lost four wickets for 107 and the follow-on was beckoning. And then Dacre, the vice-captain, joined Ken James, the wicket-keeper, and within an hour 79 had been scored. When James was out Lowry joined Dacre, and in a savage onslaught they flayed the bowlers for 115 in forty-five breathless minutes of high-class, murderous batsmanship in which no chance was offered. Both reached their centuries in ninety minutes, and if they both fell soon afterwards they had transformed the game.

Ces Dacre never did play Test cricket, but he had the great satisfaction of knowing that he had helped his country to achieve Test status. He had set a world record by making his first-class début for Auckland back in 1914 aged 14 years 7 months, and it had been a great day for him in more ways than one; not only could he now call himself a cricketer, but for the first time in his life he had worn long trousers. Stocky and strong, he was a batsman of enormous power who often scored very quickly once he got going, and he played many an exciting innings; but he was too inconsistent and too uncertain a starter to be reckoned a great player. Having started the tour with two centuries (he got one against Martineau's team) his form rather fell away, although he did come up with a splendid 176 against Derbyshire. At the end of the tour he decided to stay in England and qualify for Gloucestershire, with whom he had a family connection, and he played for them regularly until 1936; he produced some fine innings but, according to *Wisden*, never made quite the number of runs that he promised. Dick Brittenden tells a nice little story about the prelude to this innings against MCC which shows Dacre's character: when Page returned to the dressing room after being dismissed he found Dacre padded up but sound asleep. On waking up he asked what the bowlers were doing and was told that Calthorpe was swinging a bit. 'I'll give him swing', he said, and was soon marching out to put them all to the sword. Most anecdotes require lines such as 'I'll give him swing' to be in a Yorkshire accent, and it's rather pleasing to think of the gentle New Zealanders adopting such an approach.

As so often after a partnership like that the next batsman, Bernau, went for nought; but then McGirr and Merritt carried on past the MCC total and took the score to 460, scored from only 519 balls. Half an hour or so was then lost to bad light before the MCC openers, Lyon and Titchmarsh, put on an undefeated 96 by close of play, helped by below-par bowling and well-below-par fielding — Merritt saw five chances go begging from his bowling. Not until the first wicket had put on 188 did New Zealand break through next morning, but there was to be little joy for them. The first four MCC batsmen all scored heavily, Lyon and Allen recording centuries and Allen and Ashton putting on 194 for the third wicket. Chapman rounded things off by scoring 24 in 10 minutes, and when he was out Douglas declared at 426 for 4, leaving the visitors three and a half hours to score 359. Mills went early on, but they scored in more than even time to finish on 224 for 4; once again it was Lowry and Dacre who provided the fireworks, and for the last half hour Lowry and Dempster were knocking them around at almost two a minute. Allen added three more wickets to give him 10 for 156 overall and with a century as well the game was a great personal triumph for him.

A grand total of 1,502 runs had been scored in the match, a new record for Lord's — 443 on the first day, 505 on the second with half an hour lost to the weather, and 554 on the third. The game was accounted a great success; they had shown that they possessed some quality batsmen who could destroy a good bowling attack and that they could hold their own against a good MCC team. They had shown, in short, that they were more or less ready for Test cricket. Since then New Zealand have put up several excellent performances at Lord's in both Tests and MCC matches (and one or two desperate ones) but none has been nearly as important as this first one.

The best all-round performance of the tour came from Roger Blunt, and it was good enough to earn him the distinction of being the first New Zealander to be one of *Wisden*'s five cricketers of the year; he scored more runs than anyone else, 1,540 at 44, and his 78 wickets at just under 25 were surpassed only by Merritt. He was still at school when he entered first-class cricket, playing principally as a leg-break bowler — once as a youngster he hit the leg stump with a ball that was called wide — but he was soon polishing up his batting until he became a very high-class all-rounder. His batting, always stylish and elegant, sometimes quite glorious, developed so much, in fact, that he became the highest-scoring batsman in New Zealand cricket, his 7,769 runs standing as the national record until it was passed by Bert Sutcliffe in 1953. He was also the holder of the highest individual score

(Above)   *Trent Bridge, 1973.
Alan Knott held England's lower
order together with an innings of 49.*

(Left)   *Glenn Turner on his way to
his 100th century. He did it in the
grand manner, with 311 not out
against Warwickshire.*

(Right)   *Trent Bridge, 1973. Dennis Amiss on his way to 138 not out, his first Test century in England.*

(Below)   *Trent Bridge, 1973. John Parker is snapped up by England captain Ray Illingworth off the bowling of John Snow.*

(Left)   *Derek Underwood, who took 48 wickets in just eight Tests against New Zealand.*

(Below)   *Will he be out? New Zealand captain Bev Congdon watches anxiously as the ball eludes Norman Gifford.*

*Hedley Howarth, elder brother of Geoff, who for several years was
New Zealand's leading spin bowler.*

The Oval Test, 1978. Geoff Howarth steers the ball past Ian
Botham on his way to 94.

The Oval Test, 1978. Chris Old bowls, John Wright, later to
become New Zealand captain, watches.

(Right)   *Bob Taylor in front of the stumps rather than behind. Stephen Boock is the fielder.*

(Below)   *Ian Botham opts for safety as New Zealand captain Mark Burgess hits out during an innings of 68 at Lord's in 1978.*

Geoff Howarth in full flow during his innings of 123 at Lord's in 1978.

Ian Botham, England's lion, complete with mane. Not a pretty sight for an opposing bowler.

MCC v New Zealanders
Lord's 11, 12, 13 May 1927
Toss: MCC

MCC

M.D. Lyon	b Bernau	24	b McGirr		110
C.H. Titchmarsh	b Merritt	171	c James b Blunt		71
G.O.B. Allen	c Dempster b Henderson	38	not out		104
H. Ashton	c Page b Merritt	4	lbw b Page		88
A.P.F. Chapman	c Page b Bernau	18	c Dempster b Bernau		24
J.W.H.T. Douglas*	b Blunt	36			
F.S.G. Calthorpe	b Blunt	31			
H.J. Enthoven	b Merritt	0			
N.E. Haig	c James b Henderson	34			
M. Falcon	b Merritt	1			
W.B. Franklin†	not out	10			
Extras	(b15, lb8, nb1, w1)	25	(b18, lb4, nb7)		29
Total		392	(4 wickets declared)		426

Fall of wickets   68, 137, 156, 181, 305,
343, 343, 349, 392

188, 200, 394, 426

	O	M	R	W	O	M	R	W
Henderson	13.5	1	59	2	7	1	26	0
McGirr	12	1	42	0	19	1	78	1
Blunt	25	2	117	2	14	2	62	1
Bernau	17	5	45	2	18.1	1	88	1
Merritt	39	4	104	4	21	1	103	0
Dacre					2	0	8	0
Page					3	0	32	1

New Zealanders

J.E. Mills	b Allen	24	c Douglas b Allen		3
R.C. Blunt	c Calthorpe b Allen	52	c Franklin b Allen		51
M.L. Page	b Calthorpe	8			
C.S. Dempster	c Franklin b Enthoven	2	(6)not out		29
K.C. James†	lbw b Allen	33	(3)b Allen		32
C.C.R. Dacre	c Falcon b Allen	107	(4)b Falcon		37
T.C. Lowry*	b Falcon	106	(5)not out		63
E.H.L. Bernau	lbw b Allen	0			
H.M. McGirr	not out	58			
W.E. Merritt	st Franklin b Allen	40			
M. Henderson	b Allen	4			
Extras	(b11, lb9, nb2, w4)	26	(b7, lb1, nb1)		9
Total		460	(4 wickets)		224

Fall of wickets   83, 92, 106, 106, 185
300, 300, 388, 456, 460

23, 87, 102, 164

	O	M	R	W	O	M	R	W
Allen	26.3	3	120	7	10	2	36	3
Haig	27	4	105	0	10	0	39	0
Calthorpe	15	2	99	1	7	1	22	0
Falcon	8	1	56	1	9	0	41	1
Enthoven	10	0	54	1	15	0	68	0
Douglas					4	1	9	0

Match drawn

by a New Zealander, 338 not out in even time for Otago against Canterbury in 1931, another record that was to be beaten by Sutcliffe; that innings included, incidentally, a tenth-wicket stand of 184 with Bill Hawkesworth, yet the game was still lost. Blunt was to play in nine Tests without really doing full justice to himself; he topped the bowling averages in the 1929–30 series with 9 wickets at 19, and his highest score, 96 in the first Test of 1931, helped to save the game, but overall his Test record is unremarkable. It is fair to say, all the same, that his all-round skills have been bettered only by Richard Hadlee and John Reid for New Zealand. He was awarded the MBE shortly before he died in 1966.

Of twenty-six first-class matches played on that tour seven were won, five lost and fourteen drawn, many of the draws being caused by the traditional 'wettest summer in living memory' that England produces about every third year. Sussex, Worcestershire, East of England, Civil Service, Glamorgan, Somerset and Derbyshire were all beaten; of those counties only Derbyshire, admittedly, finished in the top half of the table, but the victory over them was a crushing one by an innings and 240 runs. Six batsmen scored over a thousand first-class runs, Dempster's 1,430 at 44.68 just pipping Blunt to top the averages. The bowling was the problem, especially as the faster men could get little response from the rather docile wickets they encountered, and the spinners Merritt (107 wickets) and Blunt did a lot more work than the rest. The fielding also let them down, although Ken James, the wicket-keeper, came in for much praise. Overall, though, the tour was accounted a great success, and it was clear that being admitted to Test status was the obvious next step.

*

Nothing matters more to an English cricket fan than getting one over on Australia. If things are not going well on the field, one ploy open to the Englishman is to try and establish some kind of moral superiority by contrasting the attitudes of the two countries towards New Zealand cricket. It isn't a difficult task; for decades Australia's attitude to their neighbour was, to put it politely, lukewarm, while England, even if their visits were very much postscripts to the serious business of an Australian tour, did at least repeatedly make the effort to ensure that New Zealand players were given *some* Test practice. The fact that by the time Australia condescended to play New Zealand for the second time in a Test, as late as 1973–4, England and New Zealand had played forty-three times is something of which Australia really ought to be ashamed. (For the record, by the time of that second Australian Test New Zealand had played South

Africa seventeen times, India sixteen times, Pakistan fifteen times and West Indies fourteen times.) It is not as simple as that, of course, for there have been a good many tours exchanged between the two countries at non-Test level and the Australians could argue, with some justification, that New Zealand did not assert themselves enough and were altogether too humble in their dealings with big cousin across the water. Whatever the rights and wrongs of it, whether an Englishman in the crowd at Sydney, watching his heroes stumbling to defeat, could convince those around him that England's greater responsibility concerning New Zealand put them on a higher ethical plane – that was altogether more important than any single cricket match – must be very questionable. But even as he endures the jeers he can take comfort from the knowledge that once New Zealand achieved Test status England did discharge her 'maternal' duties reasonably conscientiously.

After his triumphant tour of Australia in 1928–9 Percy Chapman left the team and went with his wife to New Zealand to visit her family. Lovely lady though Beet Chapman was, the New Zealanders would have preferred him to have brought his team and participated in some serious cricket, but he was at least able to initiate arrangements for a tour the following winter which would see New Zealand Test cricket officially launched. It was a pity that Chapman himself didn't make that tour, for, as Lowry was the automatic choice as home captain, there would have been something pleasing about New Zealand's first Test series being led by brothers-in-law.

English cricket was strong at this period and would remain so throughout the next decade, although without being able to win back the Ashes that were lost in 1930. The first Tests against West Indies and India were also played around this time (in 1928 and 1932 respectively) and India, like New Zealand, found the going tough. West Indies fared rather better, winning a Test at only the sixth attempt and in 1934–5 winning a series at just the fifth attempt. For now, though, we are in 1929–30, and for the second time (the first having been in 1891–2) there are two England teams on tour to different countries. The team that went to the West Indies, and drew the four-Test series 1–1, was undoubtedly the stronger – no fewer than six Englishmen made their débuts in the first New Zealand Test – but Harold Gilligan, the captain to New Zealand, had under him some very fine players including Woolley and Duleepsinhji. The original choice as captain had been Arthur Gilligan, but when he fell ill his brother replaced him and they remain the only brothers to have captained England.

These four games against New Zealand were Harold Gilligan's only Tests, and he made no outstanding personal contribution; in fact his ability as an all-rounder was relatively modest – his career batting average of 17 was half his bowling average – and there have undoubtedly been better players who have not felt the selectors gazing benignly upon them. Yet he was certainly a capable captain and the tour was happy and successful, with nine wins and eight draws in New Zealand. Maurice Allom and Maurice Turnbull in their *Book of the two Maurices* cheerfully sing his praises as a fine all-round leader; 'off the field he was masterly', they say. The early part of the tour had involved five games against Australian state teams which the Australians agreed to stage to help meet MCC's costs; against this sterner opposition two matches had been won and two lost. The weather had been such that they had earned themselves the title of 'Drought-breakers' – and it carried on in the same vein in New Zealand.

The great, long-awaited day was 10 January 1930, the venue was Lancaster Park, Christchurch. Lowry won the toss and Dempster and Foley walked proudly out to open for their country. By the end of the first over Foley was back in the pavilion; before long they were 15 for 3, all three wickets falling to Morris Nichols, making his début. And then his partner and fellow débutant, Maurice Allom, produced one of cricket's more remarkable overs: from the first ball Blunt was almost lbw but got a leg-bye; the second ball bowled Dempster; Lowry played and missed at the third and was lbw to the fourth; James was caught behind off the fifth and Badcock was bowled off the sixth. The pitch was fast, a strong wind was blowing, Allom was swerving the ball and New Zealand were 21 for 7. He was to play in only five Tests and take only fourteen wickets, but that over gained Maurice Allom immortality; in well over a thousand Tests only one other bowler, Chris Old against Pakistan in 1978, has taken four wickets in five deliveries – and as the third of those deliveries was a no-ball he missed the hat-trick.

From these depths some honour was saved, principally by Roger Blunt. Helped by Dickinson and Merritt his 45 not out saw his team to 112, and hope must then have flickered when England fell to 20 for 2, Matthew Henderson taking a wicket with his first ball. Duleep, Woolley and Legge then put together some runs and at the close on the first day England were 147 for 4 and coasting along. The whole of the second day, Saturday, was lost to the weather. Monday morning saw a curious time for Lowry; fine captaincy brought a clatter of wickets and England were all out for 181, with Blunt on a hat-trick at one point, but he received a lot of barracking from the crowd, presumably because he was wearing his club cap rather than the national one. In view of the historic nature of the occasion it does seem an odd thing to have done.

In the second innings only Dempster, Page and Lowry were able to give

*On their way to the record books. Jack Mills and Stewie Dempster
photographed at Wellington in January 1930 at the time of their
opening partnership of 276 in New Zealand's second Test match.*

any account of themselves. Three wickets were down before the deficit was erased, and although Lowry top-scored with 40 to try to save the game his team could total no more than 131, leaving England 105 minutes to make 63. Blunt accounted for both openers but England's eight-wicket victory was accomplished in an hour under two days. After the batting success at Lord's in 1927 it was a sad story.

The second Test at Wellington came close to being a very different story. Jack Mills had had to withdraw from the first Test but now he came into the team and played a part in two crucial aspects of the match. He opened with Dempster, and on a lively pitch it wasn't long before Dempster was getting a leg-bye for a ball that had come off his head! They stuck it out, though, and had made 113 by lunch. By tea it was 227 and both had their centuries; to Dempster fell the honour of the first century for New Zealand and to Mills that of the first century on début. They put on 276 before they were parted, 136 to Dempster and 117 to Mills, a partnership that is still the New Zealand record against England and has only once been passed in all of New Zealand's Tests (by Turner and Jarvis against West Indies in 1971–2). Scores of 67 from Page and 36 from Blunt helped the total to 440, with Woolley recording his best Test figures of 7 for 76. The two Maurices suggest that one of the very few tactical mistakes Gilligan made during the tour was not to put Woolley on earlier.

When England fell to 149 for 5 the New Zealand adrenalin must have been racing – too much, perhaps, for catches began to go down. Mills made his second important contribution to the match when he dropped a straightforward one off Nichols, and the 78 not out that he went on to make helped England avoid the follow-on, finishing with 320 on the third morning. Dempster, almost out first ball, had made an undefeated 80 when Lowry declared at 164 for 4, but with only 110 minutes left and a deficit of 284 there was only one result. A beautiful 56 not out from Duleep did at least make the closing stages watchable. Had the catching been better New Zealand could have lost their 'poor relations' tag much earlier than they did; but even without the victory that should perhaps have been achieved the game did project one player to the front of the world's cricketing stage.

Stewie Dempster is not a name with which many present-day English fans will be familiar, and that is a pity. For a few years around this time he was one of the very finest batsmen in the world, usually an opener, and posterity deserves to be taken severely to task for allowing the shadow of Bradman, Hammond and the other leading lights to obscure him. George Headley, the outstanding batsman of West Indies' early years, made his Test début the day after Dempster made his and is still spoken of with reverence and awe;

if Dempster wasn't quite in Headley's league he wasn't far from it, and is long overdue for some recognition. Fairly short and stocky, he was an orthodox, graceful batsman who hit the ball with enormous power and no little style; he loved the off-drive in particular, but hooking, cutting and glancing all came easily to him. Like all the best batsmen he saw the ball early, was quick on his feet, and excelled at finding the gaps. Confidence oozed out of him, as it must do from anyone who could score 723 runs at nearly 66 in just fifteen Test innings. This was five points higher than Headley's, although the West Indian's was sustained over a longer Test career of 40 innings. Perhaps the crucial difference between the two is that Dempster did not have the commitment to his country's cricketing fortunes that Headley did, choosing to play in England for part of his career and so rule himself out of international selection.

Born in 1903, six years before Headley, Dempster was playing for Wellington at 17 without ever having had any coaching, and was an automatic choice for the 1927 tour. This, he said, was when he really learned cricket, and he topped the averages to prove it. In 1931, despite missing several games through injury, he was to score 1,778 runs at 59 with seven centuries, one of which helped save the Lord's Test and another of which was a double-century against Essex. In his last Test against Jardine's tourists in 1932–3 he scored an undefeated 83 out of his team's total of 158 and, had he wanted to, could have boasted afterwards that his innings had delayed the sailing of a passenger liner. He was due to leave on a business trip to England, but because of his innings the captain, a keen cricket fan, announced that the boat would not be able to sail until midnight on the day the game finished. Thereafter he played in the Lancashire League and then qualified for Leicestershire, playing for them from 1935 to 1939, scoring eighteen hundreds and averaging 49. From 1936 to 1938 he was captain, heading the batting averages each year; but since the highest position the county reached in those years was fifteenth we may feel entitled to wonder whether his leadership skills matched his batting skills. Because of some family connection he even managed to represent Scotland during this period and after the War he played a few games for Warwickshire when he was past his best. No doubt the fact that he played only ten Tests is the main reason why he is not better known; had he lived in a later era he could well have been one of the all-time greats.

Jack Mills wasn't in the same class as a batsman, although he was a distinctly useful performer; by coincidence he played the same number of representative games for New Zealand (sixty) as did Dempster, scoring nearly 2,900 runs at 32. He played in seven Tests but this was his only major innings, and his average declined to 26. A left-hander, he was a fine batsman to watch, his driving and cutting aesthetic treats, although perhaps he took too many risks for a top-class batsman. He toured England in 1927 and 1931, making over a thousand runs each time, and scoring over five thousand throughout his career, a substantial figure for New Zealand cricket. If he is now unknown outside his country at least he has an honourable place in the record books.

New Zealand hopes of capitalising on this performance came up against two days of Auckland rain. Gilligan was asked if he would agree to add two days at the end, but said that instructions he had had from MCC forbade this. Just before play started on the third day, however, a message came from England telling him either to agree to an extension or to arrange an extra game, and the latter was decided upon. The formalities that were still the third Test had to be observed, though, and Lowry, having won the toss, decided to field so that the crowd could enjoy the English batting. Bowley, Duleep and Woolley duly obliged, the first two scoring high-class centuries, and in three and a half hours England reached 330 for 4 before Gilligan declared — the kind of statistic that makes a modern-day fan turn green. Even then the fireworks weren't finished as Dempster took over, rattling up 62 not out and hitting the last ball of the match into the crowd. It was all good, clean, meaningless fun.

The additional Test, also at Auckland, produced plenty of runs as Gilligan won the toss and his batsman set about consolidating the series. Only Woolley of the top six failed to make a score, and Geoffrey Legge, all sixteen stones of him, took advantage of a missed stumping chance at 47 to run up 196, his one Test century and an admirable one. Once again the runs were made quickly, 540 of them coming in 445 minutes. If the game was to be saved clearly two or three of the home team would have to put their heads down. Weir was the first to do so, helped by Dempster and Page, and by the close on the second day they were 171 for 4. Early on the last morning two wickets fell quickly, but Lowry and McGirr staved off the collapse, the captain making his highest Test score of 80. In the end the New Zealand innings lasted exactly the same time as England's; their 387 was three runs short of the follow-on target, but there was little time left and Gilligan did not enforce it. There was time, though, for England to lose three wickets for 22, including Legge for a duck.

Of the three full matches that were played, New Zealand's first Test series produced, therefore, a comprehensive defeat, an honourable draw and a draw that would probably have been a victory had the catching been better. By and large it was to become a pretty familiar pattern. Suppose, though,

The one that got away. What might the story of New Zealand's cricket have been had Clarrie Grimmett not gone to Australia?

that a certain gentleman who had been born in New Zealand in 1891 had not emigrated to Australia in 1914 after being left out of the New Zealand team. Clarrie Grimmett was to become one of the greatest of all bowlers, the first to reach 200 Test wickets and for over seventeen years, including the War, the leading Test wicket-taker with 216 victims from 37 Tests – and he didn't make his début till he was 33. He was a leg-break and googly bowler who could suddenly produce a top-spinner – a fastish ball with a late dip, that few bowlers in history have been able to match and which took him endless wickets. He had a couple of seasons with Wellington before going to seek his fortune in Australia, playing first for Victoria and then for South Australia, and making an explosive start to his Test career when he took 11 for 82 against Arthur Gilligan's team in the last match of the 1924–5 series. Partnering first Arthur Mailey and in later years Bill O'Reilly he enjoyed outstanding success, especially in the 1930s when the Australians were such a formidable power. In eight of the ten series in which he played he either took most wickets or headed the Australian averages, and for O'Reilly he was simply a genius, whose presence at the other end made the batsmen so apprehensive that O'Reilly, by his own happy admission, benefited considerably. Grimmett was just 5 feet 7 inches tall, a balding little gnome of a man, who capitalised on his shortness by bowling at eye-level, a trajectory which he insisted makes it harder for the batsman to judge where the ball will land. How New Zealand must have regretted losing him as he won Test after Test for his adopted country; had he stayed, the story of the early years of New Zealand's Test cricket must inevitably have been very different.

The two Maurices reported that a good deal of progress had been made in New Zealand cricket in the last five years. Ted Bowley, the England opener, had coached there for three years from 1925, and said that when he arrived players often turned up for matches without the proper trousers or boots. (In Percy May's book about the 1906–7 tour there are two photographs of batsmen dressed in ordinary clothes; dark trousers and waistcoat. The pictures are posed, of course, and presumably they just didn't have their whites with them when the photographer requested their presence – but it would seem that for many years 'proper' kit was not necessarily the norm in New Zealand.) That had been eradicated, and the Englishmen had found enthusiastic crowds everywhere, so that they set several new gate records. Clearly there was a new spirit abroad.

1927	Lord's	MCC 392, 426–4d;	NZ 460, 224–4d	Drawn
1929–30	Christchurch	NZ 112, 131;	E 181, 66–2	E 8 wkts
	Wellington	NZ 440, 164–4d;	E 320, 107–4	Drawn
	Auckland	E 330–4d;	NZ 96–1	Drawn
	Auckland	E 540, 22–3;	NZ 387	Drawn

1927

MCC
Best batting: C.H. Titchmarsh 171,71   M.D. Lyon 110   G.O.B. Allen 104*
Best bowling: G.O.B. Allen 7–120, 3–36

New Zealand
Best batting: C.C.R. Dacre 107, 37   T.C. Lowry 106, 63*   H.M. McGirr 58*
R.C. Blunt 52, 51

Best bowling: W.E. Merritt 4–104

Wicket-keepers: W.B. Franklin (MCC) 3 dismissals   K.C. James (NZ) 2 dismissals

1929–30 (the first Test series)

England

Batting	Innings	NO	HS	Runs	Average
M.S. Nichols	6	4	78	185	92.50
K.S. Duleepsinhji	6	2	117	358	89.50
G.B. Legge	6	1	196	299	59.80
E.H. Bowley	4	0	109	162	40.50
F.E. Woolley	6	1	59	146	29.20

Bowling	Overs	M	Runs	W	Average
M.J.C. Allom	100.1	24	194	13	14.92
F.E. Woolley	101.3	26	261	13	20.07
M.S. Nichols	84.3	22	202	8	25.25
T.S. Worthington	73.1	14	186	7	26.57
F. Barratt	95	22	197	3	65.66

New Zealand

Batting	Innings	NO	HS	Runs	Average
C.S. Dempster	6	2	136	341	85.25
H.M. McGirr	1	0	51	51	51.00
G.L. Weir	4	1	63	114	38.00
J.E. Mills	4	0	117	139	34.75
C.F.W. Allcott	1	0	33	33	33.00

Bowling	Overs	M	Runs	W	Average
R.C. Blunt	65.4	20	171	9	19.00
F.T. Badcock	82	23	153	7	21.71
G.L. Weir	16	2	50	2	25.00
G.R. Dickinson	40.5	4	134	5	26.80
M.L. Page	23.4	6	63	2	31.50

Wicket-keepers: K.C. James (NZ) 4 dismissals   W.L. Cornford (E) 8 dismissals

In the first match M.J.C. Allom took four wickets in five balls on his Test début; M. Henderson took New Zealand's first Test wicket, that of E.W. Dawson, with his first ball. In the second match C.S. Dempster became the first New Zealander to score a Test century, and J.E. Mills became the first New Zealander to score a Test century on début; their opening partnership of 276 is still New Zealand's highest for any wicket against England.

— 4 —

Playing the Game in the Truest and Best Tradition

Two earthquakes almost brought about the cancellation of the 1931 tour to England. One occurred in Hawkes Bay early in February; the other had had its epicentre in Wall Street, New York back in 1929. The depression of the 1930s hit New Zealand hard, and when the Hawkes Bay disaster compounded the difficulties serious consideration was given to cancellation. By this stage, though, matters were virtually finalised and as it would have been very expensive to call off the tour and impossible to rearrange it for several years the NZCC decided to press on. As an economy measure Tom Lowry was appointed manager as well as captain, although there were those, including the Chairman of Selectors, who disapproved of this on the grounds that the players were there to play and shouldn't be saddled with extra responsibilities. The 1927 tour had made a heavy loss, but once again a limited liability company was set up to provide the finance and twelve thousand £1 shares were issued. A lottery was also held which helped pay for the players' boat fares, a little oddity which brought Lowry some laughs when he mentioned it during a speech in England. The New Zealand people were obviously able to reflect with pride that they had played some small part in getting their country established in international cricket, and the fact that the tour was ultimately very successful despite the difficult background must have been greatly satisfying for all concerned.

The first game, against Essex, produced an innings victory. By the time of the MCC match the tourists had played three county games and Dempster had scored 451 runs at an average of 150. Almost as impressive was the record of the leg-break bowler Bill Merritt who had taken 22 wickets at 18. A cheerful and happy character, he had come over in 1927 as the youngest member of the party, aged just 18, with hardly any first-class experience and then proved to be the most successful bowler in the team with 107 wickets at under 24. After his good start in 1931 he fell away somewhat, but

New Zealand's touring team to England in 1931. Left to right:
back row – H.G. Vivian, A.M. Matheson, R.O. Talbot, I.B.
Cromb, J.E. Mills, G.L. Weir, J.L. Kerr; sitting – R.C. Blunt, M.L.
Page (vice-captain), T.C. Lowry (captain), C.F.W. Alcott, C.S.
Dempster; front – K.C. James, W.E. Merritt

still finished with 99 wickets at 26. Powerful stuff from a young leggie, but he could not match this success in Tests. In the first series he took only eight (very expensive) wickets and after the first two games of 1931 his final Test tally stood at twelve wickets at 51 apiece. However, he was a useful if unorthodox batsman, scoring 538 runs at almost 27 on the first tour and 545 runs at almost 19 in 1931. Like Dempster he then played in the Lancashire League before qualifying for Northamptonshire for whom he played just before and after the War; in 1939 his twelve wickets against Cambridge University helped his county to their first win for four years, but he found little other outstanding success. *Wisden* said that when he was hit he tried to spin the ball more so that his length duly suffered, and that he was inclined to overbowl the googly rather than the more dangerous leg-break. When things went right for him, though, he could be an undoubted match-winner and was certainly one of the best leg-break bowlers to come from New Zealand. Things were about to go very right for him in the MCC game.

Nine of the MCC team were Test players, four of them past or future

England captains. With the one exception of J.W. Hearne the team was all-amateur; it was a very capable side that must have fancied its chances of seeing off the tourists without too much bother. Six of the New Zealanders had played in the corresponding fixture four years earlier. In view of what had happened last time Lowry must have been pleased that 'Gubby' Allen wasn't playing, and in view of what was to happen this time he must have been especially pleased that MCC were captained by Percy Chapman, his brother-in-law.

After heavy rain the day before the skies were dark and ominous, the weather cold and the pitch soft; it was to turn, but only slowly. Lowry won the toss and remarked 'It's just a habit one has.' By lunchtime New Zealand were 114 for 4, only Dempster, Kerr and Talbot having achieved anything worth mention. Then the heavens opened and that was that for the day. In fact that was that until half past three on the second day when at last the frozen spectators had some pyrotechnics to warm them. Talbot came within a foot or so of emulating Albert Trott and putting the ball over the pavilion roof, and then Lowry came in to repeat his performance of four years ago. This time his century took 135 minutes and was completed just before close of play, but it was the same display of powerful, high-quality batsmanship; Jupp in particular was shown the big stick as Lowry chose to step back and hit him against the spin. From being 190 for 7 Lowry was able to declare at the overnight score of 302 for 9 thanks to the support he received from Weir and Merritt, but with only one day left the match seemed moribund.

Enter, firstly, Ian Cromb, an all-rounder from Canterbury who was a fast-medium bowler, a solid lower-middle order batsman and a fine fielder. Quite tall and loose-limbed, *The Times* likened his action to that of Maurice Tate and he could swing and cut the ball; Douglas Jardine said that he 'made the ball come at you so quickly that it hit the bat before the bat could hit the ball', but his bag for this tour was to be a relatively modest 58 wickets at 26. He was to have an inspired spell in his first Test, although like Merritt his Test record is disappointing – in five matches he took only eight wickets at 55. Dick Brittenden wrote that unlike many New Zealand bowlers he was able to work up a real dislike of the batsmen and this spirited attitude gave his bowling the whip which brought wickets. In 1935–6 he captained the New Zealanders against the touring MCC team, he played in the East Lancashire League for some years and also some good standard club cricket until well into his fifties with considerable success. Tuesday 19 May 1931, though, was one of his more memorable days.

Perhaps the most important thing Cromb managed to do was to convince the batsmen that the pitch was doing more than in fact it was, so that they contributed to their own downfall. Just for once, too, the New Zealanders held their catches, Page taking two blinders; the full-length dive to his left to dismiss Chapman first ball was described as a catch in a thousand. It gave Cromb his fifth wicket for 14 runs in 68 deliveries, and was a good example of Lowry's canny captaincy; as Chapman, a noted big hitter, came out Lowry pushed back his field and then told Cromb to bowl on a length just outside off stump. Chapman fell straight into the trap, provided the edge and Page did the rest. By lunch MCC were 86 for 7, only Jardine giving any sort of account of himself. He carried on after the break to finish undefeated on 62 out of a total of 132, with Cromb's 6 for 46 taking the honours. He didn't bowl at all in the second innings.

MCC were 170 runs behind with 170 minutes left. Survival really shouldn't have been a problem. Something, though, made Lowry give the new ball to Merritt and in his second over he deceived Hearne with a googly to which the batsman played no stroke. From that moment on he was unplayable; Dick Brittenden felicitously compared him to a Hollywood temptress, 'all curves and deceit', making some of England's best batsmen look like schoolboys. Admirably supported by Roger Blunt's leg-breaks, he took three wickets in one over, with Page again taking a catch – with his left armpit – to dismiss poor Chapman, whose reaction to trouble was always to try and hit himself out of it, for his second first-baller of the match. Each of Merritt's next three overs produced a wicket, with Jardine once again the only batsman to make any showing – in fact the only one to get into double figures. In nine overs he had figures of 7 for 28, Blunt weighing in with 3 for 13, and MCC were all out for 48 in just 65 astonishing minutes. Budge Hintz, the New Zealand journalist who covered the tour and wrote a book about it, praised Lowry's captaincy as masterly; Hintz was convinced that he came out for the second innings intent on victory, which was why he gave the ball to Merritt. Comparisons with the 1878 Australians, who had dismissed MCC for 33 and 19 to win in one day, were inevitable.

In fine weather there was a distinct carnival atmosphere at Lord's for what was scheduled to be the only Test, New Zealand's first in England. The England team, led by Douglas Jardine, was a strong one with the accent on youth; Larwood and Sutcliffe had to drop out from those selected, but their replacements, Allen and Woolley, were both to play crucial innings. Lowry won the toss and by lunchtime Mills, Dempster and Weir had rattled up 132 for 2. Then the collapse – all out for 224 to the leg-spin of Peebles and Robins, the price paid for surrendering the initiative. It was to be a good day for bowlers; before long Cromb had three wickets, including Ham-

MCC v New Zealanders
Lord's 16, 18, 19 May 1931
Toss: New Zealanders

New Zealanders

C.S. Dempster	c & b White	45
K.C. James†	lbw b Allom	1
R.C. Blunt	b Robins	5
J.L. Kerr	c Dawson b Jupp	24
M.L. Page	c White b Jupp	14
R.O. Talbot	c Crawley b White	66
T.C. Lowry*	not out	101
I.B. Cromb	c White b Robins	8
G.L. Weir	st Franklin b Jupp	12
W.E. Merritt	c Franklin b White	15
A.M. Matheson	not out	5
Extras	(lb6)	6
Total	(9 wickets declared)	302

Fall of wickets: 9, 28, 77, 83, 158, 163, 190, 262, 291

	O	M	R	W
Allom	19	2	57	1
Hearne	8	5	17	0
Robins	20	1	50	2
Jupp	31	3	106	3
White	28	7	66	3

MCC

E.W. Dawson	c Lowry b Cromb	1	(3)c Merritt b Blunt	2
J.W. Hearne	b Cromb	12	b Merritt	0
A.M. Crawley	c Page b Matheson	0	(4)b Merritt	1
D.R. Jardine	not out	62	(1)b Blunt	19
M.J.L. Turnbull	lbw b Cromb	0	st James b Merritt	2
V.W.C. Jupp	c & b Cromb	12	(7)c Lowry b Merritt	5
A.P.F. Chapman*	c Page b Cromb	0	(6)c Page b Merritt	0
R.W.V. Robins	c Blunt b Matheson	16	b Merritt	0
J.C. White	c Page b Cromb	17	not out	7
W.B. Franklin†	lbw b Merritt	2	c Kerr b Merritt	2
M.J.C. Allom	c Kerr b Merritt	0	c Weir b Blunt	9
Extras	(b6, lb3, nb1)	10	(lb1)	1
Total		132		48

Fall of wickets 3, 6, 20, 21, 41, 41,
67, 125, 132, 132

4, 15, 18, 20, 20, 28,
30, 30, 32, 48

	O	M	R	W	O	M	R	W
Matheson	11	4	16	2	3	1	6	0
Cromb	23	7	46	6				
Merritt	17.5	4	49	2	9	3	28	7
Blunt	4	1	11	0	6.1	1	13	3

The New Zealanders won by an innings and 122 runs

The immortal Frank Woolley, one of the most graceful of batsmen. He scored some useful runs against New Zealand and also took his best Test bowling figures against them — 7 for 76 at Wellington in 1929–30.

mond's, with only 31 on the board. Cromb clearly liked Lord's, for as well as his success against MCC he had had 8 for 70 in one innings against Middlesex. Duleep and Jardine repaired matters a little, but five went down for 129. Then Woolley, 44 years old, scored a masterful 80 in best Woolley fashion; but he went down before the end, and at 190 for 7 by the close the visitors could feel that they had done something to atone for their disappointing batting. Life in Britain, as in New Zealand, had become fairly hard during the Depression, but with 414 runs and 17 wickets in one day there were certainly compensations.

Next morning the New Zealanders bowled poorly and Ames – who should have been stumped the previous day before he had scored – and Allen capitalised on it in the best possible way. A total of 246 surpassed the highest Test partnership for the eighth wicket and established a world record which still stands, the oldest Test partnership record to survive. Lowry changed his bowlers rapidly, but with seventeen changes before lunch he did it too rapidly for anyone to settle down and England's eventual lead was 230. Mills's dismissal to Allen's second ball might then have triggered off a disaster, but with the pitch playing well Dempster and Weir applied themselves to the uphill battle. Weir went at 40, but Lowry came up with an inspired decision and moved Page up the order to number four. By the close the score was 161 for 2.

Three runs on the final morning took Dempster to 1,000 for the tour, and soon afterwards he had his century. When he fell for 120 Page and Blunt put on 142 in 105 minutes, Bill Voce (and his captain) getting in some practice for a not-too-distant tour of Australia by bowling fast and short to a leg-side trap. Page survived to be on 99 at lunch, during which P.F. Warner, in a prophetic moment, told Voce to 'stop trying to hit the man and pitch the ball up'. Could he but have known what was to come eighteen months later. The bowler made some amends by sending down an easy no-ball immediately after lunch; Page missed it, but the century soon came, to be quickly followed by his exit. Now it was Blunt's turn to be senior partner. With the New Zealanders needing to make runs without losing wickets Dick Brittenden wrote that Blunt 'drew up a batting balance sheet in a neat, precise hand; the team showed a spectacular profit'. He made 96 before he went, at which point the score was 404 for 7; a final collapse now and England could probably be expected to polish off the deficit in the time left. Instead, Lowry and Allcott made 63 in 50 minutes and when Lowry eventually declared at 469 for 9 ('with quiet pride', says Brittenden) England needed 240 runs in 140 minutes. His bowlers then had the best of the closing session, taking five wickets for 146.

The English press were practically dancing in Fleet Street. 'Bravo New Zealand', 'exhilarating game', 'Dempster, Blunt and Page gave as brave an exhibition of batting as ever seen in a Test' and so on and so on. There was no question that more Tests had to be arranged and Surrey and Lancashire agreed that these could be played at the Oval and Old Trafford.

Budge Hintz, in his book on the tour, speculated on what the effect might have been had New Zealand won that Test, and came to the remarkable conclusion that it was, all in all, a good thing that they did not. His argument was that since the All Blacks' successful 1905 tour of Britain Rugby in New Zealand had been unhealthily competitive, and he didn't want to see cricket going the same way. The emphasis had always been on club cricket and its enjoyment, and he believed that once winning became the top priority the game would decline. One wonders how many years it had been since such a sentiment had been expressed in England; could he *really* have expected New Zealand simply to keep playing for fun year after year and not thought that, as they fell further and further behind the other countries, the game would decline rapidly as people lost interest in it? One shudders to think what he must have made of Jardine's tactics in Australia not long afterwards.

There had been some fine rhetoric uttered after the first game; unfortunately, after the second a line of Mark Antony's from *Julius Caesar* might have been more appropriate: 'O! what a fall was there, my countrymen'. Admittedly New Zealand were without their leading batsman, as Dempster was injured. They were also entirely out of luck with the weather; Lowry lost only two tosses in his seven Tests, but this one was crucial. What the game highlighted, however, was their lack of a fast bowler on a comfortable pitch that, as Allen demonstrated, cried out for one. Nor did they hold their catches, allowing both Sutcliffe and Bakewell early lives. The Yorkshireman helped himself to a century and Duleep did likewise against bowling that was as easy as the wicket. By the close England were 312 for 3. It poured with rain during the night, but play began on time. Hammond set about the bowlers, and when his hundred came up in even time Jardine declared at 416 for 4. Before long the pitch was drying and bouncing nastily, and Allen decimated them. Off 13 overs he took 5 for 14, only Lowry with 62 and Kerr with 34 stopping a total disaster; according to Jardine, 'Lowry's was the best innings seen at the Oval for many years, because the wicket was so troublesome.'

A score of 193 all out and following on on a wicket that was still dangerous meant that there was never much chance of survival. Only Mills, Blunt, Kerr and the 18-year-old Vivian, on his début, made any runs as Tate

Herbert Sutcliffe, always immaculate, scored two centuries for England in the Tests of 1931.

and Peebles did most of the damage; by a quarter past three on the third day they were all out for 197, Lowry making a duck in what was his last Test innings. It was a good instance of the contention that Lady Luck has rarely appeared over-anxious about the welfare of New Zealand's cricketers.

This match, incidentally, saw one innovation. Via the radio-telephone link between London and Wellington, Arthur Gilligan sent an account of each day's play to the Wellington Cricket Association, who then relayed it to the local radio station. Far from being in a commentary box at the scene of play, Gilligan spoke from a bedroom of the Great Central Hotel! What a pity this had not come one Test earlier.

The anti-climax was compounded completely when the Old Trafford Test was almost totally washed out. It was after three o'clock on the last afternoon when Lowry put England in, possibly, according to *Men in White*, because it may 'have been suggested to him by New Zealand's opening batsmen that they would prefer to avoid meeting the explosive Larwood until the after-match function'. A century from Sutcliffe and 63 from Duleep entertained the crowd, and young Vivian was able to claim the wickets of Duleep and Hammond before stumps were drawn at 224 for 3. Loss of gate money on this game hardly helped the NZCC's precarious financial situation, but suggestions for a fourth Test which, given good weather, could have made quite a difference to the balance sheet, came to nothing.

As usual, the summer of 1931 was one of the wettest ever known. Maybe this year there was actually some truth in that claim, as the tourists lost twenty-eight full playing days and fourteen of their twenty-six first-class games ended in draws. Six were won and three lost, so that overall the tour was accounted a great success. As in 1927 six batsmen exceeded a thousand runs with Page missing the mark by only ten. Dempster, inevitably, was named as one of *Wisden*'s five cricketers of the year. As usual, the bowling had been the weak link, but the fielding had improved and the man behind the stumps was rated as one of the best wicket-keepers in the world.

Ken James had come to England in 1927 as second-string keeper to Lowry, but it didn't take him long to secure the position for himself, and he went on to make eighty-five dismissals during that tour. Fast, agile, dependable and very skilful, he worked particularly well with Merritt, once taking a hat-trick of catches off him in a match in Colombo; but he was also taken to task in his *Wisden* obituary for being one of the first to stand back to medium-pace bowling. In view of this, concluded the oracle, 'he must be regarded as partially responsible for one of the most questionable developments in modern cricket.' He played in New Zealand's first eleven Tests, making sixteen dismissals, and his keeping was praised in all of them as being of the highest class. His batting took time to develop and his highest Test score was only 14; in the late 1930s, however, he played for Northamptonshire – where he was joined by Merritt – and his batting improved markedly, to the extent that he finished his career with seven first-class centuries to his name. Averaging some fifty-five dismissals and scoring not far short of a thousand runs each season he was altogether a useful acquisition for a struggling team. He was one of those players who

Ken James, outstanding wicket-keeper in New Zealand's early Tests.
Prowess with the bat came later when his Test career was over.

thoroughly enjoy the game and all the work it involves, and whose enthusiasm is so valuable to a captain; not surprisingly, the writers of the time gave him much praise for the outstanding part he played in these tours.

In fact the English press praised the whole team to the skies for their sportsmanship, friendliness and general approach to the game; for, as the London *Truth* put it, 'playing the game in the truest and best tradition – a very different method from that which has been known in county cricket at times, and in Australian tours often.' (That reference to Australia must have provoked a few smiles in all three countries, especially New Zealand.) The players, for their part, were equally complimentary about the kindness and hospitality shown to them. Even the shareholders got their money back, plus six per cent interest.

Yet as the team were being congratulated after their return home there was a cloud in the sky, one that was to grow bigger in the next few years. The team had given an undertaking not to return to England as players for at least two years, but Bill Merritt had broken this by signing as professional for a Lancashire club. He was promptly barred from representing his country again; in fact he did play against the MCC tourists in 1935–6, but his Test career was finished. Moreover, Dempster, James and Cromb were all to follow him to England in various capacities before too long. As New Zealand played so few Tests before the War these losses were not as serious as they might have been, but had they not occurred the outcome of the 1937 series might just have been different.

*

In 1931–2 South Africa stopped off to play two Tests in New Zealand after their tour of Australia. Since they won both of them after having lost all five to Australia, it was hardly a confidence-boosting exercise for a New Zealand team that was mostly the same as had toured England. Some consolation could be gained from the strength of the Australians, for Bradman had scored 806 runs at 201.5 and Grimmett and Ironmonger had taken sixty-four wickets between them, but the defeats by South Africa were both substantial ones.

A year later Douglas Jardine and his team visited New Zealand after the most rancorous tour in cricket history, a description that still applies despite efforts to usurp it in Pakistan fifty-five years later. England lacked Larwood and the Nawab of Pataudi from their Australian squad, but were still a very formidable team; New Zealand lacked Lowry, Blunt, Merritt, Mills and others from 1931, and 'formidable' is not quite the adjective to describe them.

They were led by Milford Page, invariably known as 'Curly', who had been Lowry's vice-captain in 1931 and had taken over against South Africa when Lowry was unavailable. He had first played for Canterbury whilst still at school in 1920 and didn't miss a single match for them until he retired – temporarily as it happened – in 1935–6. A solid, careful batsman with a preference for the leg side, he fortified many an innings from the middle order with a responsible, if not always speedy, performance. He was an excellent slip fielder and an occasional slow bowler, although his five Test wickets proved expensive; he also played at half-back for the All Blacks. His captaincy was modelled on Lowry's – firm, but with a light touch that made him much liked and respected – and he was very popular with players and fans alike. Most important of all for him was sportsmanship, and he actually uttered the immortal words, straight from the pages of boys' public-school fiction, 'People think more of a good sportsman who loses than a bad sportsman who wins'.

In view of events that had just taken place in Australia it is hard to think of a more delightful quotation with which to introduce a few words about Douglas Jardine. His method of attacking a very strong Australian batting line-up headed by Bradman was, of course, to instruct his bowlers to bowl fast and short at the leg stump, and by placing a ring of fielders close in on the leg side to take the catches as the batsmen fended off the ball. This had made him immeasurably the most unpopular person, cricketing or otherwise, ever to visit Australia. It was legal at the time, but few have ever tried to pretend that it did not make him 'a bad sportsman who wins'. He was a very fine batsman who scored almost 1,300 runs at an average of 48 in his twenty-two games – including a century the following summer against West Indian bowlers who were giving him a taste of his own bodyline medicine – but the quality of his batting has tended to be overshadowed by his reputation as a win-at-all-costs captain, a hard, joyless man whose single-mindedness took much of the pleasure from the game. Certainly there were times when his play was very negative and the criticism he received was justified, but over the years there were plenty of others when the reverse applied. Some players would support him unswervingly, others loathed him; some observers thought his captaincy tactically very shrewd, others unimaginative. No doubt like everyone else he had good days and bad days, but he seems to have inspired more conflicting loyalties, and more controversy, than almost any other English cricketer. Maybe even today there are some English fans who are just a little ashamed of the bodyline series, and find Curly Page's dictum about sportsmanship not too comically naive.

New Zealand could hardly have made a better start to the first Test at Christchurch. Badcock had Sutcliffe caught behind off the first ball of the match, and Paynter was bowled by Smith's first ball in Test cricket with the score on 4; Wyatt then went with England on 46, and the crowd, which reached 15,000, must have wondered if . . . just possibly . . . By the close of play England were 418 for 5. Against a very ordinary attack Hammond was at his imperious best, slaughtering them for a double century, while Ames also piled up a hundred; together they put on 242 in 144 minutes for what is still the fifth-wicket record by either side in England v New Zealand Tests. Next morning Brown and Voce hammered 108 in 45 minutes, and Jardine declared at 560 for 8 at lunch-time. And then Dempster failed, leaving it to Whitelaw, Weir and Kerr to take the score to 153 for 3 overnight. The third morning saw a dismal procession of batsmen come and go, and New Zealand were all out for 223; the injured Vivian wasn't able to bat, but one suspects that he would not have made a significant difference to a deficit of 337. Following on with some three hours in which to survive Dempster and Whitelaw held out for sixteen overs before a dust storm, followed by rain and bad light, put an end to the proceedings. Maybe it wasn't the most honourable of draws, but for the home team it could have been much worse.

It was a very similar story in the second Test at Auckland. Dempster was late in getting to the ground and, officially, did not open the innings; but since Mills and Weir both fell in the second over to Bowes, with no runs on the board, effectively he did. And without his 83 not out to take his side to 158 it would have been a sorry story indeed. In response Hammond more than doubled the New Zealand score on his own, his 336 not out beating Bradman's 334 as the highest individual Test innings. It was scored in 318 minutes, the last hundred coming in 47 minutes and the 300 coming in 288 minutes, the fastest Test treble-century; his ten sixes are still a Test record. Even allowing for the ordinariness of the bowling it was an astonishing achievement, giving him an average of 563 for the two-match series, a figure that has always seemed one of cricket's more impregnable records. Bob Wyatt, captain in place of Jardine who had rheumatism, declared on 548 for 7 shortly before the end of the second day. Needing 391 runs to make England bat again New Zealand had 16 of them when, early on the third morning, it rained. Maybe this deprived Dempster of leading a heroic rearguard action that would have saved the day and brought glory to the underdogs; but on the evidence of the pusillanimous first innings, maybe the underdogs were better off settling for the escape that Lady Luck, for once, offered them.

The majestic Walter Hammond, scorer of 563 runs in two innings
in 1932–3 against New Zealand and captain against them in the
first meeting after the War.

Jardine pointed out the enormous advantage that England had had of having played regularly together for several months, and suggested that the strength of New Zealand cricket could be better measured if they excluded Hammond's exceptional performances from their reckonings. Perhaps, but it was a kind thought rather than a practical one. The New Zealand officials knew well enough that if they wanted to make their mark in Test cricket they had to learn how to deal with the outstanding players; it was finding their own outstanding players to do so that was the problem.

*

The MCC team which toured New Zealand in 1935–6 has a distinctly unfamiliar ring to the modern fan; although six of them played for England only Joe Hardstaff (jr) really 'made it' at Test level. An important aspect of the tour was to give experience to promising young players, but it seems often to have happened over the years that selection for such a tour has proved the kiss of death and this one was no exception. Happy and successful it certainly was, but it didn't produce the Test players to take on Australia the following winter that MCC hoped it would.

Bob Wyatt was offered the captaincy but declined it, and the team was led instead by Errol Holmes, whose five-match Test career, had he but known it, was already behind him. Holmes was one of the most delightful of cricket's characters, a warm and humorous man who was one of the steadily-decreasing band who believed that cricket should primarily be about enjoyment; when he took over from Jardine as Surrey captain it must have been rather like Charles II succeeding Genghis Khan . . . An all-rounder in his early years at Malvern and Oxford, he later concentrated on his batting; this matched his character – easy, fluent and entertaining – and for a while in the mid-1930s he was high in the averages. The fact that he was able to miss no less than seven years of first-class cricket during his twenties because of business commitments and still become a top batsman showed how good he was, and Jack Hobbs said he was sure that had he been able to play more often he would have won more Test caps. He didn't have much personal success on this tour, but his description of it in his autobiography *Flannelled Foolishness* – a title that says much about the man – is that it 'must surely rank as the best tour of its kind which has ever taken place . . . we were all firm friends when we arrived back in England . . . and we are still friends to this day'.

The early part of the tour had been spent in Australia, and had seen three victories, two draws and a defeat. The first game in New Zealand produced an upset as MCC lost to Wellington by 14 runs through poor batting, but after that came five victories and fourteen draws, many of them caused by the weather. The bad weather was to wreak havoc with the NZCC's finances and caused an overall loss of some £3,200.

Four unofficial 'Tests' were played, New Zealand being led by Ian Cromb as Page had (temporarily) retired. Bill Merritt was back in favour, but not for long; the first game at Dunedin was a disaster for his team and he was one of several who departed the scene. Dempster was badly missed as New Zealand were all out for 81, 'Hopper' Read taking 6 for 26. MCC replied with a mere 653 for 5 declared, scored in six hours and forty minutes; Parks, Barber and Langridge all made hundreds and Human 97 as no fewer than a dozen catches were dropped. New Zealand's second innings was once again a shambles, and only Vivian's unbeaten 87 enabled them to reach 205 for 7 before rain and bad light saved them. Holmes describes how, early in Vivian's innings, he dropped a slip catch off Read when the ball hit him just below the right thumb and hurt him considerably; next ball precisely the same thing happened, the ball hitting him on the identical spot. Furious with himself he changed places with mid-off as a self-punishment for all to see, only for Vivian to hit a skier to him which he also duly dropped. By this time his hand was very painful and in fact never properly recovered. Years later, when he told Read that he hadn't been able to write properly since dropping those catches, the bowler 'beamed all over his face, and, in a very gentle and benign manner, he commented, "Well, it serves you right." '

So often when a team has been outplayed and changes half its players for the next game they just end up deeper still in the mire. In this case, however, New Zealand came up with the goods. In the first innings they made 242 and then dismissed MCC, who were led by the Honourable Charles Lyttelton as Holmes missed the game with his hand injury, for 156. One of the replacements, Jack Kerr, then scored a fine century, putting on 190 in 139 minutes with Vivian, who made 96. Cromb was able to declare at 229 for 3, leaving two and a half hours for his bowlers to win through. Roberts and Blundell almost did it, only 61 not out from Langridge saving MCC, and at the end seven wickets were down for 130. If the score so far was actually 0–0 it was in effect 1–1. One curiosity about the game was that each side fielded a future Governor-General of New Zealand, Denis Blundell for the home team and Lyttelton, later Lord Cobham, for MCC. This had also happened in the Wellington match, when Blundell's eight wickets had proved decisive; indeed he was to make more of an impact with the ball than Lyttelton did with the bat.

The day after this match the news came through that King George V had died, which caused some disruption to MCC's itinerary. Holmes recorded that this affected the people of Palmerston North, where they happened to be at the time, every bit as much as the people of England; few back home would have realised the effect it had on people throughout the Empire and when the team attended a ceremony to mark the occasion he said that he felt very humble.

Two more 'Tests' were played at the end of the tour but both were inconclusive. The first of these was on a comfortable Auckland pitch and although New Zealand lost early wickets they reached 368 with the aid of 99 from Elmes. MCC replied with 435 including a hundred from Hardstaff, but as this was scored very slowly there was never a chance of victory and the game petered out with New Zealand 128 for 3. In the last game, at Christchurch, MCC were put out for 195, and New Zealand replied with 334; there was another hundred from Kerr and 47 from Walter Hadlee, making his representative début. At the close of the second day MCC were 142 for 2, and maybe a timely declaration could have brought about an exciting finish. As it was the weather had the last word, damaging the sight-screens and soaking the pitch; no more play was possible.

Admittedly the tourists were nothing like a full England team, but honours were just about even at the end of the series, and Cromb – 'Cranky' to his friends – was widely praised for his captaincy after the opening débâcle. Holmes found several New Zealand players about whom to enthuse as excellent prospects for the future; Kerr in particular caught his eye, as did Wallace, Roberts, Hadlee, Cowie and others. One of those others was a young batsman named Martin Donnelly who after the War was to have the scribes scratching around for fresh superlatives. Around this time New Zealand cricket fans undoubtedly had grounds for optimism.

*

In the best cricketing traditions February 1937 saw the New Zealanders arguing about the make-up of their party to tour England. Page, who had come out of retirement, was made captain, but there was a lot of support for Cromb as he had led the team well against MCC the previous season; as it was, Cromb wasn't even in the squad. Their hosts-to-be, meanwhile, were managing to lose a series against Australia after having won the first two Tests, partly because the luck with the weather which had favoured them turned sour and partly because Bradman crucified them.

It had been arranged that they would make a brief visit to New Zealand before returning home, playing three games including two unofficial 'Tests'. This, however, highlighted a problem that was always a potential

Bob Wyatt – captain of England at Auckland in 1932–3 and scorer of 144 at Wellington in 1936–7.

source of worry to New Zealand's administrators: because the game was played on an amateur basis, players were dependent on the goodwill of employers to give them leave, and these two games would have called for additional time off just before the players were about to set off on a six-month tour. If, however, a second-string team played in those games the likely defeats might lead to both loss of morale by the players and loss of interest by the British public. In the end only one representative match was played and the New Zealanders played their first-choice team.

There had been a lot of rain before the game which left the Wellington pitch slow and fairly easy for batting. MCC wickets fell steadily, though, with only Wyatt standing firm and going on to an unhurried 144, and at 162 for 5 the home team were on top. Yet one suspects there was no great optimism in New Zealand hearts; Ames and Allen were still to come and they were to New Zealand what Bradman was to England – what, in the gentlemanly language of the time, might be called a regular nuisance. Ames duly made 97, Allen 88 and MCC totalled 427. Even then Allen wasn't finished, as he and Voce took four wickets apiece to dismiss New Zealand for 265, Vivian, Page and Moloney the only ones to make a real contribution.

Following on on the last day, New Zealand needed 162 to make MCC bat again – and the first four wickets went down for 30. The crisis needed its man, and found it in young Walter Hadlee; Moloney held up one end while they put on 80 for the fifth wicket. At 132 Moloney's was the sixth wicket down, and now, with time running short, it was the turn of Eric Tindill, the wicket-keeper. The seventh wicket fell at 142, the eighth at 152 and the ninth at 158, still four short of the target. Tindill scored a single to take him to an invaluable 24 and then the last man, Cowie, swung the ball away for four and New Zealand had a one-run lead. Next ball he was stumped – and with just three minutes left on the clock there was no time for MCC to get the two runs they needed, the penalty for having scored too slowly on the first day.

Nail-biting stuff, but after all the worries about loss of morale and so on it must have left the New Zealanders distinctly concerned about the prospects for the forthcoming tour. The optimism hadn't lasted very long.

*

Shortly after the New Zealanders began their 1937 tour King George VI was crowned and Lowry, who was the team's manager, and Page, the captain, were invited to the coronation as representatives of the Empire's cricketers. *Men in White* tells of the amusement of their team-mates at

Captains in opposition in 1983. Bob Willis bowls, Geoff Howarth backs up, David Evans is the umpire.

The first win in England draws near. Wicket-keeper Ian Smith expresses his delight at catching Phil Edmonds for 0 off the bowling of Ewen Chatfield. It was one of four wickets which fell to that combination in the second innings at Headingley in 1983.

(Right)   *Richard Hadlee, 1983 vintage.*

(Below)   *Headingley, 1983. Chatfield sends Tavaré's off stump cartwheeling early in England's second innings. Only Gower, the non-striker, put up much resistance, with a fine unbeaten century.*

(Above)   Not out. Allan Lamb survived Cairns' appeal for a catch and went on to make a century (Trent Bridge, 1983).

(Left)   Nick Cook made his Test début at Lord's in 1983 and took 8 for 125.

(Above)   *Lance Cairns beats Botham at second slip off Norman Cowans (Trent Bridge, 1983).*

(Right)   *Jeremy Coney, victorious New Zealand captain in 1986. His gentle medium pace could be frustratingly deceptive.*

David Gower, scorer of over 1,000 Test runs against New Zealand.

A maiden Test century is on its way. John Bracewell was one of the heroes of the 1986 Trent Bridge Test which gave New Zealand its first series win in England.

Richard Hadlee, also a hero of the 1986 Trent Bridge Test, took yet another 10-wicket haul as well as scoring 68 runs.

*Ewen Chatfield's relentlessly accurate bowling has provided an
admirable foil to Richard Hadlee for much of the 1980s.*

(Right)   *Martin Crowe, New Zealand's star batsman of the 1980s, seen here against a TCCB XI in 1986. Warwickshire's Brian McMillan is the fielder.*

(Below)   *Mark Greatbatch celebrated his Test call-up with a century on debut in the 1987–8 series.*

seeing them in full court regalia – velvet jackets and doublets, hose, buckled slippers and swords – and then says 'unfortunately, the two became so preoccupied with a struggle to restrain their weapons when they left a taxi at the Abbey that a flask of brandy thought necessary to toast the new monarch was left behind.'

After their previous successful visits the tourists were well received by the press. Page found himself one of the first New Zealanders, and one of the first cricket captains, to be hauled in front of a television camera and required to utter one of the first dollops of sporting platitudes. Clearly the modern world had arrived.

The game against MCC was almost completely washed out, little more than an hour's drizzly play being possible. By the time of the first Test the visitors had lost five county games, all of them heavily, and beaten only Cambridge University in first-class matches. Lowry, who was available to play if needed, had done so with success and there was talk that he might play in the first Test at Lord's; this came to nothing, but they could certainly have done with him – and with Dempster too, now playing for Leicestershire. As it was, their team, which had played no Tests for four years, contained six new caps.

Len Hutton also made his début in that first Test, scoring 0 and 1. England's first innings was built around Hardstaff and Hammond who put on 245 for the third wicket with a century apiece – still the record for that wicket in England–New Zealand tests – and around Paynter, who made 74. At the beginning and end of the day, though, wickets fell, Cowie and Roberts bowling well and claiming four each by the time the innings closed next morning at 424. Encouragingly, the fielding had been very good, one of the benefits of having a young team. A steady fall of wickets, however, saw the visitors at 175 for 7 and in danger of having to follow on. Moloney and Roberts came to the rescue, putting on 104 for the eighth wicket; it was ended when there was a break in play so that the New Zealanders could meet the new king, and Moloney's concentration was dealt a mortal blow. The innings ended next morning at 295. As it was a three-day Test quick runs were obviously the order, and Barnett and Hardstaff provided them. When Robins declared at 226 for 4 New Zealand had to survive for two sessions to save the game. This did so, just. From being 15 for 3 Wallace, Donnelly and Kerr managed to stay there long enough to see the score to 175 for 8 at stumps, a defiant effort that brought praise from the press – and criticism for England for being 'unconvincing'.

The leader of this supposedly unconvincing outfit was Walter Robins, captain of a Middlesex team that finished second in the Championship for year after year before eventually winning it in 1947. He was one of cricket's most dynamic players, fast, inventive, energetic, combative, an adventurous leg-break and googly bowler, attacking batsman renowned for his speedy footwork and outstanding cover fielder. When he took over at Middlesex he shook a depressed team by the scruff of its neck and completely rejuvenated it; Alan Gibson wrote of his captaincy that it was 'in the style of Sam Woods, half a century earlier, who believed that draws were only any use for bathing in'. These three Tests against New Zealand were the only time he led England and were the last of his nineteen Tests; there would have been more had he been able to go on Jardine's tour of Australia for which he was selected, and there were some at the time who felt that his sense of humour might have provided just the right antidote to the Iron Man's single-mindedness. Perhaps, though, the incident which shows him in his most characteristic light occurred near the end of this 1937 season. Middlesex and Yorkshire were neck and neck in the chase for the Championship when, just before the end of the season, Robins sent a telegram to Brian Sellers, the Yorkshire captain, challenging him to a four-day match on a neutral ground, irrespective of who were to win the title, with the proceeds going to cricket charities. Sellers accepted, and Yorkshire, with the help of a turning Oval pitch, won by an innings. Nevertheless, the game was well supported and there were many beneficiaries. Somehow that challenge encapsulates Walter Robins.

England were not exactly over-convincing in the next Test, either. Heavy rain had made the Manchester wicket soft, thereby drawing the teeth of Jack Cowie, the visitors' fastest and best bowler, and allowing England to make a sound start as Hutton put together his first Test century. Wickets fell later on, though, and Robins declared at the overnight score of 358 for 9. He then got himself into the wars; first he split his right index finger trying to make a catch, then, fielding at slip, he contrived to tread on his right hand with his left foot, tearing the flesh with a spike. At 119 for 5 in reply it looked as though New Zealand might capitulate, but Hadlee, who had not been having much of a tour, came good with 93, an innings that ended only when he slipped and knocked over his wicket. With 281 on the board there was still plenty to play for. Indeed there was a great deal to play for next morning when they had reduced England to 75 for 7; but Freddie Brown was dropped three times early on and went on to 57, putting on 72 for the eighth wicket with Ames (who else?). A score of 187 left New Zealand 265 to get in four hours, but after a bright beginning the innings collapsed and they were all out for 134. If just one of those catches off Brown had stuck the match could so easily have produced a great upset, but there was at least one consolation for the tourists – Cowie became the first New Zealander to take ten wickets in a Test, in unhelpful conditions at that, with a splendid display of accurate and tenacious bowling. At the time he was 25; he would be almost 64 before another of his countrymen managed the same feat. There are no prizes for guessing who that was.

Most of the first day of the Oval Test was lost to rain, prompting the customary outcry against three-day Tests. Donnelly, Page and Roberts made fifties as New Zealand reached 249, which England had passed by five runs when Robins declared with seven wickets down, Hardstaff having made a hundred and Compton 65 on début. When New Zealand then fell to 107 for 6 there would have been time for England to knock off the runs had the last wickets gone quickly, but Moloney, Tindill and Dunning saw them to the safety of 187, and there was time only for England to reach 31 for 1.

It wasn't a distinguished tour, really. Of the first-class games New Zealand won nine, lost nine and drew thirteen, but only four of those victories were against counties, the others being against Minor Counties, Combined Services and suchlike. The main problem was a lack of consistency, with some fine performances being negated by some disappointing ones; tiredness, too, played its part in the closing weeks, for they were simply not used to playing so intensively. Lionel Tennyson, a former England captain, wrote that 'if they have a fault it is modesty', and one suspects that this was very near the mark; not so much an inferiority complex as a feeling that they had no right to be going around beating the top English counties. After the War Arthur Mailey, the Australian leg-spinner turned journalist who watched England's 1946–7 visit to New Zealand, wrote that in New Zealand's case 'there is something akin to accepting the idea that you are a puppet state in world cricket administration. It seems to be that England and Australia arrange a world fair and if there is a spare corner New Zealand walks nervously in and puts up a tent.'

New Zealanders have never wanted to emulate the brashness of Australians and have greatly endeared themselves to the British as a result; but there is no doubt that the brashness has stood Australian cricket in very good stead, and would most probably have done the same for New Zealand. A positive psychological attitude is important in all sports, of course, and in cricket, with its relatively slow-moving nature that allows time for thought, more than most; and perhaps New Zealand's lack of success over the years has been mainly caused by just not being able to believe that, as a bunch of part-timers, they could seriously challenge the world's top players.

The tour did, however, produce one great benefit, the emergence of Jack

Cowie as a world-class bowler. New Zealand had had other fine bowlers over the years, but Cowie was the first really outstanding one, all the more remarkable for having begun his career as a leg-break bowler before switching to speed. His 114 wickets at under 20 apiece were due reward for sustained accuracy, determination, hard work and the ability to extract life from the deadest pitch. Nineteen of those wickets came in the Tests at under 21 each, and with better catching he could perhaps have brought off a historic victory at Old Trafford. He had a late out-swinger which caught out the best batsmen and also one that came back in to them at great speed. Had he been playing today – and what a partnership he and Richard Hadlee would have made – he would probably have been in the '300 club' for Test wickets, but what with the War and New Zealand's lack of matches he played in only nine Tests, taking forty-five wickets at 21, his best figures being 6 for 40 in the game against Australia immediately after the War.

He toured England again in 1949 and turned in more fine performances; he had always been noted for his stamina – he was nicknamed 'the Bull', perhaps partly because of his name but certainly because of his strength as well – and the passing of the years seemed to have little effect. *Wisden* said of him after the 1937 tour that 'had he been an Australian, he might have been termed a wonder of the age' – a significant comment on the status of New Zealand cricket. It seems typical of New Zealand's luck, though, that the best batsman and bowler of their early years, Dempster and Cowie, should total only nineteen Tests between them and not coincide. Had they been in the same team for a few matches who knows what they could have produced.

There was one more tour before the War. In 1938–9 Sir Julien Cahn took a team to New Zealand which, strangely, played most of its games fielding teams of twelve and so not first-class. The one first-class game was against a representative New Zealand team captained by 'Sonny' Moloney – who was soon to lose his life in North Africa – but, as it happened, after weeks of sunshine the first two days were washed out. The ritual was seen through on the third day, New Zealand declaring at 170 for 5 and the visitors, who included Stewie Dempster in their number, being 163 for 7 at the close. Cahn, a wealthy sporting philanthropist, donated £100 to the NZCC to make up for the loss of gate-money caused by the rain, but also persuaded Giff Vivian to go and work for him, thereby depriving New Zealand of their best all-rounder. As Cahn had earlier lured away Dempster, the cynics in New Zealand may just have felt that the £100 was a sop to his conscience.

1931	Lord's	NZ 302–9d;	MCC 132, 48	NZ inns 122 runs
	Lord's	NZ 224,469–9d;	E 454, 146–5	Drawn
	Oval	E 416–4d;	NZ 193, 197	E inns 26 runs
	Old Trafford	E 224–3;	NZ –	Drawn
1932–3	Christchurch	E 560–8d;	NZ 223, 35–0	Drawn
	Auckland	NZ 158, 16–0;	E 548–7d	Drawn
1935–6	Dunedin	NZ 81, 205–7;	MCC 653–5d	Drawn
	Wellington	NZ 242, 229–3d;	MCC 156, 130–7	Drawn
	Auckland	NZ 368, 128–3;	MCC 435	Drawn
	Christchurch	MCC 195, 142–2;	NZ 334	Drawn
1936–7	Wellington	MCC 427;	NZ 265, 163	Drawn
1937	Lord's	NZ 56–2;	MCC –	Drawn
	Lord's	E 424, 226–4d;	NZ 295, 175–8	Drawn
	Old Trafford	E 358–9d, 187;	NZ 281, 134	E 130 runs
	Oval	NZ 249, 187;	E 254–7d, 31–1	Drawn
1938–9	Wellington	NZ 170–5d;	J. Cahn's XI 163–7	Drawn

1931 Test series

England

Batting	Innings	NO	HS	Runs	Average
H. Sutcliffe	2	1	117	226	226.00
G.O.B. Allen	1	0	122	122	122.00
L.E.G. Ames	3	1	137	195	97.50
D.R. Jardine	4	3	38	73	73.00
W.R. Hammond	4	1	100*	169	56.33

Bowling	Overs	M	Runs	W	Average
M.W. Tate	39	15	37	4	9.25
G.O.B. Allen	66	21	129	8	16.12
H. Verity	35.4	12	85	4	21.25
I.A.R. Peebles	102.4	16	325	13	25.00
F.R. Brown	45	18	90	3	30.00

New Zealand

Batting	Innings	NO	HS	Runs	Average
C.S. Dempster	2	0	120	173	86.50
R.C. Blunt	4	0	96	148	37.00
M.L. Page	4	0	102	142	35.50
H.G. Vivian	2	0	51	54	27.00
T.C. Lowry	4	0	62	97	24.25

Bowling	Overs	M	Runs	W	Average
G.L. Weir	23	3	92	3	30.66
H.G. Vivian	48.3	9	150	4	37.50
W.E. Merritt	36	2	181	4	45.25
I.B. Cromb	108	23	287	6	47.83
C.F.W. Allcott	98	18	243	2	121.50

Wicket-keepers: L.E.G. Ames (E) 5 dismissals   K.C. James (NZ) 6 dismissals

In the first match L.E.G. Ames and G.O.B. Allen made 246 for the eighth wicket, still the world Test record for that wicket.

1932–3 Test series

England
Best batting: W.R. Hammond 227; 336*   L.E.G. Ames 103   F.R. Brown 74
W. Voce 66   R.E.S. Wyatt 60
Best bowling: W.E. Bowes 19–5–34–6   W. Voce 17.1–3–27–3

New Zealand
Best batting: C.S. Dempster 83*   G.L. Weir 66   J.L. Kerr 59
Best bowling: F.T. Badcock 54–11–142–3

Wicket-keepers: K.C. James (NZ) 2 dismissals   L.E.G. Ames (E) 0 dismissals   G. Duckworth
(E) 1 dismissal

In the first match W.R. Hammond and L.E.G. Ames put on 242 for the fifth wicket, the highest for that wicket by either side in England v New Zealand Tests. In the second match Hammond made what was then the highest individual Test score, his 336 not out coming in only 318 minutes; his triple century took 288 minutes and is the fastest in Tests, his third hundred taking only 47 minutes. His ten sixes have never been equalled in a Test innings. His average of 563.00 is the record for any Test series.

1935–6
MCC

Batting	Innings	NO	HS	Runs	Average
J. Hardstaff	6	2	147*	269	67.25
J. Langridge	5	2	106*	190	63.33
W. Barber	6	0	173	365	60.83
D. Smith	4	1	48	130	43.33
J.H. Parks	6	0	100	225	37.50

Bowling	Overs	M	Runs	W	Average
H.D. Read	88.2	11	291	17	17.11
E.R.T. Holmes	6	0	18	1	18.00
A.D. Baxter	99.2	21	266	11	24.18
J.M. Sims	105.3	20	358	12	29.83
J.H. Parks	117	35	271	6	45.16

New Zealand

Batting	Innings	NO	HS	Runs	Average
J.L. Kerr	5	1	132	282	70.50
H.G. Vivian	7	2	96	289	57.80
W.A. Hadlee	1	0	47	47	47.00
J.A.R. Blandford	2	0	40	76	38.00
A.W. Roberts	4	1	75*	90	30.00

Bowling	Overs	M	Runs	W	Average
E.D. Blundell	47	11	117	6	19.50
A.W. Roberts	104	30	234	10	23.40
B.G. Griffiths	57	3	206	7	29.42
I.B. Cromb	85	9	301	9	33.44
A.M. Matheson	36	10	75	2	37.50

Wicket-keepers: J.A.R. Blandford (NZ) 3 dismissals   C.K.Q. Jackman (NZ) 1 dismissal
S.C. Griffith (E) 6 dismissals

1936–7

MCC
Best batting: R.E.S. Wyatt 144   L.E.G. Ames 97   G.O.B. Allen 88
Best bowling: J.M. Sims 4–35   W.Voce 4–50   G.O.B. Allen 4–56

New Zealand
Best batting: H.G. Vivian 88   W.A. Hadlee 82   M.L. Page 50
Best bowling: M.L. Page 2–38   A.W. Roberts 2–58   J. Cowie 2–73   H.G. Vivian 2–79

Wicket-keepers: E.W.T. Tindill (NZ) 0 dismissals   L.E.G. Ames (E) 3 dismissals

1937 Test series
England

Batting	Innings	NO	HS	Runs	Average
J. Hardstaff	5	0	114	350	70.00
D.C.S. Compton	1	0	65	65	65.00
W.R. Hammond	4	0	140	204	51.00
C.J. Barnett	6	1	83*	196	39.20
E. Paynter	3	0	74	114	38.00

Bowling	Overs	M	Runs	W	Average
J.H. Parks	21	9	36	3	12.00
C.I.J. Smith	36	9	63	4	15.75
T.W.J. Goddard	60.4	20	143	8	17.87
R.W.V. Robins	62.1	12	173	8	21.62
W. Voce	43.1	10	115	5	23.00

New Zealand

Batting	Innings	NO	HS	Runs	Average
A.W. Roberts	4	1	66*	142	47.33
H.G. Vivian	6	0	58	194	32.33
D.A.R. Moloney	6	0	64	156	26.00
J.L. Kerr	4	1	38*	76	25.33
W.A. Hadlee	6	0	93	151	25.17
W.M. Wallace	6	0	56	151	25.17

Bowling	Overs	M	Runs	W	Average
J. Cowie	139.5	30	395	19	20.78
A.W. Roberts	76.3	19	209	7	29.85
N. Gallichan	44	11	113	3	37.66
H.G. Vivian	124	27	338	8	42.25
J.A. Dunning	95.2	15	337	3	112.33

Wicket-keepers: L.E.G. Ames (E) 7 dismissals   E.W.T. Tindill (NZ) 5 dismissals

In the first match J. Hardstaff (jr) and W.R. Hammond put on 245 for the third wicket, still the highest third-wicket partnership by either country in these Tests. D.A.R. Moloney and A.W. Roberts put on 104 for the eighth wicket, still the New Zealand record for that wicket against England.

1938–9

Sir Julien Cahn's XI
Best batting: C.S. Dempster 44   N. Oldfield 42*
Best bowling: J.E. Walsh 4–67

New Zealand
Best batting: W.M. Wallace 54*   J.A. Ongley 35
Best bowling: J. Cowie 3–46

Wicket-keepers: E.W.T. Tindill (NZ) 1 dismissal C.R. Maxwell (Cahn's XI) 2 dismissals

— 5 —

The Golden Forty-niners

There were first-class games in New Zealand during the War just as in England, but no full Plunket Shield competition. One outstanding player, Bert Sutcliffe, was to make his début for Auckland at this time, but Australia didn't let New Zealand, any more than England, in on the secret of how to produce a whole crop of top-class players out of a war, a trick they were in the process of pulling for the second time. Thus it was that when early in 1946 Bill Brown brought along an Australian team they made mincemeat of the New Zealanders, including dismissing an inexperienced home team for a two-innings total of 96 runs in what was subsequently recognised as the first Test between the two countries. The one-sidedness of the matches on this tour was an important reason why almost four decades had to elapse before the Australians would condescend to play another Test against their neighbours.

England didn't fare much better against the Australians the following season, losing the Test series 3–0 before rounding off the tour in New Zealand. MCC beat Wellington and Auckland with ease, but the game against Otago proved a cliff-hanger; Sutcliffe scored 197 and 128 as MCC were set 218 to win in two hours; when time ran out they were 216 for 9. The one Test at Christchurch, however, was not so fortunate. Only four of the home team, Hadlee, Wallace, Tindill and Cowie, had played before the War; Dempster, now 43, was chosen but had to drop out at the last moment with an eye injury, and Donnelly was studying at Oxford. Hammond, the England captain, put New Zealand in and watched them compile 133 for the first wicket, Sutcliffe making 58 on début and Hadlee, the captain, going on to his only Test century. Wickets fell steadily after that until Cowie and Burtt put on 64 for the ninth wicket, Cowie's 45 being his highest Test score. Hadlee declared at 345 for 9, whereupon Hammond, in his final Test, was given three cheers as he came out to bat. The following year his arch-enemy Bradman was given an emotional welcome to his last innings and promptly fell second ball, but Hammond displayed no such weakness; his

79 was in fact his team's top score and helped them to reach 265 for 7 by the close, Cowie having bowled splendidly to take 6 for 83 from thirty overs. Hammond then declared despite the deficit of 80, but next day it rained; an extra day was added but it rained throughout that too. It meant an anti-climactic end to Hammond's Test career; this most majestic of batsmen had had a wretched time in Australia, with his captaincy especially disappointing. He had allowed his personal problems to distract him, he had been aloof from his players, and in what he saw as his final showdown with Bradman he had come off disastrously. For a Test career as glorious as his to end at such a low ebb simply seems wrong.

*

1949 is a special year in England's cricket history. If you insist on being prosaic you could say that a fine touring team, blessed with good weather, played some excellent cricket with some exciting finishes and left everyone happy. Some writers, though, have portrayed it as a throwback to the Golden Age, a final fling of the age of innocence before the 1950s ushered in the thousand natural shocks that cricket's flesh has proved heir to; and since there is already sufficient prosaicness in the world let us defer to these romantics. The sun shone every bit as endlessly as in Compton and Edrich's glory year of 1947, and the New Zealand tourists did not lose a single full day's play to the weather. They brought a splendid team rich in batting talent and with some decent bowlers as well, and they grandly entertained a nation still suffering from rationing, still in the process of restoring normality after the upheaval. They gave endless pleasure, made endless friends and left behind endless golden memories. If that sounds over the top then so be it; 1949 was a summer of hyperbole.

The leader of these happy cavaliers was Walter Hadlee. To refer to Walter Hammond as 'Wally' always sounds so sacrilegious, so Olympian was he; yet on Hadlee the familiar form sits much more happily, and he was invariably 'Wally' to his team. Perhaps this little comparison has most impact when considering their styles of captaincy; for Hammond tended to be aloof and unempathic, especially in the disastrous series of 1946–7 in Australia, while Hadlee was a warm, just, humanitarian leader much loved and respected by his men and by all who knew him. New Zealand have had some fine captains but he was undoubtedly one of the best. If he was fortunate to coincide with a good team and a lovely summer, everyone knew that it was he who must take most credit for what that team achieved.

Tall and bespectacled, he was a batsman with plenty of strokes who could score quickly and attractively or, if necessary, put up the shutters to

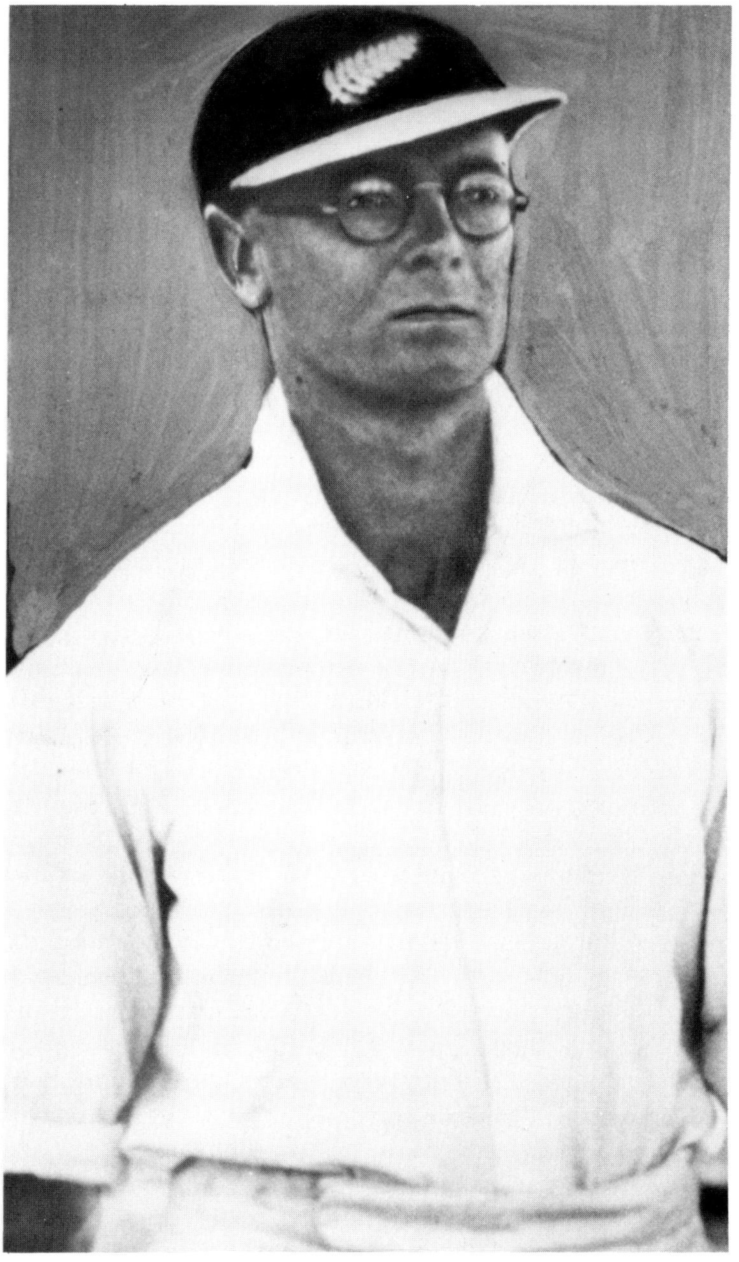

Walter Hadlee, the accountant who ended the 1949 tour of England very much in credit.

hang on for a draw. He made only one century in his eleven Tests but contributed many useful knocks to finish with an average of 30 and set very high standards for his players with his fielding. He had scored over 1,200 runs on the 1937 tour and was to score over 1,400 on this one, despite some injuries; Alan Mitchell, who travelled with the team throughout the tour and wrote a book about it called *Cricket Companions*, considered his most attractive shot to be the cover drive, 'either off his back foot or with both feet planted firmly down the pitch with the bat flashing a graceful arc.' Of his captaincy Mitchell wrote that he 'was determined, with his well-trained mind, his innate fairness, sense of fun, and kindly good nature that springs from the heart, that the team should be a success . . . He knew the strength and weaknesses of the various players, very often far better than they did themselves; and despite his air of gentleness off the field, he could be, and was occasionally, quite ruthless with his team on the field. Yet he drove himself hardest of all; to the extent that, after a trying innings in the heat of a burning day at Derby, he was on the verge of a nervous breakdown when he reached Northants, and was ordered to rest by a doctor.'

An accountant by profession, he still managed to remain in the administration of the game after he stopped playing and had three separate spells as a national selector. He became Chairman of the NZCC and was President at the time of the Packer schism. Over the years he has done many a noble service for his country's cricket and in 1950 was awarded the OBE; but perhaps none was more important than giving it his son Richard.

Hadlee's vice-captain must also take his share of the plaudits for the success of the tour. Merv Wallace had made his début with Hadlee in 1937 and was a good enough attacking batsman to finish with a career average of almost 44, although his Test average was disappointing at just under 21. On a good day he could be a joy to watch, pulling and hooking with great gusto and cover-driving gloriously. He started the tour magnificently and made 910 runs before the end of May; a persistent injury hampered him after that, but he still finished with 1,722 runs at 49. He was one of those players for whom cricket was never more than a game and he never had any idea about his own run-making statistics. 'Yet,' wrote Mitchell, 'if asked about the ability of any particular player, his merits or demerits as a batsman, fielder or bowler, or the characteristics of any wicket, he would give an incisive commentary.' He led the team four times in Hadlee's absence and won all four; but perhaps his most important contribution was as a coach, for at this he was a 'natural' and several players benefited considerably from his advice. Enormously enthusiastic, good-humoured and uncomplaining, he played a prominent part in New Zealand's cricket affairs for several years, and along with Hadlee and Jack Kerr had been one of the selectors of this tour party.

Three of the first five games were won, with some big scores accumulated, and the interest for the MCC game was such that 28,000 came to Lord's on the first day. They saw New Zealand bowl an average of twenty-six overs an hour – this was the final fling of the age of innocence, after all – but also saw a strong MCC batting line-up, with ten Test players, perform rather laboriously. Edrich, Simpson, Compton and Watkins got half-centuries, and at the close MCC were 311 for 6. They took the score to 379 next morning, with six wickets for Burtt, but in reply New Zealand collapsed for the first time on the tour; Bailey held a magnificent catch and then dismissed three leading batsmen to reduce the visitors to 94 for 6. The heroes of the hour were Rabone and wicket-keeper Mooney, who by stumps had taken the total to 237 for 6 and largely averted the danger; the following day Mooney was to go on to a century on his first appearance at Lord's, Rabone just missing out on 92. That last day was curtailed by the weather, however, and after New Zealand reached 313 there was just time for MCC to lose one wicket for 34 before the end.

The original plan had been for three four-day Tests, but for financial reasons this was changed, at Hadlee's suggestion, to four three-day Tests, the last appearance of this anachronism anywhere in the world. The prolonged good weather did mean that the profit from the tour would be substantial – £16,800 – and no doubt this was bigger than it would have been had the Tests been fewer and longer, but in view of the batting strength of both teams it seems sad that financial expediency was allowed to triumph over cricketing common sense. Four-day Tests could have produced a riveting series to crown this golden summer. When the amendment was agreed, Hadlee said 'Well, that means we can draw all four', and there can't have been many to disagree with him.

After the MCC game New Zealand played an Oxford University team good enough to beat both Yorkshire and Middlesex, who were to share the Championship, and lost their only match of the tour. This happened principally because after Oxford had batted first heavy overnight rain made the pitch extremely difficult, twenty-two wickets falling on the second day for just 160 runs. They came back with a good win over Sussex, though, and after two more draws were ready for the first Test at Headingley.

England's captain for the first two Tests was George Mann. When appointed captain for the previous series in South Africa, Mann had become the first player to lead England whose father had also held the same honour; curiously, both had only short Test careers (five games for Frank in

1922–3 and seven for George) and were captain in all of their Tests. Both were attacking batsmen and outstanding fielders, both were natural leaders who were highly popular and respected – no one could have been surprised to learn that George's distinguished war record stamped him as a brave and resourceful officer – and both led Middlesex to the title (in George's case shared with Yorkshire). In the fifth Test against South Africa the previous March he had scored his only Test century, 136 not out at a time when England were in some trouble, enabling his team to go on to an enthralling last-minute victory; and it was during this series, when he was dismissed by South Africa's slow left-armer, 'Tufty' Mann, that John Arlott was able to come up with his lovely comment about 'Mann's inhumanity to Mann'. After two Tests he indicated that he would not be available for the tour to Australia the winter after next because of the demands of the family brewing business – and that proved the end of his Test career. It was by no means the end of his connection with the game, though, for he acted as honorary secretary to Middlesex, served on the TCCB, being chairman from 1978 to 1983, and was president of MCC in 1984. Happily, the ideas of both Mann and Freddie Brown, his successor, accorded well with the New Zealanders' idea of enjoyment and the Tests were played in an excellent spirit. If only they could have had an extra day to make them meaningful . . .

During the first day of the first match at Headingley New Zealand bowled 114 overs and England made 307 for 5, a scoring rate which was criticised as too slow for a three-day Test. Hutton and Compton both made hundreds, but there was praise for tight bowling and good fielding from the tourists. Next morning the rest of the wickets went within an hour for 65 runs, Cowie and Burtt finishing with five apiece; but when the visitors fell to 80 for 4 there seemed to be trouble ahead. They were rescued by Donnelly and Brun Smith who put on 120, Smith going on to fall just four short of a century in his second Test. Lower down the order Mooney contributed 46, putting on 57 with Cowie for the last wicket, both of these partnerships being New Zealand records at the time. The innings closed on the third morning with New Zealand just 31 behind and with six wickets for Trevor Bailey on début, but with Cowie injured and unable to bowl. Washbrook made a century, Edrich got 70 and Mann hammered 49 in 24 minutes; by declaring at 267 for 4 he deprived himself of a possible place in the record books, missing the chance to beat Jack Brown's fastest Test fifty made in 28 minutes in 1894–5 in Australia. The declaration set a target of 299 in 150 minutes, and Sutcliffe and Scott made a fast start; but it was never really on, and at the end New Zealand were 195 for 2, Sutcliffe having made 82. It

*Len Hutton, front foot right out to the pitch of the ball, drives
Cave through extra cover during his century at Leeds in 1949.
Mooney is the wicket-keeper and Scott is at slip.*

had been a well-fought game, but the pleas from the press for longer Tests went unheeded.

At Lord's New Zealand enjoyed their best game against England, and the best they were to put up for some time. Only Compton with a century and Bailey with 93 gave any substance to England, putting on 189 in 145 minutes for the sixth wicket out of a total of 313; astonishing as it may sound, Bailey actually gave Compton a start of seventy-eight minutes and then caught him up when they were in the seventies, having scored his first 50 in forty-eight minutes. Mann then made history by declaring on the first day of a Test, without anyone realising at the time that this was not allowed in Tests under the current regulations. Mann duly apologised, and fortunately no New Zealand wicket fell during the fifteen minutes they batted that evening, but the visitors said they were more concerned about the spirit of the game than a minor breach of the law. After Sutcliffe and Scott had made a good start, the next day belonged chiefly to Martin Donnelly; by stumps the score was 372 for 7 and he had 126 of them, treating the crowd to a display of quality batsmanship, cutting and driving with power, grace and certainty. For the first time New Zealand had a first-innings lead over England and Hadlee ordered drinks for the entire press-box to celebrate.

In ninety minutes next morning the score went to 484, Donnelly being on 197 when the last man came in; Mann offered him singles to get Cowie on strike and he refused several easy runs. The crowd watched spellbound as Cowie, experienced and calm, faced a number of balls without failing his partner, and then Donnelly pushed Hollies to mid-off and, wrote Mitchell, 'he and Cowie sprinted as though the devil were on their tails'. Frank Mooney, the wicket-keeper, had in fact offered Cowie half a crown if he could stay there until Donnelly got to 200, and Cowie was so confident of his ability that he took the coin and batted with it in his pocket. (Cowie had once, batting for Auckland against Otago, come in at number eleven when his friend Bill Carson was on 46, to be asked anxiously by Carson if he could hold on while he reached his fifty. Some time later Cowie asked Carson the same question, by which time Carson had a century. Cowie got his fifty.) Donnelly – Dick Brittenden referred to him as Prima Donnelly – finally holed out for 206, at the time the highest New Zealand Test innings by a long way and still their only double-century against England, and the crowd acclaimed him nobly. If the rest was an anti-climax England could still, theoretically at least, have lost had they collapsed. Hutton and Robertson averted that danger by putting on 143 for the first wicket, Robertson making a hundred, and the game ended gently with England 306 for 5.

That innings was the peak of Martin Donnelly's glorious but all-too-brief career. He played in only the seven Tests of the 1937 and 1949 tours, scoring 582 runs at almost 53; in this series alone he was to score 462 at 77, and to head the tour averages with 2,287 runs at nearly 62. After showing great promise as a youngster – he caught the eye of Errol Holmes in 1935–6 – for a few years after the War he brought enormous pleasure to many thousands of war-weary people by the grace, style and sheer completeness of his batting. Left-handed and slightly below average height, he was extremely fast on his feet and, the mark of the quality batsman, always seemed to have time to play whatever stroke he wanted.

What might New Zealand have achieved had Martin Donnelly not retired so early? Dick Spooner watches another ball being sent on its way.

War service saw him in North Africa and Italy as a tank commander. In England at the end of the War he played for the New Zealand Services team and made an unbeaten century against Walter Hammond's XI, following this soon after with a splendid 133 for the Dominions against England in a wonderful high-scoring match which Dominions won with a few minutes to spare. He then went to read history at Oxford, having already graduated from University College, Canterbury, and performed deeds for the university which those writers who saw them insist they will never forget. In two years, 1946 and 1947, he scored 2,400 runs for Oxford, with nine centuries, at an average of almost 65 – a higher average than anyone else from either university who totalled over 2,000 runs. In the first year his six centuries equalled the record, culminating in 142 in under three hours against Cambridge to set up a victory. In the second year he captained them and although he could not bring off another victory in the varsity match he did score 162 not out for the Gentlemen in just three hours. With his double-century in the 1949 Test, therefore, he emulated Percy Chapman by scoring centuries at Lord's in the university match, Gentlemen v Players and a Test. He was also a good enough Rugby player to win his blue and a cap for England, his speed of movement making him, too, one of the greatest cover fielders the game has known. In 1948, now working for Courtaulds, he played several games for Warwickshire but without really distinguishing himself and he then made it clear that 1949 would be his last full first-class season. In the game at Oxford, the one that New Zealand lost, he was cheered all the way out to his first innings and, cricket being what it is, duly made 0 on a rain-affected pitch. For all his greatness as a batsman he was always modest about his deeds, a friendly man who enjoyed a good joke, had a fancy for shaggy-dog stories and insisted that cricket was just a game that had to be enjoyed. England, as well as New Zealand, mourned his departure to business in Australia.

New Zealand notched up four more victories before the third Test, which saw two significant débuts. For New Zealand John Reid played the first of his fifty-eight consecutive games, a career that was to see him as one of her finest all-rounders and as captain in her first three Test victories; and Brian Close became, at 18 years 149 days, the youngest man ever to play for England, a record one suspects he will hold forever. Close didn't have an especially happy match, taking 1 for 85 in all and not troubling the scorers in his only innings. The fact that he took his captain's instructions literally may just have had something to do with the latter misfortune; Close had gained a reputation for himself as something of a six-hitter, and as England already had a lead of over 120 when he went in Freddie Brown told him to 'have a look at a couple' before letting go. Which is precisely what he did, sending the third ball he received soaring towards the rope, to be caught by Rabone; for years after he insisted that if he hadn't hit it at the 'tallest bugger in side' he would have opened his Test account with a six.

Freddie Brown had succeeded Mann as England captain, a burly, genial all-rounder who that season had taken over at Northampton and transformed them after years of languishing at the foot of the table. He had played a few Tests before the War, but was one of those amateurs who would undoubtedly have been a top-line player had he been able to devote more time to the game. His batting was hard-hitting and carefree, and his leg-spinners and googlies, and later in his career medium-pace cutters, were good enough to bring him over 1,200 wickets. He went on to lead the tour to Australia in 1950–1 which was lost 4–1 but which, with a little more luck going England's way, could have been won 3–2, and he helped make it one of the happiest of all series. Enormously popular wherever he went, especially Australia, it was appropriate that he should have led England in this joyful summer for he was one of the last senior players for whom cricket was primarily about enjoyment rather than winning. He was a genuine throw-back to the Edwardian days when all those dashing amateurs were serving up rich entertainment throughout endless days of golden summer, and that his captaincy should coincide with the visit of a team of very gifted amateurs from New Zealand in another golden summer suggests that history was trying to make some belated amends for what had occurred earlier in the decade.

On winning his first toss as England captain Brown put New Zealand in as there had been a lot of rain beforehand and he hoped conditions would suit his bowlers. He was rewarded with four wickets down for 82 before lunch, after which Donnelly and Reid put on 116 for the fifth wicket, with Reid making 50 on his début. By close of play they were 276 for 8, and there were those who felt that they had been playing for a draw from the start. They were all out next morning for 293 in front of an Old Trafford crowd of no less than 38,000, the biggest attendance at a post-War Test in England. Hutton and Washbrook put on a century opening partnership, but proceedings were not as fast as the crowd would have liked; Simpson took a long time to get going, but then after a slow half-century scored his second fifty in twenty-eight minutes. Bailey at this time was scoring runs in an altogether different fashion from his later ten-an-hour grinds, and he and Simpson put on 105 in the last hour to see England to 363 for 5. Brown declared on the last morning at 440 for 9, a lead of 147. Having used seven bowlers in New Zealand's first innings he now used ten in their second, only

Early in his Test career Trevor Bailey actually scored runs quickly.
He subsequently abandoned this practice.

Evans missing out; he also missed out on a chance to stump Donnelly when he had made only 22, which could have swung the match irrevocably to England as Donnelly went on to make 80 – and with Sutcliffe reaching his maiden Test century the game was easily saved, New Zealand finishing on 348 for 7. The fact that Simpson, Washbrook and Hutton bowled a few overs says much about the interest left in the game.

That century brought to the fore the other outstanding New Zealand batsman of the post-War years. Six years younger than Donnelly and like him left-handed, Bert Sutcliffe was to become one of the real immortals of New Zealand cricket and enjoy a long career that saw him break several records. He too tasted war service in North Africa and Italy, after which he began to show his skills for Auckland and Otago, particularly with the 197 and 128 in one game against MCC in 1946–7. As a schoolboy in 1933 he had watched Hammond's 336 not out and once thrown back the ball after a six; on his own Test début that year he was to catch the great man and bring his last Test innings to its end, having already opened his own account with 58. In these 1949 Tests he was to score 423 runs at 60. For the whole tour his figures were 2,627 runs at just under 60, an aggregate for a tourist that has only been exceeded by Bradman, and a performance that earned him a place as one of *Wisden*'s five cricketers of the year. Fair of hair, wiry of build and cheerful of disposition, he was initially an opener although he dropped down the order in later years. His batting, always serene and apparently effortless, managed to combine style and artistry with adventure, splendid driving being mixed with determined hooking and pulling. He could also score extremely quickly; twice on this tour matches were won at the last gasp because he and Donnelly scored 'impossibly' fast to snatch a victory.

During the previous home season, playing for Auckland against Canterbury, he and Don Taylor had made 220 and 286 to provide the first instance of double-century opening stands in both innings of one match. In 1949–50 he was to make 355 against Auckland and three years later 385 against Canterbury, a score that remains the highest ever first-class innings by a left-hander. In forty-two Tests he was to score 2,727 runs at 40, with five centuries, the highest of which was 230 not out against India. Had he not had to bear the responsibility of being the leading batsman in a weak batting team for much of the 1950s his total would almost certainly have been significantly higher; and if it is idle to speculate what he and Donnelly might have achieved together had the latter not retired it is still irresistible, even allowing that the rest of the batting was weak. He captained New Zealand twice against West Indies and twice against South Africa but with little success; his man-management talents lay more in coaching, and

Bert Sutcliffe, one of New Zealand's true immortals.

having at one point been a physical training instructor he later became official coach in Otago. Not surprisingly he was very fast in the field, and also during this tour discovered an aptitude for slip-catching. It was sad that after all his efforts he was not in the team that gained New Zealand's first Test win, but by the time he retired – and he was in the Test team as late as 1965 – he had broken Roger Blunt's record aggregate of runs for a New Zealander, and had also scored more centuries – forty-four – than any other of his countrymen.

Sutcliffe came close to another century on a comfortable pitch at the Oval in the fourth Test, a match whose pattern followed that of the previous game quite closely. Hadlee won his first toss of the series and batted, with only Reid of the top batsmen failing. Sutcliffe's 88 was top score, with the total at stumps being 320 for 8, which was taken to 345 next day. England's bowling line-up now looks almost unbelievable: Bailey, Bedser, Edrich, Wright, Laker, Hollies and Brown, with Compton sending down a few as well; these were to claim 824 Test wickets between them and Brown, spoilt for choice, seemed hardly to know whom to use next. The second day, though, belonged to Hutton, Edrich and Simpson. Hutton and Simpson put on 147 in better than even time for the first wicket. Hutton took some three-and-a-half hours to reach his century but then scored another one in eighty-five minutes with some breathtaking batting that silenced those critics who called him too machine-like. He was out for the same score as Donnelly at Lord's, 206, after which Edrich followed him to three figures; at the close England were 432 for 4. The rest of the wickets fell for 50 runs on the third morning, Cresswell finishing with 6 for 168. Facing a deficit of 137, New Zealand lost four wickets before they passed it during the afternoon. The wicket was now turning and Brown had some rather useful spinners to call on, but Reid and Wallace stuck it out, Reid going on to an excellent 93. Near the end there was a break for bad light, after which Hadlee declared on 308 for 9 and everyone then called it a day.

One player who had had a particularly good tour was the wicket-keeper, Frank Mooney, who had made 66 dismissals and scored 774 runs at almost 23. His inclusion in the party had almost caused a strike in Dunedin, where the Watersider Workers' Union were incensed that the Otago wicket-keeper-batsman George Mills had been left out, believing his exclusion to have been caused by the fact that he was a watersider (docker). Thus there was extra pressure on Mooney to do well, but he was an easy-going character and it did not affect him – especially as Mills was ruled out on medical grounds anyway. He began in fine style by making six dismissals in one innings in the second game, and went on to claim ten victims in the first

Frank Mooney – quiet and serious on the field and a great extrovert off it.

three Tests, only to miss the last Test with a badly bruised finger. On the field he was neatness and efficiency personified, concentrating intensely, rarely speaking or smiling, and appealing only when virtually certain; off the field he was a cheerful extrovert, always ready for an evening's entertainment. This earned him the nickname of 'Starlight', the theory being that his character changed when the stars came out. His batting was limited but often effective, rarely more so than in the MCC match when his century – one of only two that he scored in his entire career – saved his team.

He went on to play in a total of fourteen Tests and make thirty dismissals, and even the Dunedin watersiders had to agree that he really was rather good.

This was the most successful English tour New Zealand were to have until 1986. Eight batsmen scored 1,000 runs, two of whom passed 2,000, and five bowlers took 50 or more wickets. The leading bowler by a long way was Tom Burtt, a slow left-armer of solid build and cheerful personality who bustled his way through more than 1,200 overs and took 128 wickets at under 23, seventeen of them in the Tests. Always accurate and with great heart and stamina, he got his wickets – in a fine summer when few pitches gave him much help – by bowling to his field for long spells, one of those bowlers who simply loved his craft and never wanted to stop; and when he did find a suitable pitch he was lethal. In all he played in ten Tests but was rather less successful in some of the others, finishing with thirty-three wickets at 35. He was also a useful batsman with a Test average of 21, who favoured a cross-bat wallop which he called his 'hockey shot' and which brought him quite a few runs. Warm, friendly, uncomplaining, tireless and a very fine cricketer, he was a touring captain's dream.

One other person who made an enormous contribution to the success of the tour deserves a mention. Jack Phillipps worked extremely hard to ensure that everything ran smoothly and was universally praised for his efficiency and friendliness. He was not involved in team selection but took responsibility for just about everything else, and relieved Hadlee of many duties to enable him to concentrate on the cricket. His job was made easier by the fact that the players were without exception amenable and easy-going, with no trouble-makers among them and no tendency to form cliques; to present-day English fans, used to repeated allegations of drugs/ booze/orgies and so forth being levelled at their heroes, such innocence will sound, depending on one's outlook, either laughable or paradisal. A pleasant source of amusement would be to imagine tabloid journalists trying to make something out a group of cricketers who didn't smoke, didn't drink and went to bed at half-past ten each night, as most of the New Zealanders did. Phillipps was to return as manager nine years later, when the story, on the field at least, would be very different. For now, though, with the tour over and plaudits being showered upon the team by everyone, he presented the Duke of Edinburgh, the President of MCC that year, with a china plate inscribed in gold with the tourists' autographs; as a reminder, he said, 'that seventeen New Zealanders thought it was a great thing to be in England in 1949'.

*

The arrangement whereby England tagged a few matches in New Zealand on to the end of an Australian tour meant that for decades the New Zealand public saw only a rather tired bunch of cricketers, most of whom now wanted little more than to get home to their families. On those few occasions when the Ashes had been won the euphoria did perhaps counteract the tiredness to a certain extent, but New Zealand fans have rarely been treated to the sight of a full-strength England team fresh and eager for the challenge. The unfairness of this to the fans was shown clearly in the first Test of 1951. Freddie Brown and Lindsay Hassett, two of the warmest and most genial of captains, had just combined to produce perhaps the most good-natured of all Ashes series; England had lost 4–1, but with more luck it could have been very different. None of the state games had been lost, and since arriving in New Zealand MCC had beaten Auckland and Otago convincingly, leading perhaps to a feeling among the English players that, despite New Zealand's good performances of 1949, not too much effort need go into the Tests. These were, incidentally, New Zealand's first four-day Tests.

A dead Christchurch pitch gave little help to the bowlers but didn't encourage stroke-making either. Sutcliffe and Reid put on 131 for the second wicket, the former making a century before becoming Brian Statham's first Test victim, but it was slow going and only 247 runs were scored in the day. By tea the following day Hadlee was able to declare at 417 for 8, but the Press were less than amused by the goings-on. The *Daily Mail* said that it 'was more like a backyard frolic than a Test. The English players made no attempt to conceal their feelings at the scoring rate. The fielding was shabby, with Compton signing autographs between balls when he was fielding in the deep. Players posed for photographs between overs.' E.W. Swanton saw this not as taking the opposition lightly but as 'a natural, if not inevitable, reaction to the long tour of Australia'. If it were really inevitable then some fairer arrangement should have been made, such as playing the New Zealand leg first in alternate Antipodean tours. It never happened, of course.

When England had a go their scoring rate was slightly worse. Washbrook, Simpson, Compton, Bailey and Brown all scored half-centuries, Bailey taking 270 minutes over his first fifty, before accelerating and going on to his only Test century. When England were at last all out for 550 there was time only for thirteen overs of New Zealand's second innings; these were bowled by England batsmen at New Zealand bowlers, Simpson's two wickets and Washbrook's one being their only Test victims. All good stuff if you enjoy farce.

In the Wellington Test the first day was lost to rain, after which New Zealand found themselves up against a pitch on to which water had seeped under the covers. Doug Wright in particular discovered that he liked this and his 5 for 48 helped to put the home team out for 125. Three England wickets fell cheaply that evening, but next day Hutton and Brown, helped by several dropped catches, averted any collapse and the innings made 227. On the last morning Tattersall reduced New Zealand to 105 for 7 with figures of 6 for 44, but Scott, batting down the order because of an injured leg, and Moir helped take them to 189, leaving England to get just 88 in 145 minutes. Cresswell and Burtt bowled very tightly and runs came very slowly. Moir found his way into the curiosities book by becoming the second player (after Warwick Armstrong in 1921) to bowl two consecutive Test overs, the last before tea and the first after. In the end four wickets were down before the match was won with fourteen minutes to spare.

There was a good deal of criticism of the poor cricket the Tests produced. It was strange that two such captains as Hadlee and Brown couldn't have managed something better, but as neither pitch was conducive to good cricket they were distinctly hampered; after the next series four years later Len Hutton was to say that New Zealand's pitches were the slowest in the world. Alex Bannister wrote that 'Test match psychology has come to New Zealand with a vengeance. Inglorious, time-wasting tactics as Tuesday's play faded out were in sad contrast to the country's tradition of bright, even if unorthodox, cricket.' Since Walter Hadlee was in charge one can't help wondering how much of an over-reaction this was, for journalists can get tired at the end of tours just as much as players. Clearly, however, something of a nadir had been reached.

*

Yet it wasn't a patch on the nadir that was reached next time around in 1954–5. Len Hutton – who said afterwards that he thought it would be better for MCC to visit New Zealand before Australia – and his team had just seen off Australia 3–1 with some fine performances and were obviously a much stronger outfit than New Zealand. In Cave, MacGibbon and Reid the home side had at last found a decent bowling attack, and their fielding was steadily improving – but now the batting was going through a lean spell and only Sutcliffe and Reid seemed able to get any runs. Since England's previous visit New Zealand had lost 1–0 at home to the West Indies, 1–0 at home to South Africa and 4–0 away to South Africa, so morale was obviously low. The Press complained that the standard of their domestic cricket was more mediocre that it had been for many years, with the batsmen allowing themselves to be kept on the defensive rather than trying to dominate the bowling and inevitably this attitude found its way into the national team. It was a rapid decline from the heights of 1949.

The first Test was the inaugural one at Dunedin, which, Errol Holmes had written, 'is, of course, merely another way of saying Edinburgh'. It didn't receive an auspicious baptism as with a wet outfield New Zealand, put in by Hutton, struggled to just 125 all out, still their lowest total in a full day's play and one which would have been sorry indeed without Sutcliffe's 74. Despite this, 16,000 people turned up on the second day and saw MacGibbon, Reid and Cave put in a good day's work and restrict England to 209 for 8 by the close. This was New Zealand's first five-day Test, but when the third and fourth days were both lost to rain this simply meant that they had the opportunity to lose on the fifth. Sutcliffe and Reid between them scored 63 out of their team's miserly 132, and England had plenty of time to knock off the 49 they needed for victory.

Few sporting encounters can be said to be truly historic, but perhaps the second Test at Auckland could claim to be one of them. For two and a half days it was a good game. The quick bowlers got some lift from the pitch, but the outfield was fast and with 49 from Sutcliffe and 73 from Reid New Zealand made 200 in their first innings. 30,000 people turned up on the second day, and in showery conditions that saw some time lost they watched as Simpson, May, Cowdrey and Hutton engaged in a fine battle with the bowlers. At the close England were 148 for 4. On Monday morning the eighth wicket fell with a lead of just one run, but Tyson and Statham took them to 246. At three o'clock on 28 March 1955 New Zealand began their second innings, still very much in the game having just bowled very well. At tea they were 13 for 3, Leggat and Reid having scored one each and Poore having completed a 'pair'. Sutcliffe was to be the top scorer on this sad day with 11 but his dismissal was dreadful, a mighty swipe at Wardle's third ball of which he was no doubt even more mightily ashamed. Appleyard spun the ball prodigiously into the middle order and with some fine close catching dismissed four of them, finding himself on a hat-trick for the second time in the match; 22 for 8. The crowd, hardly able to believe their eyes, had one more horror to come; Rabone appealed against the light, and they expressed their displeasure accordingly. The appeal was turned down, Rabone was lbw to Statham next ball and, an hour and three-quarters after the innings began, the last wicket fell with the score on 26. It is still the lowest total ever recorded in Test history.

There were no outstanding English performances in either game, Tyson,

Frank Tyson's speed was too much for the Australians and the New Zealanders.

Statham, Wardle and Appleyard sharing the wickets and Hutton's 53 being the highest innings. It was his 138th and last innings for England, taking him to 6,971 Test runs and, after the pressures that had attended his appointment as England's first official professional captain, one of the best-earned of sporting retirements. He is, of course, one of cricket's immortal batsmen, his Test average of 56 placing him as one of the very best – and this despite an accident during the war which resulted in his left arm having to

*Geoff Rabone in action against Warwickshire during the 1949
tour. The bowler is A.H. Kardar.*

be shortened by an inch or so. For years he and Denis Compton, with their differing styles, were way above any other English batsmen, and if Hutton's perfection was sometimes criticised as too machine-like it was only because people failed to understand the essential Yorkshireness in his character. When he was appointed captain there were those antiquated old bodies who were appalled, thereby increasing the pressure on an already very sensitive man; but apart from being unduly cautious at times and introducing the slowing down of the over-rate as a tactical weapon, for which posterity has little cause to be grateful to him, he did his job well and successfully, undoubtedly being one of England's best captains since the War.

It was also the end of the Test line for his opposite number, Geoff Rabone. In many ways Rabone is the archetypal New Zealand Test cricketer; an intelligent, friendly, sporting and courageous man, he played in twelve Tests, averaged 31 with the bat including one century, and took sixteen rather expensive wickets with off-spin which he occasionally varied with leg-spin or medium pace. New Zealand has produced many fine players who were just not quite fine enough for their country to make a real impact and Rabone was just such a one. As captain on the initial tour to South Africa he enjoyed his best Test spell with the bat, scoring 254 runs at 50 in the first three Tests before being injured. One draw and four defeats in his games as captain may not be much of a record, but he was much liked and respected by his players and was unfortunate to coincide with a weak side. It can't have been easy to go through life knowing that you were the captain of the team that recorded the lowest ever score in a Test innings.

After the game it was announced that vandals had removed the covers from the wicket during the previous night, but as there had been no rain the wicket had not been damaged. There was, regrettably, no hiding place for New Zealand, and the reaction of Press and public may safely be left to the reader's imagination.

1946–7	Christchurch	NZ 345–9d;	E 265–7d	Drawn
1949	Lord's	MCC 379, 34–1;	NZ 313	Drawn
	Headingley	E 372, 267–4d;	NZ 341, 195–2	Drawn
	Lord's	E 313–9d; 306–5;	NZ 484	Drawn
	Old Trafford	NZ 293, 348–7;	E 440–9d	Drawn
	Oval	NZ 345, 308–9d;	E 482	Drawn
1950–1	Christchurch	NZ 417–8d, 46–3;	E 550	Drawn
	Wellington	NZ 125, 189;	E 227, 91–4	E 6 wkts
1954–5	Dunedin	NZ 125, 132;	E 209–8d; 49–2	E 8 wkts
	Auckland	NZ 200, 26;	E 246	E inns 20 runs

1946–7 Test match
England
Best batting: W.R. Hammond 79   J.T. Ikin 45   W.J. Edrich 42
Best bowling: A.V. Bedser 39–5–95–4   R. Pollard 29.4–8–73–3

New Zealand
Best batting: W.A. Hadlee 116   B. Sutcliffe 58   J. Cowie 45
Best bowling: J.Cowie 30–4–83–6

Wicket-keepers: E.W.T. Tindill (NZ) 1 dismissal   T.G. Evans (E) 2 dismissals

W.R. Hammond, playing in his last Test, took his Test aggregate to the then record figure of 7,249 runs.

1949 Test series

England

Batting

Batting	Innings	NO	HS	Runs	Average
R.T. Simpson	2	0	103	171	85.50
C. Washbrook	3	1	103*	157	78.50
L. Hutton	6	0	206	469	78.16
T.E. Bailey	5	2	93	219	73.00
W.J. Edrich	6	0	100	324	54.00

Bowling	Overs	M	Runs	W	Average
D.C.S. Compton	33	2	126	5	25.20
J.A. Young	62.4	13	158	6	26.33
A.V. Bedser	85	19	215	7	30.71
T.E. Bailey	158	22	599	16	37.43
W.E. Hollies	175	54	385	10	38.50

New Zealand

Batting	Innings	NO	HS	Runs	Average
F.B. Smith	3	1	96	173	86.50
M.P. Donnelly	6	0	206	462	77.00
B. Sutcliffe	7	0	101	423	60.42
J.R. Reid	4	0	93	173	43.25
W.A. Hadlee	7	1	43	193	32.16

Bowling	Overs	M	Runs	W	Average
G.F. Cresswell	41.2	6	168	6	28.00
J. Cowie	147.1	23	451	14	32.21
T.B. Burtt	195.3	50	568	17	33.41
G.O. Rabone	87	22	327	4	81.75
B. Sutcliffe	26	2	95	1	95.00

Wicket-keepers: T.G. Evans (E) 12 dismissals   F.L.H. Mooney (NZ) 10 dismissals   J.R. Reid (NZ) 2 dismissals

In the second match M.P. Donnelly became the only New Zealand batsman to score a double century against England. In the third match D.B. Close became the youngest man ever to play for England, aged 18 years 149 days. In the fourth match L. Hutton emulated Donnelly's score of 206, his third fifty coming in only 35 minutes.

1950–1 Test series

England

Best batting: T.E. Bailey 134* R.T. Simpson 81 D.C.S. Compton 79 F.R. Brown 62 C. Washbrook 58 L. Hutton 57

Best bowling: R. Tattersall 21–6–44–6 D.V.P. Wright 19–3–48–5

New Zealand

Best batting: B. Sutcliffe 116 W.M. Wallace 66 V.J. Scott 60 J.R. Reid 50 W.A. Hadlee 50

Best bowling: A.M. Moir 56.3–16–155–6

Wicket-keepers: F.L.H. Mooney (NZ) 2 dismissals T.G. Evans (E) 3 dismissals

In the first match B. Sutcliffe and J.R. Reid put on 131 for the New Zealand record second-wicket partnership against England.

1954–5 Test series
    England
    Best batting: L. Hutton 53   P.B.H. May 48
    Best bowling: R. Appleyard 6–3–7–4   F.H. Tyson 12–6–16–4   J.B. Statham 17–9–24–4;
                     17.4–7–28–4

    New Zealand
    Best batting: B. Sutcliffe 74 and 35; 49   J.R. Reid 73
    Best bowling: A.M. Moir 25.1–3–62–5   J.R. Reid 27–11–36–4

    Wicket-keepers: I.A. Colquhoun (NZ) 4 dismissals   T.G. Evans (E) 4 dismissals

In the second match New Zealand's second innings score of 26 is the lowest in all Tests.

— 6 —

The Reid
is as the Oak

If 28 March 1955 was the low point in New Zealand's cricketing history 13 March 1956 was the high, when at Eden Park, Auckland they beat the West Indies by 190 runs to record their first ever Test victory. If the reaction to the 26-run disaster is easily imaginable, how much more so is the sheer sweetness of this moment after twenty-seven years of waiting. Many stories were told of the way people were affected; Geoff Rabone, for instance, kept saying over and over again 'I'm so bloody pleased, I'm so *bloody* pleased.' It doesn't take much effort to put oneself in his position.

That victory came at the end of the most sustained period of Test cricket New Zealand had ever played. In five months they toured Pakistan and India, playing eight Tests, and then entertained the West Indies, playing four and gaining their win in the last one. They then played no more until the 1958 tour of England, a delay which, now that they had broken their duck, must have been particularly galling. Only five of the players who had beaten West Indies were in the first Test of 1958, and clearly any impetus that the victory might have given them had long since been lost.

Thinness of batting talent was still a problem for the selectors and they decided to go for young players who appeared promising rather than more experienced ones who hadn't been playing too well. John Reid, the captain, didn't go along with this idea and when he came to write his autobiography he complained that he had not been consulted about the make-up of the squad. He wrote: 'One looks for experience to burn in an international touring team. This one had inexperience to burn.' In fact five of the sixteen were uncapped, but in the event the youngsters didn't perform too badly – outside the Tests, that is. A full programme of five five-day Tests had been arranged – the only time so far that this has happened – but against a very strong English team it was a disaster matched only by the appalling weather. Twenty-nine full playing days were to be lost in one of the wettest summers since the tour of 1931, depriving the tourists of much-needed practice – the glorious weather of 1949 stands out as an aberration.

Yet again the ball lands in the crowd. The mighty John Reid, challenged only by Richard Hadlee as New Zealand's greatest all-rounder.

John Reid was to captain New Zealand thirteen times against England and thirty-four times in all. It was his third game in charge which saw the first Test victory, but his other thirty-one matches produced only two more wins, both in the 1961–2 series in South Africa; the one prize he wanted most of all, a victory over England, always eluded him. As a captain he was better able than most to lead by example as he was one of the great all-rounders, and as he grew into the job he became a very able tactician who would handle his bowlers well and get the best out of them. His players had the greatest respect and affection for him, and there can be no doubt that with a stronger team he would have achieved great things.

He was a very strong man who used his power to fine effect as a batsman, always looking to drive, cut or hook the bowling as much as possible. He played many excellent Test innings including six centuries, but so often had he to carry the weight of the batting that his Test average of 33 is markedly lower than his career average of 41. His peak was undoubtedly in South Africa in 1961–2 when he scored 1,915 runs at 68 to break all records for a touring batsman; 546 of these at an average of 60 were scored in the Tests, and he headed the Test bowling averages as well with 11 wickets at under 20. On tour eight years earlier he had become the first player to score 1,000 runs and take 50 wickets in a South African first-class season. His medium-fast outswing was usually highly accurate and he possessed an off-cutter which deceived many a batsman. He was also an outstanding close fielder and deputy wicket-keeper; fulfilling that role in only his second Test, he came close to becoming only the second wicket-keeper-batsman, after Les Ames, to score a century when he made 93. When he retired he possessed a remarkable collection of New Zealand Test records: played in most Tests (his 58 consecutive games, which constituted his entire career, were a world record); scored most runs (3,428); taken most wickets (85); made most centuries (6); held most catches (43); most Tests as captain (34, still the record). His performances become even more outstanding when one remembers the overall weakness of the sides in which he played, and one can only guess at what he might have achieved had he had less responsibility in terms of carrying the team. A song in Shakespeare's *Cymbeline* contains the words 'the reed is as the oak' which, with a slight alteration in spelling, will serve admirably to illustrate his importance to his country's cricket.

England's captain had considerably fewer problems. Peter May had led his country since 1955 and would go on to an England record of forty-one Tests as captain, winning twenty and losing ten. Until the disastrous tour of Australia the following winter not a rubber was lost, for this was a period when English cricket was strong. One of its strengths was May's batting, and he is still widely regarded as the best English batsman to emerge since the War, with over 4,500 runs at nearly 47 from sixty-six Tests. He had taken over the captaincy from Len Hutton and had also inherited his cautious approach, sometimes declining to press for a victory if there was the least risk of losing – and he did cricket fans no favours by persisting with the practice started by Hutton of slowing down the over rate as a tactical ploy. A quiet, fastidious, mild-mannered man, he was perhaps too reserved to be able to communicate intimately with his team, yet he seemed to have few problems with man-management as they all liked and respected him. Obviously he was lucky to coincide with a powerful team, but the shambles in Australia in 1958–9 suggests that he didn't have the character, ability or whatever to pick his side up when being beaten by a better outfit. By that time, though, the demands of the job were taking their toll on his health, and when at the end of the 1961 series against Australia he announced his retirement there was much sadness among English cricket followers. His wife, incidentally, is the daughter of Harold Gilligan, England's captain in those first Tests against New Zealand.

The tour got off to a splendid start. Of the ten games played before the first Test six were won and the only defeat was by mighty Surrey, then in their seventh consecutive Championship-winning season. The most exciting of these games was against a strong MCC team that fielded ten Test players. New Zealand batted first and at one point were 146 for 2 with good knocks from Lawrie Miller and Noel Harford; Appleyard and Tyson then got going and they were all out for 190. By the close, though, MCC were 68 for 4 and were all out for 164 next morning. Once again the tourist's batting centred on Miller and Harford before 66 not out from MacGibbon on the final morning allowed Reid to declare at 266 for 8. With a target for a strong batting line-up of 293 in 275 minutes, it was a declaration that might have come from a match in Utopia. Stewart and Milton put on 72 for the first wicket and then Mike Smith and Parks carried on. At tea they were 162 for the loss of three wickets. Smith fell at 200 and when the fifth wicket went down there was an hour left with 82 still required. When Tyson departed there was half an hour to score 40; then two more wickets fell quickly. When the ninth fell 19 were needed in six minutes. Swetman, who had made 48 while his partners were falling, hit a four – and in trying to score another was caught behind. New Zealand had won by 13 runs with two minutes to spare. Johnny Hayes, so unlucky with injury in 1949, took 7 for 49 to add to his 4 for 40 in the first innings. The only black spot was that Sutcliffe broke a wrist fielding and missed six games including the first Test.

MCC v New Zealanders
Lord's 17, 19, 20 May 1958
Toss: New Zealanders

New Zealanders

B. Sutcliffe	c Swetman b Moss	9	lbw b Tyson		8
L.S.M. Miller	c Milton b Appleyard	76	c Richardson b Appleyard		65
N.S. Harford	c & b Appleyard	52	c Milton b Tyson		59
J.R. Reid˙	c Stewart b Appleyard	10	(5) b Allen		18
W.R. Playle	b Appleyard	0	(4) c Swetman b Allen		21
J.T. Sparling	c Stewart b Allen	5	c Swetman b Moss		4
A.R. MacGibbon	b Tyson	9	not out		66
J.C. Alabaster	c Swetman b Tyson	3	c Stewart b Tyson		1
E.C. Petrie†	run out	2	run out		10
R.W. Blair	b Tyson	12			
J.A. Hayes	not out	0			
Extras	(b7, lb1, nb4)	12	(lb5, nb9)		14
Total		**190**	(8 wickets declared)		**266**

Fall of wickets: 18, 117, 146, 146, 158, 173, 175, 176, 190, 190

36, 126, 152, 170, 182, 190, 198, 266

	O	M	R	W	O	M	R	W
Tyson	13	1	72	3	21	4	59	3
Moss	7	0	43	1	18	3	71	1
Appleyard	23.1	11	36	4	13	2	40	1
D. Smith	8	5	12	0				
Allen	10	4	15	1	28.1	9	82	2

MCC

M.J. Stewart	c Petrie b Hayes	6	c sub (Meale) b Hayes		46
C.A. Milton	c Petrie b Hayes	12	lbw b Hayes		22
M.J.K. Smith˙	c Petrie b Hayes	7	c & b MacGibbon		70
J.M. Parks	c Petrie b MacGibbon	18	c Harford b Sparling		41
D.V. Smith	lbw b Reid	39	(11) not out		0
D.W. Richardson	b MacGibbon	34	(5) c sub (Meale) b Hayes		15
R. Swetman†	c Petrie b MacGibbon	3	(6) c Petrie b MacGibbon		48
F.H. Tyson	c Reid b Sutcliffe	10	(7) c & b Hayes		9
M.H.J. Allen	not out	16	(10) c Sparling b Hayes		7
A.E. Moss	c Sparling b Hayes	9	(8) b Hayes		4
R. Appleyard	c sub (D'Arcy) b Alabaster	2	(9) c Alabaster b Hayes		0
Extras	(lb6, nb2)	8	(b3, lb11, nb3)		17
Total		**164**			**279**

Fall of wickets: 11, 18, 33, 51, 100, 120, 120, 146, 161, 164

72, 75, 159, 200, 211, 253, 266, 266, 274, 279

	O	M	R	W	O	M	R	W
Blair	12	4	33	0				
Hayes	25	12	40	4	24	8	49	7
MacGibbon	20	5	31	3	27.1	5	90	2
Alabaster	19.2	6	37	1	20	2	58	0
Reid	5	2	5	1	14	0	49	0
Sutcliffe	2	1	10	1				
Sparling					4	1	16	1

The New Zealanders won by 13 runs

The evening session of the opening day of the first Test at Edgbaston saw the turning point of the tour. Thereafter the only match won was against Scotland; there was a thrilling tie in the last first-class match against T.N. Pearce's XI, defeat in a second match against Surrey, a very one-sided Test series and draw after rain-affected draw against the counties. During the first two sessions of the first Test, though, only May and Cowdrey, with 84 and 81, averted English ignominy; 17 from number eleven Loader was the next highest score in a total of 221, MacGibbon taking 5 for 64. Trueman was to take five wickets too, at a cost of only 31, with a fine spell of bowling; by lunch on the second day New Zealand were 73 for 9, the follow-on (then enforceable if the deficit was 150 or more) being avoided only by the last pair, Cave and Hayes, who took the score to 94. Even at this early stage of the series what followed had an air of predictability. In showery weather May declared at 215 for 6 with 100 from Richardson and 70 from Cowdrey, whereupon New Zealand collapsed again for 137, the match finishing on the afternoon of the fourth day and the winning margin being 205 runs. For the New Zealanders things were to get worse.

One of the duties of the historian is, of course, to record events, but it would be a sad business if he or she were not able to display a spot of humanitarianism along the way. We shall, therefore, dispose of the rest of this series with some alacrity and if any fervently patriotic and/or xenophobic English readers feel cheated out of a wallow in the triumphs of their heroes that is simply bad luck.

At Lord's New Zealand bowled well on a good pitch to restrict England to 237 for 7 on the first day, only for prolonged rain to present Laker and Lock with a dream wicket. Admittedly the tourists then batted very poorly to be all out for 47, but they were desperately unlucky. Further rain meant that the pitch was no easier second time round and they were dismissed for 74, Lock's match figures being 9 for 29. Only Jack D'Arcy had shown any application in these two matches and the papers duly applauded him, but he then faded and played in no more Tests after this tour.

Bad weather then seriously curtailed the visitors' next matches, depriving them of much-needed practice. The Headingley Test did not start till the afternoon of the third day and when Reid won his first toss of the series he had a difficult decision as the pitch was still damp. He decided to bat – and they were soon all out for 67. Next day the weather was fine; Milton, on début, and May both scored undefeated centuries. May declared with a lead of exactly 200, Lock took seven wickets to finish with 11 for 65 and New Zealand were all out for 129. Arthur Milton became the first Englishman to remain on the field throughout a Test, and the first player to do this on

Arthur Milton, last man to play for England at both football and cricket and first man to remain on the field throughout a Test for England. Here, playing for Gloucestershire against Warwickshire in 1959 he has a lucky escape as the ball slips through Cartwright's hands.

début. England, having lost only two wickets, won by an innings and 71 runs.

In the fourth Test at Old Trafford New Zealand did at least manage to bat throughout a full day, reaching 220 for 6 before being all out for 267 next morning. MacGibbon made 66 and was supported by Sparling, Petrie and Sutcliffe, Petrie retiring hurt after being hit on the head by a Trueman bouncer. Reid kept wicket in Petrie's place and made one stumping, but the bowling was rather innocuous and May got another century as much time was lost to the weather. By the fourth evening the wicket was drying and the ball was flying, so May declared with a lead of 98 – and yet again the weather made life difficult for New Zealand. Overnight rain followed by a drying wind helped Tony Lock to his best Test figures of 7 for 35 as the visitors were all out for 85, only Sutcliffe making any resistance. An innings and 13 runs this time.

England's first Test whitewash had to wait another year, however, when India were the visitors, as only some twelve hours of play were possible at the Oval. New Zealand made 161 thanks mainly to 41 not out from number ten Moir, his best Test score, and then for the first time the weather went in their favour. Even so, almost all the England batsmen got in before getting out and they managed to total 219, leaving New Zealand the task of not capitulating for under 58 in less than three hours. Even then there were early alarms, but Sutcliffe and Reid saw them home for the draw.

The main mitigating factor in all this was that the weather was desperately unkind to them; not only did the luck go against them almost throughout the Tests, but they were unable to get the practice they so badly needed in the county games. The pattern of weather in the Tests helped Lock to get 34 wickets at 7.47 with Laker taking 17 at 10.17, and as innings after innings crumbled the tourists were pilloried by the Press who, with a few exceptions, showed little appreciation of their problems. It was notable that what sympathy they did get came largely from ex-cricketers such as Hutton and Compton who had been through the mill themselves against a strong Australian team and knew what it was like. At least there was a financial profit from it all when it had seemed likely at one point to end in a loss. A total of £4,000 made some small inroads into the disappointment.

One big problem was that neither Sutcliffe nor Reid was in anything like their true form in the Tests, and there was no one else with the ability or experience to mount the rescue campaigns. Only one player, in fact, came out of the series with real credit. Tony MacGibbon was a 6 feet 5 inches fast-medium bowler who could make the ball move either way and, with his height, get good lift even from unresponsive pitches. He had made his début against England in 1950–1 and had been the mainstay of the team's bowling during the 1950s, this series being his swansong since he decided to stay in England to read civil engineering at Durham University. He began the series with five wickets on the first day and ended with 20 at 19.45 to beat Cowie's 19 of the three-match 1937 rubber to set a new record for New Zealand against England; his value to his team can be seen from the fact that he bowled almost twice as many overs and took more than three times as many wickets as anyone else. He also took more on the tour than any of his colleagues, 73 at 21.35. He ended his twenty-six Tests with 70 wickets at just under 31, and added to that a batting average of almost 20, helping to bolster a weak batting team; his 66 in the fourth Test was the highest from New Zealand in the series. He was also a fine slip fielder, and New Zealand's loss was very much Durham's gain.

*

Six months later England were in New Zealand, having just come a monumental 4–0 cropper to Richie Benaud's Australians in a series that many had expected them to win. One reason for the failure had been that the batsmen didn't give the bowlers a strong enough base from which to operate; there had been complaints about illegal Australian bowling actions, but in truth Benaud, Davidson and Meckiff had been too good for them. New Zealand's bowlers, unfortunately, posed much less threat, especially now that MacGibbon had gone. In fact only six of the home team, which was the same for both Tests, had been in England the summer before, most of the newcomers being batsmen. Half a dozen of the MCC party did not make the trip to New Zealand, but the team that did was still a powerful one. And the story really just continued from where it had been interrupted the previous August.

In the first Test England batted first and wickets fell steadily. At one point they were 224 for 7 and New Zealand seemed to have done a good job. Ted Dexter, however, was having one of those days when he looked the most majestic batsman in the world and today his first Test century was looming. In the end he made 141, England totalled 374, and with the pitch responding to Reid's off-cutters Lock was ready to resume where he too had left off the previous summer. His barren tour of Australia would soon be just a bad memory. In twenty-six overs he took 5 for 31 as New Zealand were all out for 142, 31 of which came from the massively-built last man Hough, on début, including 16 in his first over from Trueman. Following on, Guy made 56 but Lock again bowled magnificently, taking 6 for 53 this time; all out 133 to lose by an innings and 99 runs. One shudders to think what the full Australian team might have done to their neighbours at this time. There was, incidentally, one little curiosity about this game to appeal to the quiz enthusiast; Eric Tindill, the wicket-keeper just before and after the War, had played international Rugby as well as Test cricket and had also refereed Rugby internationals. By standing in this Test at Christchurch he became the only man to play and also referee/umpire in official internationals at both sports.

The Auckland Test was ruined by the weather. Strong winds several times blew off the bails and in the first hour only eight runs were scored for the loss of two wickets, with Trueman bowling seven maidens before conceding a run. More wickets fell, and only Sutcliffe, with 61, made any impact on the bowling or the conditions. A wag of the tail took the score to 181. In response Richardson and Graveney gave the England innings a decent base, and although a few wickets fell May went on to a fine century and was 124 not out at the close – the close of the match, in fact, since the other two days had been completely washed out.

In the last seven Tests, the only games he played against New Zealand, Tony Lock had taken 47 wickets at 7.81. Somehow it always seemed surprising that Lock was a slow bowler, for his temperament was that traditionally associated with the fiery fast men – aggressive, combative, at times rash; the contrast with the phlegmatic Jim Laker, for so long his 'spin twin' for Surrey and England, could hardly have been greater. Where they coincided was that both would invariably give their all, two superb attacking spin bowlers who played vital parts in Surrey's and

Tony Lock – 47 wickets at 7.81 in just 7 Tests against New Zealand.

England's success of the 1950s. Lock was not yet 17 when he made his début in 1946, and his first appearance for England came six years later. By this time he had developed a faster ball to help him on the slow turning pitches at the Oval. Although it was often lethal and made him a very dangerous bowler it had a question mark against it; he was called occasionally over the years and it attracted a good deal of criticism so that eventually, during this tour of Australasia, he abandoned it. In 1956, at the age of 26, he became the third-youngest bowler to reach 1,000 wickets, although he was later to be pushed down one place by Derek Underwood. His total Test bag was 174 victims at 25 each from 49 matches, and as well as being a useful tail-end batsman he was one of the greatest close fielders in the history of the game, his reactions at short leg being beyond belief at times. His career was unusual in that at an age when some players would be thinking of retiring he went to Western Australia, first as player-coach and then as captain; and, making an enormous contribution as a player as well as proving a fine captain who played attractive, attacking cricket, he led them to their first ever success in the Sheffield Shield. For some years he also returned to England each summer to play for Leicestershire, captaining them in 1967 and 1968 and taking them to third place in the table. It was a commuting lifestyle that made him one of the first of cricket's jet-setters, and was altogether in character for an altogether remarkable player.

Where, though, was New Zealand cricket to go from here? An inordinate number of players had been tried over the last few years and discarded after just one or two Tests, and clearly the selectors had to reconsider their policy of choosing youth rather than experience. As ever, the problems stemmed from being part-timers up against professionals; a series of newspaper articles by Bert Sutcliffe highlighted the difficulties they faced, some of which the ordinary fan might not have realised – by going on tour, for instance, they were likely to risk losing promotion and possibly even their jobs. Better practice facilities were needed, he said, and faster, more even wickets to allow the young batsmen to develop. He suggested too that Christchurch should cease to be the sole administrative centre of the game and that each of the major cities should share this responsibility in rotation.

As it happened New Zealand played no more Tests for almost three years, yet when they did so had their most successful series thus far.

*

In 1960–1, for the first time since Errol Holmes's tour, MCC made a proper tour of New Zealand, although only ten of the twenty-two games were first-class. There was no England tour that winter, but it was a long way from being a full-strength squad; the captain was Dennis Silk of Somerset, five of the players had Test experience and six more would later win caps, but it didn't have the air of an outfit to strike fear into the Australians or West Indians, who had produced their wonderful tied Test shortly before this tour began. There were three unofficial four-day 'Tests' but no official ones, and one of the aims was to visit as many centres as could be managed in order to create as much widespread interest as possible. Obviously this meant that travel costs would be high and to offset this the players stayed with various families to cut down on hotel bills. This didn't apply in the cities where the 'Tests' were to take place, but not surprisingly it didn't do much to foster team spirit. As it happened the weather was poor and the trip made a loss of over £1,500. Of the first-class games MCC won four, lost one and drew five, but were hampered by a string of injuries and a lack of practice caused by the weather. MCC were managed, incidentally, by Jack Phillipps, who had done such good work for the New Zealanders in 1949 and 1958.

Silk injured his hand early on and missed several games, including the first two 'Tests'. The team was led in his absence by the most experienced of the players, Willie Watson, who had earned himself immortality in 1953 when, with Trevor Bailey, he had kept the Australians at bay in the Lord's Test after defeat for England had seemed inevitable. The opening day of the first match was washed out and he then inserted the opposition, only to see them total 313 for 7 as Harris and Sparling both scored over 70. By the end of the third day MCC had put together 277 for 5 in better than even time, with Parks and Prideaux the main contributors, at which point Watson declared in order to make a game of it. New Zealand duly obliged in this undertaking next morning by losing wicket after wicket, eight going down for 110, but then Dick Motz, not yet a Test player and destined to just the occasional sparkle at that level with the bat, hammered 60 in eighty minutes, including three sixes in one over from David Allen. It proved crucial, for when the last wicket fell at 169 MCC needed 206 in 145 minutes. Russell and Stewart began well, putting on 77 in just over an hour, and when the second wicket went down 85 were needed in fifty minutes. And then suddenly four wickets fell and the chance was on for New Zealand. The time had clearly come for the shutters to go up and Watson obliged, the visitors being 167 for 7 at the end.

In the second match the opening day was again lost to rain and Watson again sent New Zealand in. This time the ploy worked. Motz once more top-scored, he and Harris salvaging something from the wreckage of 43 for 5 and, with 89 in seventy minutes, helping the total to 148. MCC were 34 for 1 overnight; next morning Cameron picked up three quick wickets, Motz took four more, and soon after lunch MCC were all out for 111, Motz finishing with 5 for 34. New Zealand then made a sound start with 89 for the first wicket; four then fell quickly, but Reid was still there and on the final morning he pushed on to 83, helping the total to 228. MCC's target was 266 in 250 minutes, but they got nowhere near it. Jack Alabaster was the hero, taking the first four wickets with the help of Reid at slip and finishing with 5 for 71 as MCC fell to 132 all out. It was New Zealand's first victory over a touring MCC team since 1907 and Reid's captaincy was widely praised. He led by example with his batting, bowling and five catches, orchestrated his bowlers and field-placings splendidly and ensured his team didn't surrender the advantage. It was the first time New Zealand had gone into the last game of a series knowing they could not lose the rubber, and he described the sensation as 'happy and unusual'.

Unfortunately the third game was then badly affected by the weather. Silk returned as MCC captain, won the toss and batted, but before long play was washed out for the day. Next morning six wickets were down for 119 before Watson, with a broken bone in his hand, and David Smith put on 93. The last wickets then fell quickly, leaving MCC 223 all out. In reply New Zealand struggled to 143 and 7 before Motz, Alabaster and Bartlett, all of whom had bowled well, took the score to 249 for 8 when Reid declared. With a day and a bit left MCC had a deficit of 26, Stewart and Watson injured and Larter in hospital with appendicitis; they made 45 for 1 by the close, but the last day was then washed out completely. New Zealand had won their first series, even if the 'Tests' were unofficial.

For MCC injuries and the weather had combined to render the tour less than a resounding success, although it was accounted an enjoyable one. Prideaux and Padgett were the leading batsmen and Larter the most successful bowler, at least in the first-class games, but there were several disappointments. Silk, like Hutton before him, insisted that New Zealand's most pressing need was for faster wickets, since the dead ones they had encountered everywhere encouraged only the defensive batsmen and actively discouraged the attacking players from making their strokes.

There was, too, some controversy at the end of the tour when English writers suggested that young Gary Bartlett might have a suspect action; he was the first genuinely fast bowler New Zealand had produced and these allegations naturally upset his confidence. Partly through this and partly through injury he was never really to fulfil his early promise.

*

Two years later in 1962–3 England went to New Zealand after drawing the series in Australia 1–1. It was a rubber that perhaps they really should have won, one batting collapse costing them the Ashes, and as in the past they took out their annoyance on the poor old part-timers – with a vengeance.

England's batting line-up at this period was quite formidable, although the bowling, at least against a strong batting side, was less so. Only the year before New Zealand had enjoyed their finest series to date when they drew 2–2 in South Africa, and the core of that successful team now faced England; but if a week is a long time in politics a year is certainly a long time in sport. Any optimism the New Zealanders may have felt after their success was destined to last only until the first afternoon of the initial Test in Auckland. The record books were about to start showing another solid block of convincing England victories.

England were led by Ted Dexter, famed as one of the most attractive attacking batsmen since the War. In sixty-two Tests he was to score 4,500 runs at an average of nearly 48, one of those fortunate players who performed better on the grander stage than in the bread-and-butter of county cricket. His batting had a splendid imperiousness to it that earned him the nickname of 'Lord Ted' and when he was really on song the bowler appeared to be little more than a servant delivering balls to his master in a country-house match. He was also a good enough medium pacer to take 66 Test wickets. He captained England thirty times, winning nine and losing seven, a good captain but not an outstanding one. Like many of the captains of his time he was not confident in his use of the spinners, and he was sometimes rather unadventurous – which was surprising in one who enjoyed gambling and generally leading an exciting life. He had a reputation for being a theorist and puzzling spectators with his ploys and also for not always concentrating one hundred per cent on the match in hand. A dominating personality, he could occasionally upset people; but in a humdrum period of cricket he stood out as a sparkling individualist.

By lunch-time on the first day the New Zealanders must still have been optimistic, for they had taken three wickets for 74. Then Barrington and Cowdrey put on 166, with the former getting a century, after which Parfitt and Knight took a liking to the bowling and put on 240 in 215 minutes, both scoring hundreds and setting a record for England's sixth wicket in all Tests. When Dexter declared on the second afternoon the score was 562 for 7, Parfitt 131 not out. In response New Zealand managed seven runs in the first half-hour at the cost of three wickets; Reid, who the previous month had struck a world record fifteen sixes in one innings (he scored 296), made an attempt to stop the rot with 59, but the only other decent scores came

Colin Cowdrey is the leading English run scorer against New Zealand with 1,133 runs at almost 60 from 18 Tests. He scored centuries at Wellington in 1962–3 and Lord's in 1965.

Fred Trueman had several happy days against New Zealand, but none more so than at Christchurch in 1962–3 when he became the leading Test wicket taker.

from Yuile and Motz, the numbers eight and nine, with 64 and 60 respectively. They took the score to 258 and the follow-on began in the last session of the third day; by the close they had subsided to 42 for 4, three wickets going down at that score. After just over an hour of the last morning the misery was ended; all out for 89 and defeat by an innings and 215 runs.

The second Test in Wellington just two days later saw the same old story. Dexter put New Zealand in, and without the contribution from the number nine, in this case Blair, who was unbeaten with 64, it would have been a sorry tale; as it was they reached 194. New Zealand's reply was to bowl well and field excellently in cold and windy conditions, restricting England to 276 for 8 by tea on the second day. Cowdrey, however, had dropped down the order because of a damaged hand, and when he was joined by Alan Smith, the wicket-keeper, they proceeded to set a new world Test record for the ninth wicket, an unbeaten 163 in even time which has only been bettered once since. When Dexter declared next morning on 428 for 8 the lead was 234 and there were almost two days left. Playle hung on to make 65 and Sinclair and Dick got to the 30s, but that was the lot; 187 all out to the spinners Titmus and Barrington; defeat by an innings and 47 runs.

As it happened, Christchurch saw much more of a match and produced an outstanding performance from two players. New Zealand batted first and Dowling and Sinclair put on 80 for the second wicket; when Trueman dismissed Sinclair he passed Brian Statham's record of 242 Test wickets. Trueman was to take 7 for 75 in this innings, and the nine wickets he took in the match were to see him to 250 in all, but before that Reid was to have something to say. In the first innings he scored an attacking 74, the total eventually reaching 266. Once again the New Zealanders then bowled and fielded well and this time there was no major stand to thwart them; four English batsmen got into the forties but not beyond, and early on the third morning the last wicket fell at 253. Luxury – a first-innings lead! It didn't last long, however, as two wickets were down for only 17, but for Reid it was to be a day to remember. Against a bowling attack that went through his team-mates like the proverbial knife through butter he scored exactly a century, his 100 out of 159 being almost sixty-three per cent of the team's total, the third highest individual percentage in any Test innings. Sad that it was all in vain, as England polished off the 173 needed to win during the last afternoon for the loss of only three wickets. As so often, one wonders what Reid might have achieved if he had had some high-class support.

*

In February 1965 New Zealand embarked upon one of the most ambitious and, it has to be said, one of the least successful of all cricket tours. Four Tests in India and three in Pakistan were followed by a trip to England for three more Tests and a string of county matches. Astonishingly, though, no preparation games were arranged in India or Pakistan; only Sutcliffe, back in the Test team after a five-year gap, and Reid had any experience of subcontinental conditions, yet within four days of leaving home they were playing in the first Test at Madras. Since their luggage, in the best Indian tradition, had gone to Calcutta, they had even been denied the opportunity to practise. In the event they did quite well, usually batting solidly and losing only the last Test, with the Indian umpiring not being above criticism. Of the three games in Pakistan two were then lost, the first one on a clay wicket at Rawalpindi about which Reid, playing a record fifty-third consecutive Test, had some strong words to say.

They had experienced the usual crop of illnesses to add to the usual crop of injuries, but when they arrived in England their problem was a new one, at least to them. From the extreme heat of the subcontinent they found themselves in a chilly English April, and they may well have wondered what Robert Browning had found to get so enthusiastic about. This year saw the introduction in England of the system of two touring teams each playing a three-match series, New Zealand sharing the summer with South Africa. The only previous occasion England had entertained two sets of tourists in one year had been the triangular tournament of 1912; that had been afflicted by some dreadful weather and 1965 wasn't much better.

A draw, a defeat and a victory over Gloucestershire and the MCC match was upon them, against a strong team of whom all but one were past or future Test players. Without a doubt it was New Zealand's game. Congdon and Dowling put on 130 for the first wicket, Congdon going on to make 136 on his Lord's début. There was a fine 63 from Sinclair, and at close of play Reid declared at 318 for 7. Next day they bowled well and only Cowdrey and Parfitt made any runs; Cameron took 4 for 46 and MCC were all out for 196. Time was lost to the weather on both the second and third days, but with Congdon and Sinclair scoring unbeaten half-centuries Reid declared at 122 for 1, leaving MCC to make 245 in two-and-a-half hours; they reached 175 for 3 with Hampshire and Cowdrey the chief contributors. Just enough time was lost to the weather to spoil it, for if New Zealand had had time to build a bigger second innings they may well have won.

In theory this should have inspired the tourists to great deeds, for they had both bowled and batted well. As it was they avoided defeat at Nottinghamshire by only one wicket and drew with Cambridge University through a good second innings after following on. This proved to be the pattern of the first Test – except England had more time than Cambridge to polish off the runs needed for victory.

Miserable weather – on the second day coffee was brought on during the drinks breaks – and a bland pitch at Edgbaston made things difficult in the field for the New Zealanders. Dexter made a half-century, but Barrington was in one of his less inspired moods and ground slowly away for hour after hour. In seven-and-a-quarter hours he had scored 137 when he was the last man out, a performance for which he was rewarded by being dropped for the next Test. Cowdrey, meanwhile, had made 85 and England totalled 435, Motz taking 5 for 108. New Zealand began well enough in reply and were 54 for 0 at one point, but on the third morning Titmus managed to extract some turn from the pitch and the wickets began to fall. Sutcliffe was hit on the ear by a Trueman bouncer and retired, but the others simply played poorly and fell to bad shots. The total eventually reached 116 all out – a deficit of 319 – and another abject defeat was staring them in the face. Instead, they showed what they were really capable of; only Sinclair failed as seven of them scored over forty. Sutcliffe made 53 in his last Test innings and put on 104 for the seventh wicket with Pollard, who had not been born when Sutcliffe began his first-class career. Pollard was not out 81 when the visitors were all out for 413, leaving England needing 95 to win which they reached for the loss of just one wicket on the last morning.

At Lord's, after little more than an hour, New Zealand were 28 for 4, all the wickets going to Rumsey, and by lunch they were 62 for 6. Pollard and Taylor got together and made 92, each getting a half-century, but the remaining wickets soon went and they were all out for 175. England then built their innings around Dexter, Cowdrey and Mike Smith, the captain. Cowdrey, despite a back injury, was the century-maker, but the last six wickets fell for 36 runs, Collinge taking 4 for 17 in one spell. All out 307, New Zealand erased the deficit for the loss of only one wicket. Dowling and Sinclair batted delightfully for a while on the third afternoon, but after a few wickets fell the spinners tied them down; 261 for 7 at the close. Much of the last two days was then lost to the weather. Pollard made another half-century before the innings finished on 347, and at stumps England were 64 for 1. The rain left them less than three hours to get the 152 they needed, but Dexter was always at his best when presented with a challenge such as a race against the clock, and he and Boycott put on 126 in almost even time; Boycott didn't quite see it through but England got home by seven wickets with a quarter of an hour to spare.

For the third Test at Headingley John Edrich returned to the England

John Edrich in action during his 310 not out at Headingley, one of only eleven triple centuries in Test history.

team. He had made his début two years earlier against the West Indies and been in and out of the team since then, with one century against Australia his only substantial score in eight games. He had been playing for Surrey since 1959, scoring two centuries in only his second championship match, and his performance in this Test would see him installed as a more or less permanent fixture in the team. Short, strong and left-handed, he was to go on to become one of England's most reliable batsmen, patient, watchful, very consistent, probably at his best when his team were staring down the gunbarrel. He had plenty of strokes, perhaps the ball played late off his toes through square leg being the most characteristic, and although he was more of an accumulator than a crowd-pleaser he could, in the right conditions – such as the coming match – attack with the best.

With Boycott Edrich was to form one of England's most dependable opening partnerships since the War, both of them noted for their great self-discipline and ability to concentrate totally. As it happened they both made their hundredth century within a few weeks of each other in 1977, and there can't have been many people who were surprised that Edrich's was much the quieter of the two, coming in a match against Derbyshire at the Oval rather than in a Test against Australia as Boycott's did; for he was one of the most unexcitable of cricketers, his approach to the game always calm and phlegmatic. Edrich played in seventy-seven Tests, scoring 5,138 runs at 43 with twelve centuries, and in all made nearly 40,000 runs at 45 with 103 centuries. Towards the end of his career he came up against the fire of Lillee and Thomson and Roberts, Holding and Daniel and battled through in his own dogged way, leading Ted Dexter to compare him to a wartime bomber pilot – 'someone who faced a lot of flak and lived to let someone else tell the tale'. He captained Surrey between 1973 and 1977, leading them to second place in the championship in his first year and to the Benson and Hedges Cup in 1974; but he was not one of nature's captains, being generally too cautious and not really the type to inspire his men to noble deeds. At Headingley, though, he was about to write his name into the record books.

On a fine batting wicket Edrich and Barrington took the first-day score to 366 for 1, and when they were parted next morning they had put on 369 together, the highest partnership by either country in England–New Zealand Tests. Barrington made 163, but Edrich just kept going and was 310 not out when Smith declared at 546 for 4. This was England's only treble-century since the War, the highest score by an Englishman at Headingley, and contained the highest number of boundaries of any Test innings – five sixes and fifty-two fours. It took almost nine hours and wasn't flawless as there were several periods when he kept playing and missing and seemed to

Bryan Yuile – left-arm spinner who found more success with the bat than the ball in his Tests against England.

be floundering; but always he came through and found the middle of the bat again, and was on the pitch throughout the game. The rest of the story was familiar; only Reid, Pollard and Yuile could get anywhere as New Zealand were out for 193. Following on, it wasn't really clear whether the showers were interrupting the fall of wickets or vice versa; Pollard made a half-century, Dowling got a few, but that was about it. Titmus bowled an over that took wickets with the first, third, fourth and sixth balls, leaving one to fall on the last morning. After a quarter of an hour of that last day Pollard duly went and as the players were leaving the field the rain came down for good. England's victory was by an innings and 187 runs.

The England leader in this little whitewash was Mike Smith and he was also to captain them in New Zealand early the following year. One of the

*Fred Titmus – four
wickets in one over at
Headingley in 1965.*

most popular of captains with his players, he was a batsman who rarely did
himself full justice at international level; his Test average of 31 was a full ten
points lower than his career average, but partly this was because in any
sticky situation he would always put the needs of the team before thoughts
of his own average. He captained Warwickshire from 1957 and 1967 with
mixed fortune, once taking them to second place in the table, and led
England twenty-five times. Five of these games were won and three lost,
leaving a very high proportion of draws that says much for the way cricket
tended to be played in the 1960s; the fact that Dexter, Cowdrey and Close
were all contending for the captaincy at around this time may have made
him all the more cautious and anxious not to lose. Perhaps he lacked that
hard streak that so many successful captains have had, and perhaps, too, he

Mike Smith (right) opens the innings with Peter Richardson on his Test début at Edgbaston in 1958. 0 and 7 didn't get his Test career off to a good start. Richardson made a century in the second innings.

would have had more success had he known how to handle his spinners better – although having said that, Titmus was by some way the most successful bowler against New Zealand. Yet he was a highly intelligent man who knew very much what he was about and whose players would do their best for him, because they always knew just where they stood with him. When he retired, John Woodcock wrote in *Wisden* that he was one of the few players of whom it could be said, after a long and distinguished career, that he had made no enemies.

John Reid, now aged 37, had announced before the game that this would be his last Test. If his captaincy record looks dismal on paper – three wins, thirteen draws and eighteen defeats – he was nevertheless an excellent leader who was simply destined to be in charge of outclassed troops. As well as being an outstanding performer in every department he was an expert tactician who knew how to handle his bowlers and set the best fields for them. The fact that his batsmen and fielders so often failed must have been more frustrating for him than any outsider could ever begin to understand.

On the entire tour New Zealand – having gone home via Holland, Bermuda and California! – won only four matches, against Gloucestershire, Scotland, Ireland and a one-day game in Los Angeles. Naturally it was all very disappointing, but Dick Motz, at least, was to find some consolation when he was named as one of *Wisden*'s five cricketers of the year. He had taken 54 wickets at just under 23 with some fine fast bowling; he could move the ball off the pitch and had a good outswinger and great stamina, assets that were to see him become the first New Zealander to take 100 Test wickets at 31 apiece – exactly 100, in fact, as injury caused him to retire after reaching the milestone. His best Test performance was 6 for 63 at Christchurch in 1967–8, the match in which New Zealand gained their first win over India, and he took five wickets in an innings five times in all. A late-order batsman who loved to hit out, he made some useful scores and had one first-class hundred to his name, although his Test average was only 11. One of the best-loved characters in New Zealand cricket, his early retirement in 1969 at the age of 29 was much lamented. He is now the landlord of a pub – and tips the scales at twenty-two stones.

1958	Lord's	NZ 190, 266–8d;	MCC 164, 279	NZ 13 runs
	Edgbaston	E 221, 215–6d;	NZ 94, 137	E 205 runs
	Lord's	E 269;	NZ 47, 74	E inns 148 runs
	Headingley	NZ 67, 129;	E 267–2d	E inns 71 runs
	Old Trafford	NZ 267, 85;	E 365–9d	E inns 13 runs
	Oval	NZ 161, 91–3;	E 219–9d	Drawn
1958–9	Christchurch	E 374;	NZ 142, 133	E inns 99 runs
	Auckland	NZ 181;	E 311–7	Drawn
1960–1	Dunedin	NZ 313, 169;	MCC 277–5d, 167	Drawn
	Wellington	NZ 148, 228;	MCC 111, 132	NZ 133 runs
	Christchurch	MCC 223, 45–1;	NZ 249–8d	Drawn
1962–3	Auckland	E 562–7d;	NZ 258, 89	E inns 215 runs
	Wellington	NZ 194, 187;	E 428–8d	E inns 47 runs
	Christchurch	NZ 266, 159;	E 253, 173–3	E 7 wkts
1965	Lord's	NZ 318–7d, 122–1d;	MCC 196, 175–3	Drawn
	Edgbaston	E 435, 96–1;	NZ 116, 413	E 9 wkts
	Lord's	NZ 175, 347;	E 307, 218–3	E 7 wkts
	Headingley	E 546–4;	NZ 193, 166	E inns 187 runs

1958 Test series
England

Batting	Innings	NO	HS	Runs	Average
C.A. Milton	2	1	104*	140	140.00
P.B.H. May	6	1	113*	337	67.40
M.C. Cowdrey	4	0	81	241	60.25
P.E. Richardson	5	0	100	242	48.40
W. Watson	2	0	66	76	38.00

Bowling	Overs	M	Runs	W	Average
G.A.R. Lock	176	93	254	34	7.47
J.C. Laker	131	67	173	17	10.17
T.E. Bailey	66	24	93	7	13.28
F.S. Trueman	131.5	44	256	15	17.06
J.B. Statham	67	20	130	7	18.57

New Zealand

Batting	Innings	NO	HS	Runs	Average
A.M. Moir	3	2	41*	74	74.00
J.T. Sparling	5	2	50	79	26.33
A.R. MacGibbon	9	0	66	175	19.44
B. Sutcliffe	8	1	41	122	17.42
J.R. Reid	10	1	51*	147	16.33

Bowling	Overs	M	Runs	W	Average
A.R. MacGibbon	175.4	50	389	20	19.45
J.C. Alabaster	46.5	17	127	5	25.40
J.R. Reid	84.2	28	187	6	31.16
J.A. Hayes	89	18	225	6	37.50
A.M. Moir	25	4	99	2	49.50

Wicket-keepers: T.G. Evans (E) 7 dismissals   E.C. Petrie (NZ) 14 dismissals

In the second match New Zealand were dismissed on a rain-affected pitch for 47 in 100 minutes, their lowest total in England. In the third match C.A. Milton became the first England player to be on the field throughout a Test, and is the only player in all Tests to achieve this on début. G.A.R. Lock's total of 34 wickets is the record for either side in these Tests.

1958–9 Test series

England

Best batting: E.R. Dexter 141   P.B.H. May 71; 124*   P.E. Richardson 67

Best bowling: G.A.R. Lock 26–15–31–5 and 28.2–13–53–6

New Zealand

Best batting: B. Sutcliffe 61   J.W. Guy 56

Best bowling: J.R. Reid 18.1–9–34–3   K.W. Hough 39–11–96–3; 38–12–79–3
A.M. Moir 28–4–84–3

Wicket-keepers: E.C. Petrie (NZ) 3 dismissals   R. Swetman (E) 5 dismissals

1960–1

MCC

Batting	Innings	NO	HS	Runs	Average
D.E.V. Padgett	2	1	54	67	67.00
R.M. Prideaux	6	1	76	194	38.80
W. Watson	5	1	61	125	31.25
W.J.P. Stewart	5	1	39	110	27.50
J.M. Parks	4	0	82	85	21.25

Bowling	Overs	M	Runs	W	Average
J.D.F. Larter	77	19	159	9	17.66
R.W. Barber	106.4	30	272	12	22.66
D.A. Allen	62	28	156	6	26.00
D.R. Smith	112.5	26	260	9	28.88
D.M. Sayer	85	19	189	6	31.50

New Zealand

Batting	Innings	NO	HS	Runs	Average
J.T. Sparling	5	1	75*	158	39.50
R.C. Motz	5	0	60	184	36.80
J.R. Reid	5	0	83	146	29.20
P.G.Z. Harris	5	0	78	139	27.80
J.C. Alabaster	4	1	57*	82	27.33

Bowling	Overs	M	Runs	W	Average
L.C. Butler	21	11	22	2	11.00
F.J. Cameron	38	19	65	5	13.00
J.R. Reid	61	30	100	7	14.28
R.C. Motz	89	30	196	10	19.60
J.C. Alabaster	103.5	22	290	12	24.16

Wicket-keepers: E.C. Petrie (NZ) 3 dismissals   J.T. Ward (NZ) 1 dismissal
J.T. Murray (MCC) 10 dismissals

1962–3 Test series
England

Batting	Innings	NO	HS	Runs	Average
M.C. Cowdrey	4	2	128*	292	146.00
K.F. Barrington	4	0	126	294	73.50
B.R. Knight	4	1	125	208	69.33
P.H. Parfitt	4	1	131*	166	55.33
E.R. Dexter	3	0	46	84	28.00

Bowling	Overs	M	Runs	W	Average
F.S. Trueman	88	29	164	14	11.71
R. Illingworth	45	20	73	5	14.60
B.R. Knight	78.4	21	152	9	16.88
F.J. Titmus	132	54	227	13	17.46
K.F. Barrington	30.3	8	89	4	22.25

New Zealand

Batting	Innings	NO	HS	Runs	Average
J.R. Reid	6	1	100	263	52.60
R.W. Blair	4	1	64*	69	23.00
R.C. Motz	4	0	60	90	22.50
B.W. Yuile	4	0	64	78	19.50
M. Shrimpton	4	0	31	77	19.25

Bowling	Overs	M	Runs	W	Average
R.W. Blair	69	26	157	5	31.40
F.J. Cameron	122	31	301	8	37.62
J.C. Alabaster	75.3	15	234	5	46.80
R.C. Motz	81.5	20	199	3	66.33
J.R. Reid	68	17	171	2	85.50

Wicket-keepers: A.E. Dick (NZ) 7 dismissals   J.T. Murray (E) 2 dismissals
A.C. Smith (E) 7 dismissals

In the first match P.H. Parfitt and B.R. Knight put on 240 for the sixth wicket, still the England record for that wicket in all Tests. In the second match M.C. Cowdrey and A.C. Smith put on 163 for the ninth wicket, still the England record for that wicket in all Tests and at the time the world record. In the third match F.S. Trueman passed J.B. Statham's Test record of 242 wickets and became the first bowler to reach 250 Test wickets.

1965 Test series
England

Batting	Innings	NO	HS	Runs	Average
J.H. Edrich	1	1	310*	310	—
K.F. Barrington	2	0	163	300	150.00
E.R. Dexter	4	2	80*	199	99.50
M.C. Cowdrey	4	1	119	221	73.66
G. Boycott	4	1	76	157	52.33

Bowling	Overs	M	Runs	W	Average
T.W. Cartwright	19	9	26	2	13.00
F.J. Titmus	171	85	234	15	15.60
R. Illingworth	35	14	70	4	17.50
J.D.F. Larter	50.1	16	120	6	20.00
J.A. Snow	35	6	80	4	20.00

New Zealand

Batting	Innings	NO	HS	Runs	Average
B. Sutcliffe	2	1	53	57	57.00
V. Pollard	6	1	81*	281	56.20
G.T. Dowling	6	0	66	197	32.83
B.W. Yuile	2	0	46	58	29.00
J.R. Reid	6	0	54	148	24.66

Bowling	Overs	M	Runs	W	Average
R.C. Motz	136	31	389	11	35.36
R.O. Collinge	110	21	292	8	36.50
J.R. Reid	21.5	7	54	1	54.00
B.R. Taylor	75	12	259	4	64.75
R.W. Morgan	18.5	1	90	1	90.00

Wicket-keepers: J.M. Parks (E) 11 dismissals   A.E. Dick (NZ) 8 dismissals
J.T. Ward (NZ) 2 dismissals

In the first match B. Sutcliffe and V. Pollard put on 104 for a New Zealand record seventh-wicket partnership against England. The second match saw the end of F.S. Trueman's Test career, his final total of 307 wickets remaining a record for over ten years. In the third match J.H. Edrich scored the only Test treble-century by an English batsman since the Second World War, his five sixes and 52 fours the record number of boundaries in any Test innings. With K.F. Barrington he put on 369 for the second wicket, the highest by either side for any wicket in England v New Zealand Tests. F.J. Titmus took four wickets for no runs in one over.

— **7** —

Some Near
Run Things

A few months later the teams were again in opposition, England having just drawn 1–1 in Australia for the second consecutive visit in the middle of a long spell where they couldn't quite regain the Ashes. With Reid and Sutcliffe having left the scene New Zealand looked even weaker than they had the previous summer, with only Pollard, Sinclair and perhaps Congdon apparently of real Test class among the batsmen. To general surprise Murray Chapple was appointed captain; he had been an able enough leader of Central Districts, but the surprise was that he was actually in the team. He had played fourteen Tests over almost as many years, had a highest score of 76 and an average under 20. In the event this was to be his last Test, as a pulled leg muscle forced him to miss the next one and he was then not brought back for the third game. He did, however, go on to show himself a very capable touring team manager.

New Zealand made a good start to the first Test, taking four wickets for 47 on a rain-softened Christchurch wicket. Smith and Parfitt then put on 113, both making half-centuries, before David Allen came along with his highest Test score, 88, to help the total to 342. The home reply centred on Congdon, whose maiden Test hundred took five and a half hours; Petrie and Motz brightened things up with rather more attractive fifties, and for only the fifth time ever in Tests New Zealand took a first innings lead over England – by all of 5 runs. Cowdrey, when he caught Chapple, became the second non-wicket-keeper after Walter Hammond to take 100 Test catches. On the last day – these were still four-day games – Smith declared at 201 for 5, having made 87 himself, leaving New Zealand 140 minutes to get 195. They made no attempt to reach the target, but simply collapsed. Higgs took 4 wickets for 5 runs from 9 overs, and only Pollard dug in, rattling up an undefeated 6 runs in an hour and a half. Cunis top-scored with 16, and at the close they were 48 for 8, a sorry state that was self-inflicted through a defensive approach by the main batsmen.

Chapple's injury gave Barry Sinclair the chance to captain his country. A very small man, he impressed *Wisden* in 1965 for his 'daintiness and grace' and was one of the more dependable batsmen of his time. In twenty-one Tests he managed three centuries with a highest score of 138 against South Africa, but in view of his ability his average was surprisingly low at 29; the result, perhaps, of playing in a weak batting team. He had previously captained a team in only one first-class match and he was to lead New Zealand only three times, drawing these two against England and losing one, two years later, against India.

The second Test at Dunedin was badly affected by the weather, several hours being lost on the first and third days. Sinclair chose to bat in miserable weather and wickets soon fell; early on the second day they were 100 for 7, and only Motz gave the innings any respectability with his 57 — of which twenty-two came in one over from Allen (three sixes and a four) to set what was then a Test record for runs in a six-ball over, a record that was to stand until 1981 when it was beaten, oddly enough, by another bowler, Andy Roberts. With New Zealand all out for 192 their bowlers again performed well, chipping away steadily at the wickets. Cowdrey, suffering from flu, managed to stay there and compile 89 not out, and Murray supported him with 50, but England could total only 254 for 8 when Smith declared at lunch on the last day. Remarkably, New Zealand then lost 7 wickets for 100 once more, just as in the first innings, and when Puna, the last man, came to the wicket there would still have been time for England to get the runs had he or Petrie capitulated. Instead, they put on an unbeaten 35 to take the score to 147 for 9 at the close to salvage something from yet more wreckage.

At Auckland in the last Test New Zealand actually had a chance to beat England and seemed not to believe that they could do it. Sinclair set it up with 114, and with 54 from Congdon they made 296. At the end of the first day Edrich had gone down with appendicitis and England, batting one short, allowed themselves to be bowled out for 222, only Russell and Cowdrey making decent scores. With a lead of 74, both New Zealand openers fell without a run on the board; the rest of the innings was painful in the extreme, 129 runs being squeezed out of 103.3 overs. The pitch was as slow as ever, but to surrender the initiative in the way they did seemed inexcusable. England were left with 272 minutes to score 204 runs, without the help of Edrich and with Brown suffering from a back injury. New Zealand bowled tightly but with little penetration on the dead pitch, and England made no attempt to reach the target. Sinclair seemed reluctant to attack and go for the win, persisting with a medium-pace attack in the last session rather than risking the spinners and there must have been many who wished John Reid was back in charge to strain every fibre for the one thing he had wanted most of all, a victory over England. The match duly meandered to a meaningless draw as England ground to 159 for 4, only 806 runs being scored in 1,440 very tedious minutes. The local Press were not impressed.

*

By the time of the 1969 tour New Zealand had reason to hope that their batting was beginning to emerge from the doldrums. Congdon and Hastings had made good scores, Dowling had made a double-century as well as other good knocks and they now had a young man named Glenn Turner who was clearly going to provide them with a great deal of runs. They also had an experienced pace-bowling line-up of Motz, Collinge, Cunis and Taylor, although they were short on spin-power. They were encouraged by victories over India and the West Indies; the three-match rubber with the latter was drawn 1–1, although the four Tests against India had been lost 3–1. England, meanwhile, had beaten West Indies 2–0 in a three-match series in the first half of the summer – their last successful series against them to date, only one of the subsequent thirty-seven Tests having been won – and were now ensconced in what was to be their longest run of Tests without defeat, twenty-six in all. Most of these were under the leadership of Ray Illingworth.

Had he still been in the ranks when Cowdrey was injured early in 1969 Illingworth may not have been asked to lead England, but at the beginning of the season he had moved to Leicestershire as captain after many years at Yorkshire. He had been in and out of the national team for years, competing for a place with several other spinners, but once he was appointed it was immediately clear that the selectors had hit the jackpot. He proved himself a natural captain, a canny old pro who knew just how to manage his men and whose grasp of tactics was unrivalled, and he became one of the best England – and Leicestershire, come to that – have ever had. Courageous, devoted to his players, shrewd as they come, he was one of the toughest opponents anyone could hope not to encounter. Through his influence a fairly ordinary group of players became a very good team, good enough to go to Australia in 1970–1 and come back with the Ashes. He was in charge for thirty-one games, winning twelve and losing only five, and if there was any criticism to be made of his captaincy it was that he didn't bowl himself enough; partly because of this he finished with the relatively modest haul for such a fine bowler of 122 wickets at 31 from his sixty-one Tests. The responsibility of captaincy, though, saw his batting blossom, and time after time he produced fine innings to rescue his side, including two

Ray Illingworth, captain in three series against New Zealand. Here he is compiling 65 at Headingley in 1973, watched by Ken Wadsworth.

centuries. Only Brearley, a very different character, vies with him for the title of best England captain since the War.

His opposite number was – but not just yet – to take over from Reid as the New Zealand captain with most Test victories. Graham Dowling had been a regular in the team since 1961 and was to go on to play in thirty-nine Tests and score 2,300 runs at 31, usually as an opener. He was a steady,

*Graham Dowling led
New Zealand to four
Test victories and began
the process of casting
off the mantle of
permanent underdogs.*

methodical, determined batsman, courageous and altruistic, with a good defence and the ability to attack if necessary and also a superb close fielder. (His fielding was such, in fact, that not long afterwards he was asked to keep wicket in a match against Australian Universities, only to damage a finger so badly that it had to be amputated.) He took over as captain from Sinclair at home to India in 1967–8 and in his first game in charge hit 239 to set up a victory, following this with the squared series against West Indies. After this 1969 rubber in England he took his team to India and Pakistan; the first series was drawn 1–1, with the weather robbing them of a victory in the last Test, and then, amid great rejoicing back home, New Zealand finally won a Test series when they beat Pakistan 1–0. Dowling's captaincy was much praised in this achievement, for he was an intelligent man (like Walter Hadlee he was an accountant by profession) who gave much thought to the game and to his responsibilities. He led his country nineteen times in all, losing seven and beating Reid's three wins by just one, until back problems forced him into early retirement. His influence was not yet finished, though, for in 1981 he became Secretary of the NZCC, moving up to Executive Director in 1984.

These triumphs in India and Pakistan must have been undreamed of during the English part of the tour, for the hopes that had been entertained for the batting didn't really materialise. They were not helped by plenty of adverse weather, losing some eight full days play in all, and beat only Scotland, Minor Counties, Warwickshire and T.N. Pearce's XI. There was no MCC match that year, but as the villain of the piece in the first Test at Lord's was the wicket perhaps this was just as well. New Zealand bowled and fielded extremely well in England's first innings of the opening Test and Illingworth had to perform one of his rescue acts as the wickets tumbled; at lunch they were 68 for 5, but in the end his half-century helped them to 190. Next day, though, on a pitch of variable bounce that gave the spinners too much help for that stage of the match, Illingworth and Underwood took four wickets apiece and dismissed the visitors for 169, only Dowling and Congdon getting forties.

New Zealand's lack of a top-class spinner was then highlighted as Boycott and Edrich put on 125 for the first wicket, Edrich going on to a century. Neville Cardus, however, was not impressed; he wrote in the *Guardian* that he 'departed from Lord's last Saturday, bored to limpness, because I had seen Boycott and Edrich compile, or secrete, 100 runs from 56 overs, bowled by game, enthusiastic, inexperienced New Zealand crick-eters.' Now by no stretch of even Cardus's imagination could Motz and Taylor, with forty-four caps between them before this game, be called inexperienced, but there must have been many watching who agreed whole-heartedly with his sentiments. There was then a middle-order collapse as five wickets went down for 25 runs, but from 259 for 7 Knight saw England to 340 all out early on the fourth day.

New Zealand's target was 362 with nearly two days to do it, but on that pitch it was never a possibility – and certainly not against Underwood. He took 7 for 32 to record the best bowling figures in England–New Zealand Tests, with only Turner able to survive against him. For Turner it was in fact a notable triumph, for he became the first New Zealander (and at 22 years 63 days the youngest player ever) to carry his bat through a completed Test innings. When the innings ended after 253 minutes he had scored 43 by exercising total concentration, although he was criticised by *Wisden* for not doing more to shield his partners from Underwood. It was a feat he was to repeat two and a half years later against West Indies (although then he scored 223) and he remains the only New Zealander to achieve it. The match was over with half an hour to spare of the fourth day; had New Zealand managed to hang on till next morning they would have got a draw, for that last day would have been completely washed out.

When Dowling won the toss in the Trent Bridge Test it was after nine consecutive wrong calls; but as *Men in White* says, 'with the prospect of facing a very quick attack on a lively wicket, New Zealand's top-order batsmen were not wholly convinced that Dowling chose the right time' to do it. With Turner out through injury, the innings centred on a third-wicket stand of 150 between Congdon and Hastings, supported later by a useful knock from Dayle Hadlee lower down the order which helped the total to 294. And then, for once, the medium-pacers let them down, bowling very poorly and being caned for it by Edrich and Sharpe. Most of the Saturday was lost to the weather, and by the Monday the conditions had become hot, humid and generally in the bowlers' favour. The big partnership was worth 249 when it was broken – Edrich's 155 took him to 25,000 first-class runs and coincided with the arrival of his first son – and for the rest of the day there were both runs and wickets to entertain the crowd, Illingworth declaring near the end at 451 for 8. Much of the rest of the time was washed out, however, and the game was abandoned with New Zealand on 66 for 1.

The Oval Test was dominated once again by Underwood, the man who the year before had beaten Australia with a couple of minutes to spare after a deluge had flooded the ground on the last day. There were no deluges this time but there was enough rain to freshen the wicket and make him almost unplayable; he took six victims in each innings for match figures of 12 for 101. Turner's 53 was New Zealand's best effort as they were all out for 150, but in reply only Boycott, Edrich and Sharpe fared much better. The dismissal of Sharpe was historic, as it gave Motz his hundredth wicket, the first New Zealander to the landmark. Ward and Snow walloped 40 for the last wicket to take England to 242. In their second innings four of the visitors got in and then got out, only Hastings with 61 making much impression, and their score of 229 left England 138 to win and over a day to do it. Despite more time lost to the weather this was comfortably achieved for the loss of the two openers.

Another disappointing series for New Zealand, but the real problem was that they had neither an Underwood nor an Edrich. If their batting fell away after a promising start, so did England's. There had been the usual part-successes and part-failures that occur on every tour; it was just that, once again, the latter had outnumbered the former. Happily, the tour to India and Pakistan was altogether more satisfying.

Basil d'Oliveira on his way to a century at Christchurch in 1970–1.

*

England's recovery of the Ashes in 1970–1 was not without its unsavoury moments. In the last Test Illingworth led his team from the field after some of the crowd took a dislike to John Snow for his short-pitched bowling, and there were various other unpleasantries. Yet it had been an exciting time, and when they reached New Zealand the poor weather and thin crowds made for something of an anticlimax. Always there was the problem for the New Zealand cricket authorities that Rugby held a much higher place in the national consciousness and interest in the summer game suffered accordingly.

The England players were tired, too, although no doubt felt rather better after dismissing the home team for 65 in the first Test. The Christchurch pitch had been viewed with suspicion before the game, and Underwood continued where he had left off in the previous series, taking 6 for 12 from 11.6 eight-ball overs. England, though, were soon in trouble at 31 for 3, and were saved only by a century from d'Oliveira with support from Hampshire and Illingworth; 231 all out. New Zealand's second innings was built around a very patient 76 from Turner and a half-century from Congdon, but there were too many failures for them to be able to save the match. Underwood, for the fourth consecutive innings against New Zealand, took 6 wickets, this time for 85, to lower the record for match bowling figures in England–New Zealand Tests that he had set at the Oval, and to pass 1,000 first-class wickets. The home team's 254 left England needing only 89 to win, and just two wickets went down as they made it.

Derek Underwood was 25 at the time, and only Wilfred Rhodes and George Lohmann had reached 1,000 wickets at a younger age. He made his début for Kent in 1963 when only 17 and became the youngest player to take 100 wickets in his first season – and they cost under 20 apiece at that. From the start his left-arm bowling was highly individual, a flat-footed approach of about eight paces preceding a delivery with an uncommonly flat trajectory – normally slow-medium, but sometimes slower and sometimes faster – that was so invariably accurate that he soon gained the nickname 'Deadly'. On a helpful pitch he could extract prodigious turn, while on a good batting track he could keep the best batsmen quiet, often getting wickets because of the frustration he induced; it is probably fair to say that he is the best one-day bowler England has yet produced. For some time he was less effective abroad than at home as his trajectory tended to be too flat for the different conditions he encountered, but as he learned more he was to play a match-winning part in many a Test. After eighty-six games his Test

New Zealand found Derek Underwood altogether too 'deadly' for them in 1969 and 1970–1.

career, which had already been interrupted once when he joined Packer's World Series Cricket, came to an end when he went on the rebel tour of South Africa early in 1982, leaving him stranded on 297 wickets taken at under 26 each. Financially, of course, both of these excursions were well worth his while, although naturally his fans – who didn't have to pay his bills – were disappointed to lose him; but such was his popularity and likeableness that there can have been few who criticised him for his 'infidelity'. A thoughtful, intelligent, disciplined player, he was, simply, one of the best-loved England cricketers since the War.

In the second game Dowling put England in and some early breakthroughs were made, but Cowdrey and d'Oliveira produced half-centuries before Alan Knott, who had dropped out for the previous game to allow Bob Taylor to win his first cap, scored his maiden Test century, and with Peter Lever put on 149 for the seventh wicket, helping the total to 321; Cunis took his best Test figures of 6 for 76. Dowling and Turner gave the home team a good start with 91, but this was followed by something of a collapse. It was halted by Burgess and Shrimpton, who made 141 for the fifth wicket, with Burgess, on his home ground, reaching his second Test century. Happily there was a good crowd to applaud it, for this was the first Sunday of Test cricket in New Zealand, an experiment which was not without its opponents as there were some players, such as Pollard and Murray, who would not play on a Sunday. The score was 313 for 7 when Dowling declared, and by the close of the third day England were 78 for 4. Looking back now it seems astonishing that four-day Tests were still being played in the 1970s, but such was the case (the last ones, in fact, were two years later in New Zealand's next home series against Pakistan). Had this game been played over five days it could have been a very memorable one, for England were then dismissed for 237, which might just have enabled New Zealand to gain a victory. Knott made 96 to come desperately close to being the first wicket-keeper to score a hundred in each innings of a Test, but he had little support. When the innings finished there was just time for the openers to score 40 without loss.

*

1973 saw the end of Ray Illingworth's tenure of the England captaincy, although there were triumphs with Leicestershire still ahead. His last series, against West Indies, was to be a 2–0 defeat, but before that the early part of the season was spent entertaining New Zealand. As Dowling had retired because of a back injury, they were now captained by Bevan Congdon.

*Roope and Knott watch as Bev Congdon presses relentlessly on to
175 at Lord's in 1973.*

Only Richard Hadlee has played more Tests for New Zealand than Bev
Congdon; not a bad claim to fame for someone who didn't play his first Test
till be was almost 27. As a young man he had been a trumpet player in a
dance band, an image that sits very incongruously with the patient,
determined batsman that he became. Usually he batted at number three,
making himself into a top-class player by much hard work, refining his
technique so that he became very difficult to dislodge. He wasn't a free-
scoring stroke-maker of the kind to set the crowd aglow, but he had a wide
range of shots and was a fine timer of the ball. His sixty-one Tests produced
3,448 runs at 32, just 20 more than John Reid and still the record aggregate
for his country; his seven centuries were also a record until passed by
Martin Crowe. Perceiving that if he had a bowling string to his bow his Test
place would be more secure he made himself into a handy medium-paced
back-up bowler who could swing the ball both ways, becoming good
enough to take 59 Test wickets; he was also an excellent fielder. As a
captain his main failing was an inability to win the toss — only four successes
out of seventeen really isn't good enough. Partly because of this, no doubt,

his record isn't outstanding, with one win and seven defeats; but that win was a good one against Australia and must have been unutterably sweet. As we shall see, he came pretty close to beating England at Lord's, but the fact that he was not able to press home his advantage suggests a question mark of some kind against his tactical acumen; or, at least, against the total psychological control which a Test captain needs in modern cricket.

There was always something of the lean and hungry look about Congdon, and the same qualities that characterised his batting were brought to his captaincy. He was a pragmatist – outside cricket he has been a very successful businessman – and his captaincy reflected it. Maybe he could sometimes be a little aloof, but if he wasn't one for jollifications no one ever questioned his commitment to the team. He was tough and straightforward, never one for any frills, always very fair, canny and thoughtful, a man determined to develop Dowling's good work that had seen New Zealand begin to cast off the mantle of permanent underdogs and under this added responsibility he made some of his best scores. In due course he was to relinquish the captaincy to Turner, who passed it on to Burgess, but happily he was still in the team when England were finally beaten for the first time in 1977–8 and made an important contribution to the first innings. Having made his Test début against Pakistan early in 1965, he eventually retired at the age of 40 after the 1978 tour of England, when his form was below par.

The game against a very strong MCC team was ruined by rain. Turner and Parker put on 211 for the first wicket before the latter went for 88, Turner remaining unbeaten on 153 when Congdon declared at 259 for 1. With time lost to the weather MCC declared on 146 for 2, whereupon New Zealand declared on 63 for 4, leaving MCC eighty-five minutes to score 177. If there were any naive souls in the ground who thought this might be attempted they were soon disillusioned; 37 for 2 at the close.

Those 153 runs took Glenn Turner to 799 for the tour, with eight playing days left before the end of May. In the next match, at Derby, he led the team in Congdon's absence and, after making only 2 in the first innings, declared in the second innings when he was on 66 to try to force a result. Against Leicestershire he scored 30 and 10 not out, leaving two playing days and 93 to get. The game at Northampton didn't begin till mid-afternoon because of the weather, and by the close Turner was unbeaten on 70. Next morning, with rain threatening, he was almost run out on 80; but eventually the moment arrived as he cut a ball from Bishan Bedi and the celebrations began. The fact that this was the first time 1,000 runs by the end of May had been achieved since 1938, and that only Graeme Hick in 1988 has since emulated him, puts his milestone very much in perspective.

Glenn Turner on his way to 1,000 runs before the end of May in 1973. Here he is making 153 not out against MCC at Lord's.

Glenn Turner was a slightly-built man who made himself into one of the world's best batsmen by sheer professionalism, and was, in fact, New Zealand's first full-time professional cricketer. As such he was something of an iconoclast in his country's cricket and the modern players who earn good money can thank Turner for paving the way for them. As a young man he had obvious ability and great dedication but a limited number of strokes and very little speed; he was recommended to Warwickshire by Billy Ibadulla, who had been coaching in New Zealand, but was taken on instead by Worcestershire; over many years he repaid them for their faith by producing a mountain of runs. Naturally serious-minded, he devoted himself to perfecting his technique by basing it squarely on the coaching manual, extending his repertoire until it included every stroke in the book and a few more besides – and learning how to score quickly as well. The result was one of the most complete and consistent batsmen of the modern period, who reached the apotheosis of his career at Worcestershire's New Road ground on 29 May 1982 when he became only the nineteenth player to score a century of centuries.

He had begun that season with a run of low scores, but the opponents that day were Warwickshire, a team against whom he always scored heavily as a reminder of their rejection of him. It was a fine day, eminently suitable for glorious deeds, and he climbed his Everest in the most splendid style, first scoring a century before lunch and then going on to make 311 not out, the highest knock of his career. As it happened, his old mentor Billy Ibadulla was at the ground and as the century approached he and Ken Kelly, the photographer, conspired to produce one of the season's happier pictures. When the hundred came up Ibadulla walked on to the field carrying a celebratory gin and tonic, mindful of the fact that Kelly was waiting with his camera on the square leg boundary; in the following year's *Wisden* the resulting photograph made a pleasant contrast to Lillee and Javed Miandad squaring up to each other, David Bairstow being doubled up by a short-pitched ball from Sylvester Clarke and others that were symptomatic of modern-day cricket's problems.

His Test début came against West Indies in 1969, but he played in only forty-one matches. In 1978 he upset some people by preferring to concentrate on his own benefit season rather than join his compatriots in their tour of England; he also chose to commentate on some games that most people felt he should have been playing in, a rather surprising decision in view of his earlier commitment to the New Zealand cause. In the end he fell just short of the 3,000 runs mark, making 2,991 at nearly 45, and taking the record for the highest New Zealand score, 259 against West Indies in 1971–2. Earlier in the same series he had scored 223 not out to carry his bat through a complete Test innings for the second time. He captained his country on ten occasions, no more successful with the coin than was Congdon as he won only twice; he beat India in one game at home, but lost six of the others and then resigned after a disagreement with officialdom. Never one to court popularity for its own sake he upset plenty of people by speaking his mind; his professionalism had never enjoyed an easy relationship with the amateur approach of his country's officials, but perhaps he was not really the stuff of the natural captain anyway. Certainly he was a fine team-man and he made some good scores whilst captain, but he somehow lacked the magic touch. He didn't captain New Zealand against England and nor, to his regret, were any of his seven Test centuries against

England. In 1973, after reaching 1,000 runs in May, he was in fact to have a disappointing Test series, until in the last innings he made 81 and was the last man out; had he been able to hang on he would have become the only man in Test history to carry his bat through a completed innings three times.

By the time of the first Test at Trent Bridge New Zealand had recorded victories over Glamorgan and Lancashire and a clutch of draws. After a good start by the England openers wickets fell to Taylor and Dayle Hadlee and only a last-wicket stand of 59 between Knott and Gifford – the record for either side in these games – saw the score to 250 all out. New Zealand's innings then lasted less than 42 overs as Greig, Snow and Arnold ripped them out for 97, the biggest contribution coming from extras with 20; obviously the bad old days were not consigned to the past. Before long they had sent back four Englishmen for 24, but next morning Greig and Amiss took them apart, both scoring centuries as they put on 210 for the fifth wicket. When Illingworth declared at 325 for 8 New Zealand faced a total of 479 to win. There was only going to be one result.

Tony Greig (left) and Dennis Amiss, having scored their maiden Test centuries on tour the previous winter, recorded their first hundreds in a home Test at Trent Bridge in 1973. Amiss made 138 not out, Greig 139.

Both the openers went at 16 and Congdon was hit in the face by a ball from Snow. Next morning, despite fears that he might not be able to bat, he was there; but he soon lost Hastings, and when Burgess departed the score was 130 for 4. He was joined by Pollard, a man who was in the team primarily for his batting but who had never scored a hundred in twenty-nine previous Tests. Together they took the score to 307 before Congdon fell, defeated as much by tiredness as anything, for his 176 – the first century by a New Zealander in England since 1949 – had taken 409 minutes. It might not have been all that aesthetically pleasing to watch, but he had given no chance, determined to salvage some pride out of the wreckage of the first innings. At the beginning of the last day New Zealand were 317 for 5 and Pollard and Wadsworth took the score to 402 before the wicket-keeper went for 46. Pollard had ground away for 437 minutes to score 116, but he fell with the score on 414, and although Taylor and Dayle Hadlee did their best they could not quite make it. New Zealand's 440, 39 short of their target, was then the second-highest total in the fourth innings of a Test and the highest fourth innings by a losing team in a Test; it had the Press in raptures. One little story from this says much about Congdon's character; after he was out he sat reading a C.S. Forrester novel while his team-mates watched in agony – not because of a lack of emotion, but because, with nothing more to be done, his reaction was to withdraw inside himself.

England at this time still regarded themselves as something of a force in world cricket and there is no doubt that they had been thoroughly frightened to be on the receiving end of one of the great fightbacks in the history of the game. They were even more frightened after the Lord's Test. Congdon actually won the toss and, on a humid day, put England in. Boycott, Fletcher and Greig made half-centuries, the last-named with no shortage of good fortune, but wickets were falling regularly and early on the second day they were all out for 253. Both New Zealand openers then went with only 10 on the board; but Congdon simply carried on from where he had left off last time and together with Hastings weathered a strong attack to put on 190 for the third wicket, Hastings falling on 86. Just before the close he reached another century, and next day, supported by nightwatchman Howarth and by Burgess, he took his score to 175 before eventually succumbing; after his score in the first game this prompted, naturally enough, Press remarks such as 'Congdon's weakness was that he tired in the 170s' and 'England have now got Congdon's measure – they know how to get him out in the 170s'. When he went the score was 330 for 5; Burgess and Pollard took it to 447 before the former fell for 105, after which Pollard and Wadsworth took

*Geoff Boycott caught and bowled by Hedley Howarth 8 runs short
of a century (Lord's 1973).*

it to 523 before the seventh wicket fell. In the end Congdon declared at 551 for 9, New Zealand's highest Test score; and with Pollard 105 not out this was the first occasion on which three batsmen had made centuries in one Test innings for New Zealand.

Faced with a deficit of almost 300, Boycott and Amiss put on 112 for the first wicket. Boycott then fell for 92, but by stumps on the fourth day Roope and Fletcher had taken the total to 224 for 2. On the last morning Roope went for 51 and Greig went cheaply, but Illingworth kept Fletcher company for a crucial two hours. Thereafter Fletcher almost ran out of partners, and when Arnold, at number nine, joined him England's lead was only 70 and there was time for New Zealand to get the runs if they could take the last two wickets. Pollard bowled to Arnold, beat him twice outside the off stump, and then found the edge – only for Wadsworth, normally so reliable, to put him down. Fletcher's response to this

Vic Pollard averaged 100.66 in the Tests of 1973. Here at Trent Bridge he hits a boundary which Norman Gifford can do nothing about.

reprieve was to flay the bowlers, and with Arnold he put on 92 in 87 minutes to put the game beyond New Zealand's reach. When he was eventually out for 178 England had reached 463 for 9 and the match was over. It was the closest New Zealand had ever come to beating them, and it prompted Press speculation that, faced with the possibility of a victory, they had almost psyched themselves out of it. It did seem as though that were the case.

These two matches were the highlight of Vic Pollard's Test career, the first centuries he had scored after twenty-nine previous games in which he had promised without quite fulfilling; there had been half a dozen fifties in that time, but rather too many failures for someone who was clearly very gifted. A short, stocky player, his batting had a good range of strokes but sometimes seemed to lack flair and in thirty-two matches he totalled only 1,266 runs at 24. In his young days it was thought that his spin bowling was stronger than his batting, but in the event he took only 40 Test wickets at an expensive 46 apiece, perhaps because he was never as effective abroad as at home. His desire had been to be a fearsome fast bowler, but because of his lack of inches he became a spinner, although some of his deliveries were uncommonly fast for a slow bowler. A Baptist lay-preacher, he was opposed to playing cricket on Sundays and missed the Test against England in 1970–1 as a result. These 1973 Tests were in fact his swansong, for he retired from international cricket afterwards, no doubt pleased to have gone out on a high note – although when he was finally out for 116 at Trent Bridge he was disgusted with himself, since the match could still have been won. The pity was that one of the centuries was not scored at Old Trafford as he had been born in Lancashire and then gone to New Zealand as a child; that would have rounded off his career particularly neatly.

What would the Headingley Test produce after this, a real triumph for New Zealand or a reaction? When three of their wickets fell with the score at 24, including Congdon for a duck, one felt that one knew. Burgess and Pollard repaired the damage to some extent with 106 for the fifth wicket and Dayle Hadlee swung his bat a bit, but in the end they were all out for 276. Much of the second day was lost to rain, and by the third morning the bowling conditions should have helped the tourists get back into the game. Instead they persisted in bowling short rather than tossing the ball up and letting the pitch help them and Boycott and Fletcher took full advantage. The Yorkshireman, on his home ground, finally scored the century against New Zealand that had always eluded him, giving him a full clutch of hundreds against all the Test-playing countries. Illingworth also contributed 65, helping the total to 419 when the last wicket fell. And then the New

*Bruce Taylor played his last Tests in 1973, finishing his career as
the leading New Zealand wicket taker.*

Zealand reaction set in properly; when Turner was the last man out for 81
his colleagues had amassed only another 41 between them. All out for 142,
a defeat by an innings and one run. In view of what might have been earlier
in the series, it was a sad finale.

It was also the end of the Test road for one of New Zealand's stalwarts,
Bruce Taylor. An all-rounder standing 6 feet 3 inches, he bowled right-arm
fast-medium with plenty of swing and bounce and batted left-handed,
attacking whenever he could. He was more prone than most to extremes of
performance, one minute batting very gracefully and the next getting
himself into all kinds of tangles, or sometimes bowling fluidly and sweetly
and at other times plodding heavily through an over. Even his fielding was
unpredictable, spectacular close catches alternating with fluffed easy
chances. He made a sensational entry into Test cricket against India at
Calcutta in 1965, scoring 105 (his first first-class century) in 158 minutes
and putting on 163 with Sutcliffe for what was then New Zealand's record
seventh-wicket partnership. When India batted he then took 5 for 86, to
become the first player to score a hundred and take five wickets in an
innings in his maiden Test. He played thirty Tests in all, passing Motz's

record of 100 wickets and finishing with 111 at 26, as well as making almost 900 runs at 20, with two centuries. He seemed not to find England happy opposition for his record against them is modest, with a top score of 51 and best bowling of 4 for 47; but the West Indies in particular must have been glad to see the back of him after some of his performances against them. A cheerful extrovert who enjoyed his cricket and life in general, he made a come-back to the first-class game in the late 1970s and although he played no more Test cricket it was by no means an unsuccessful return. It was a pity that he had so little one-day cricket, for it would undoubtedly have suited his approach to the game.

This tour saw, as it happened, the first one-day internationals played between the two countries, England winning the first and the second being washed out. These various defeats by England were the only reversals of the tour, three of the counties being beaten and the rest of the matches drawn. For New Zealand it could easily have been a spectacular tour; the fact that by no stretch of anyone's imagination did they deserve to lose the Tests 2–0 is not, unfortunately, something that is mentioned in the record books.

1965–6	Christchurch	E 342, 201–5d;	NZ 347, 48–8	Drawn
	Dunedin	NZ 192, 147–9;	E 254–8d	Drawn
	Auckland	NZ 296, 129;	E 222, 159–4	Drawn
1969	Lord's	E 190, 340;	NZ 169, 131	E 230 runs
	Trent Bridge	NZ 294, 66–1;	E 451–8d	Drawn
	Oval	NZ 150, 229;	E 242, 138–2	E 8 wkts
1970–1	Christchurch	NZ 65, 254;	E 31, 89–2	E 8 wkts
	Auckland	E 321, 237;	NZ 313–7d, 40–0	Drawn
1973	Lord's	NZ 259–1d, 63–4d;	MCC 146–2, 37–2	Drawn
	Trent Bridge	E 250, 325–8d;	NZ 97, 440	E 38 runs
	Lord's	E 253, 463–9;	NZ 551–9d	Drawn
	Headingley	NZ 276, 142;	E 419	E inns 1 run

1965–6 Test series
England

Batting	Innings	NO	HS	Runs	Average
J.M. Parks	4	2	45*	117	58.50
D.A. Allen	3	1	88	104	52.00
M.C. Cowdrey	5	1	89*	196	49.00
M.J.K. Smith	5	0	87	209	41.80
P.H. Parfitt	5	1	54	137	34.25

Bowling	Overs	M	Runs	W	Average
K. Higgs	128	50	157	17	9.34
I.J. Jones	122.3	40	242	14	17.29
P.H. Parfitt	28	9	58	3	19.33
D.J. Brown	61	14	126	6	21.00
D.A. Allen	190.5	72	359	13	27.62

New Zealand

Batting	Innings	NO	HS	Runs	Average
B.W. Sinclair	6	0	114	218	36.33
B.E. Congdon	6	0	104	214	35.67
R.C. Motz	6	0	58	148	24.67
E.C. Petrie	6	1	55	115	23.00
R.S. Cunis	6	3	16*	55	18.33

Bowling	Overs	M	Runs	W	Average
B.R. Taylor	33	10	66	5	13.20
V. Pollard	25	6	61	4	15.25
G.A. Bartlett	76.2	12	177	6	29.50
R.S. Cunis	121.5	32	248	7	35.43
R.C. Motz	114	27	271	7	38.71

Wicket-keepers: E.C. Petrie (NZ) 4 dismissals J.M. Parks (E) 11 dismissals
J.T. Murray (E) 4 dismissals

In the first match M.C. Cowdrey became the second non-wicket-keeper to hold 100 Test catches. In the second match R.C. Motz hit 22 runs off an over from D.A. Allen, then the record for the most runs by one batsman off a six-ball over. In the third match Cowdrey passed 6,000 Test runs.

1969 Test series
England

Batting	Innings	NO	HS	Runs	Average
J.H. Edrich	5	0	155	376	72.20
P.J. Sharpe	5	1	111	270	67.50
B.R. Knight	3	1	49	96	48.00
B.L. D'Oliveira	4	0	45	95	23.75
R. Illingworth	4	0	53	90	22.50

Bowling	Overs	M	Runs	W	Average
D.L. Underwood	150	70	220	24	9.16
R. Illingworth	101.3	43	154	10	15.40
A. Ward	73.5	15	210	10	21.00
B.L. D'Oliveira	53	21	77	2	38.50
B.R. Knight	35.5	8	83	2	41.50

New Zealand

Batting	Innings	NO	HS	Runs	Average
G.M. Turner	4	1	53	126	42.00
B.F. Hastings	5	0	83	188	37.60
B.E. Congdon	6	1	66	179	35.80
D.R. Hadlee	3	1	35*	55	27.50
B.A.G. Murray	4	1	40*	70	23.33

Bowling	Overs	M	Runs	W	Average
B.R. Taylor	63.5	17	155	10	15.50
R.S. Cunis	30	6	85	5	17.00
D.R. Hadlee	55	10	179	6	29.83
H.J. Howarth	166	67	313	8	39.12
R.C. Motz	123.1	34	310	7	44.28

Wicket-keepers: A.P.E. Knott (E) 11 dismissals   K.J. Wadsworth(NZ) 8 dismissals

In the first match G.M. Turner became the first New Zealander to carry his bat through a completed Test innings, and at 22 years 63 days he is still the youngest Test player to achieve this. In the second match the third-wicket partnership of 150 between B.E. Congdon and B.F. Hastings was then the New Zealand record for any wicket in a Test in England. In the third match R.C. Motz became the first bowler to take 100 Test wickets for New Zealand.

1970–1 Test series (In this, the 1974–5 and the 1977–8 series the overs were of 8 balls)
England
Best batting: B.L. D'Oliveira 100; 58   A.P.E. Knott 101 and 96   P. Lever 64
                  M.C. Cowdrey 54 and 45
Best bowling: D.L. Underwood 11.6–7–12–6 and 32.3–7–85–6; 38–12–108–5

New Zealand
Best batting: G.M. Turner 76; 65   M.G. Burgess 104   G.T. Dowling 53 and 31*
Best bowling: H.J. Howarth 19–7–46–4   R.O. Collinge 19–6–41–4

Wicket-keepers: K.J. Wadsworth (NZ) 9 dismissals   R.W. Taylor (E) 3 dismissals
                 A.P.E. Knott (E) 0 dismissals

In the first match D.L. Underwood took his 1,000th first-class wicket and recorded match figures of 12 for 97. In the second match A.P.E. Knott and P. Lever put on 149 for the seventh wicket, an England record against New Zealand.

1973 Test series
England

Batting	Innings	NO	HS	Runs	Average
G. Boycott	5	0	115	320	64.00
D.L. Amiss	5	1	138*	250	62.50
K.W.R. Fletcher	5	0	178	309	61.80
A.W. Greig	5	0	139	216	43.20
N. Gifford	3	2	25*	35	35.00

Bowling	Overs	M	Runs	W	Average
C.M. Old	75.5	12	225	11	20.45
G.G. Arnold	161	48	351	16	21.93
A.W. Greig	74.5	15	185	8	23.12
J.A. Snow	135.1	27	320	13	24.61

New Zealand

Batting	Innings	NO	HS	Runs	Average
V. Pollard	5	2	116	302	100.66
B.E. Congdon	5	0	176	362	72.40
M.G. Burgess	5	0	105	236	47.20
H.J. Howarth	3	2	17	40	40.00
B.F. Hastings	5	0	86	128	25.60

Bowling	Overs	M	Runs	W	Average
R.O. Collinge	135	32	289	12	24.08
V. Pollard	55	18	98	4	24.50
H.J. Howarth	113	36	230	7	32.85
D.R. Hadlee	106.1	16	340	10	34.00
B.R. Taylor	136	24	395	9	43.88

Wicket-keepers: A.P.E. Knott (E) 12 dismissals   K.J. Wadsworth (NZ) 9 dismissals

In the first match New Zealand's second innings score of 440 runs was at the time the second-highest fourth innings total in all Tests and the highest by a losing team. B.E. Congdon and V. Pollard put on 177 for the New Zealand fifth wicket record against England and A.P.E. Knott and N. Gifford put on 59 for the tenth wicket, the record for either side in England v New Zealand Tests. In the second match New Zealand scored their highest total in Tests, 551, and three New Zealand batsmen scored a century in the same innings for the first time; B.E. Congdon and B.F. Hastings put on 190 for the third wicket and M.G. Burgess and V. Pollard put on 117 for the sixth wicket, both records for New Zealand against England. In the third match G.M. Turner almost became the first batsman to carry his bat through a completed Test innings three times, being the last batsman out in the second innings.

— **8** —

The Golden
Forty-eighters

Eighteen months later England walked into Lillee and Thomson – and rather wished they hadn't; asked what he felt about the torrid business that the 1974–5 Ashes series had become, John Edrich summed up the feelings of many of the English batsmen: 'One tour too many, mate, one tour too many.' The year before, New Zealand had beaten Australia – lacking the terrible twins – for the first time; then in February 1975 they had beaten England in a one-day match in Melbourne, although because England were playing as MCC it was not recognised as an official international. When England arrived in New Zealand a week or so later for two Tests and two one-day games there was, therefore, a certain amount of optimism abroad that the fateful hour of victory over them was not far away.

The burden of having lost the Ashes in such devastating fashion cannot be an easy cross for Mike Denness, the England captain, to bear. Yet he was not at all a poor leader, taking a fine Kent side to a string of trophies in the early 1970s, and it is difficult to see what any captain could have done against Lillee and Thomson – especially as the Australian team under Ian Chappell were at this time perfecting the art of destroying the batsman's concentration by 'sledging' (subjecting him to a barrage of abusive language). Denness had nineteen Tests in charge and still finished in credit, winning six and losing five, and in 1973–4 was the last England captain to beat the West Indies. He was a good, orthodox batsman, especially strong against the spinners, but, like many of his team, vulnerable against extreme pace; in his twenty-eight Tests he scored 1,669 runs at just under 40. He was a quiet, sensitive, rather withdrawn Scotsman who didn't enjoy the best of relations with the Press; and they, as is their wont, contrived to make things worse for him by not always tempering their criticism with balanced judgements. It is true that he was not noted for his ability to empathise with his troops and didn't have much of a knack of being able to pick them up when they were down; but he was a tremendous fighter who showed his real qualities in an innings of 188 in the last Test – when Thomson was absent and Lillee was injured early on — the highest score ever made by an England captain in Australia. Ominously for New Zealand, as it turned out, he had been partnered during that innings by Keith Fletcher, who made 146.

Three of the England party had gone home after leaving Australia and Barry Wood was summoned from the Caribbean to join the team. After a sixty-three hour journey he was out first ball, soon followed by Amiss. Edrich and Denness took the score to 153 before Edrich went, and Fletcher joined his captain. When they were parted the next morning they had put on 266, a new fourth-wicket record for these Tests. Denness made 181 (like Congdon in the 170s, he evidently had a weakness in the 180s) but Fletcher pressed on and scored his first Test double-century, making 216. With Greig also contributing a half-century Denness was able to declare at 593 for 6, the highest total by either side in England–New Zealand Tests. Four of the top home batsmen then failed, but a painstaking century from Parker in six hours, supported by 58 each from Morrison and Wadsworth saw them to some respectability at 326 all out. Respectable it might have been but it wasn't enough to avoid the follow-on and then the performance really wasn't very respectable at all. Morrison made another 58 and Geoff Howarth, on début, scored an undefeated 51, but they subsided to 184 for 9 as Underwood helped himself to another five wickets.

Thirteen of these runs had come from Ewen Chatfield, also making his début; he had batted sensibly for seventy-five minutes and was looking a very capable tail-end batsman. Peter Lever, having bowled just three short balls in the previous forty-five minutes, two of which had hardly risen to waist height, moved his gully in closer with the intention of trying to get Chatfield caught off the glove. He then bowled a ball which was straight and not especially short; it hit Chatfield on the glove well enough, but it ricocheted up and struck him on the side of his head. He collapsed unconscious and began to convulse and turn purple, and for several seconds his heart stopped beating. Bernard Thomas, the England physio, and a St John Ambulance Brigade officer raced on to the pitch and by heart massage and mouth-to-mouth resuscitation succeeded in saving his life; he had a hair-line fracture of the skull but made a full recovery. Poor Lever was utterly distraught and could only kneel on the pitch in anguish while Chatfield was being attended to; but the New Zealanders made it quite clear that he had in no way been responsible for dangerous bowling and that it had simply been an accident. He said afterwards that he had been so sick that his first thought had been to retire from cricket; he was in fact approaching the end of his career anyway, and in his last couple of seasons it was noticeable that he restricted his use of the short ball considerably. The irony that this should happen to a man who must have a fair claim to be the least malicious of all fast bowlers did not go unremarked and coming after the carnage inflicted by Lillee and Thomson simply compounded that irony. The books show that England won the match by an innings and 83 runs, but there can't have been many who were really bothered about that.

As it happened, the next Test was to be the last that Ken Wadsworth played against England, for a reason every bit as tragic as the accident to Chatfield might have been; in August 1976, just six months after he played his final Test against India at Wellington, he died of cancer at the age of 29. It was an enormous blow to New Zealand cricket, for not only had he made himself into a fine wicket-keeper but he was a very useful attacking batsman and an ideal person to have in the dressing-room to instil some pep and confidence into the rest of the team; he was the kind of splendid team man who really believed they would win and never failed to tell everyone so. Powerfully built, with a mop of fair hair that made him a distinctive character, he was a very keen and determined cricketer who was not put off by early disappointments but worked enormously hard to make himself into a Test keeper. He made his début against England in 1969 and became a regular member of the team, playing in thirty-three Tests; he scored just over 1,000 runs at 21 – his last first-class innings was an aggressive century – but was denied the honour of becoming the first New Zealander to make 100 Test dismissals as he finished just four short of the mark. His career total of 292 dismissals was also his country's record for first-class cricket. There was every reason to believe that he would hold his Test place for years, and although that was taken well enough by Warren Lees the gap that his death left in the dressing-room was much less easily filled.

That second Test at Christchurch was destroyed by the weather and the English over-rate. The first two days were washed out – these were, incidentally, the first five-day Tests England had ever played in New Zealand – and it was agreed to play on the rest day to make up for it. Denness won the toss, put New Zealand in and saw Morrison go first ball, but Turner and Congdon battled on against the conditions. Congdon made 64 and next day Parker supported Turner for a while. The 98 he made here was the closest Turner ever got to a hundred against England, and it was scored in the face of a desperately slow over-rate that must have taxed the batsmen's powers of concentration to the limit; even the gentle Walter Hadlee, Chairman of the NZCC, criticised England for their performance. Wadsworth, Cairns and Dayle Hadlee chipped in lower down the order and the score went to 342 all out, not at all bad in the circumstances. The

England innings belonged primarily to Amiss; he had had a horrendous time against Lillee and Thomson, but now he made 164 not out to help restore his belief in himself. The match was washed out, though, when England were 272 for 2, and the rain annihilated the one-day internationals as well. England were no doubt only too pleased to get home alive after all the drama of the previous months; but as they were faced with the prospect of another encounter with Lillee and Thomson maybe some felt that it would not be at all a bad idea to stay in New Zealand and watch the rain.

*

For the first time since 1929–30, England's tour of New Zealand in 1977–8 was not an appendage to a visit to Australia; from now on New Zealand would be given a tour in its own right. After so many years of receiving weary and travel-stained cricketers it was about time the New Zealanders got a better deal – yet even then their opponents had spent two months playing on lifeless pitches in Pakistan. Mike Brearley, the captain, had had his arm broken in a one-day match, and so for the last Test against Pakistan and the three in New Zealand Geoff Boycott took over.

Boycott's achievements as a run-scoring machine need little elaboration; that he lies eighth in the all-time aggregates list and was for a while the leading Test run-maker tell their own story. Any present-day cricket fan will know of the intense passions which he has aroused by his single-minded pursuit of runs, with his defenders insisting that his genius was indispensable and his detractors insisting that he batted far too selfishly far too often for the good of the team. It's very hard to be objective about Boycott; of course his single-mindedness and his dedication were admirable, but there was always the feeling that they were taken to unnatural extremes. Of course he rescued Yorkshire and England countless times by applying himself to a difficult task, but there were countless other times when he scored desperately slowly, clearly content simply to occupy the crease and to hell with the spectators who had paid good money in the hope of watching better entertainment than he provided, and whose frustration was made greater by the knowledge that he could bat attractively when he so wanted. Many a time has he been accused of playing for his average rather than being concerned with the state of the game, and many a time has this and the other criticisms been refuted, both by himself and by his supporters.

Yet if his batting inspired conflicting loyalties, there has been an argument or two over his captaincy as well. From 1971 to 1978 he led Yorkshire, a period which saw them devoid of a trophy of any sort. Obviously his captaincy was by no means the only reason for this, but many

Geoff Boycott in characteristic pose, placing the ball through the covers with pin-point accuracy.

Mark Burgess played some very attractive innings for his country, but none that could have given him so much pleasure as leading his team to their first victory over England.

people believed it to be one of the most important, especially in view of some of the stories of disharmony that emanated from the dressing-room; the general feeling was always that he was too intense and self-absorbed to be a good captain, and had very little to offer as a 'man manager'. Always the England captaincy was the prize he coveted most, but because of the controversy his leadership aroused he was passed over in favour of Denness and then Greig – and went away and sulked as a result. In the end the honour came to him only because of the injury to Brearley and he led England in just these four games. Whether Brearley's presence would have changed the result of the first Test at Wellington we can never know, of course – but the anti-Boycott brigade will always have their opinion.

His opposite number in this series was a much less controversial character. Mark Burgess was a fine and attractive batsman with a range of attacking strokes – Dick Brittenden described him as 'a natural' – especially strong on the drive, and with a warm and friendly personality that made life much easier for him than ever Boycott's intensity has done for him. (To which the Boycott fan replies 'Ah, but look at the difference in the batting record', and so the argument rolls on.) Burgess played in fifty Tests, scoring 2,684 runs at 31 with five centuries, and on his day could be a delightful batsman to watch, although his batting generally declined under the responsibility of captaincy. He has been described as a dedicated amateur cricketer in a professional age, one of the fortunate band for whom the game is not a matter of life and death. His captaincy record of one win, six defeats and three draws is identical to Turner's, but he was a more easygoing leader; Turner, incidentally, was back in England organising his benefit. An experienced Test cricketer, Burgess knew, for all his so-called 'amateurishness', very much what the game is all about and he was very popular with his team-mates. Can he really have believed that, with his first shot at the captaincy, he was about to gain himself a place in his country's sporting history?

One aspect of the new touring arrangement was that there was more time for matches other than Tests, and England – now England rather than MCC – played three first-class games before the first Test, drawing two and, with the help of Central Districts, providing only the second tie in a first-class game in New Zealand, the first having come over a century earlier. Ominously, the batting had sometimes looked rather frail in these matches. Boycott won the toss in the first Test, put New Zealand in, and John Wright, on his début, survived a very confident appeal for a catch behind off the first ball he received. Wright later admitted that he had touched it but that he wasn't going to walk, especially in his first Test. He was to go on to

Chris Old – 6 for 54 at Wellington in 1977–8.

55, his team's top score. It was to be a slow-scoring match, with New Zealand 153 for 3 at the close. Next morning Old, bowling superbly into a very strong wind, chipped away at the wickets, only Congdon and Richard Hadlee making much impression on the scorebook, and finished with 6 for 54 as New Zealand were all out for 228. When the match was over Boycott received some criticism for putting New Zealand in, but this was patently unfair; dismissing a team in a Test for 228 must vindicate an insertion – and anyway Burgess said that he would have done the same in the conditions.

Collinge then became the third New Zealand bowler to take 100 Test wickets when he had Rose caught behind; rather pleasing that he should choose such an important match to do it in. By the close on the second day England had crawled to 89 for 2, Boycott having taken 277 minutes to reach his fifty. He was to go on to 77 and take 422 minutes about it, enthralling the crowd with a steady 11 runs per hour; yet it was a highly responsible performance from a leading batsman who knew just how easily his team-mates could collapse and whose fears were to be proved only too well-founded. With Roope he put on 57 for the fifth wicket, but that was the biggest partnership of the innings and after they departed in quick succession the tail subsided to Richard Hadlee (who finished with 4 for 74) and Congdon – England were all out for 215.

How many times had New Zealand taken a first-innings lead – admittedly usually only a modest one – and then failed to capitalise on it? Could there really have been much optimism in the home ranks at this point, even when Anderson, Wright and Howarth got the innings off to a reasonable start, with 82 on the board before the second wicket fell? Surely there would be a collapse? Yes, of course there was. Along came Bob Willis, on one of his memorable days, to exploit a deteriorating pitch and finish with 5 for 32 as New Zealand were all out for 123. Gloom and despair. Only 137 to win. Same old story. Another chance thrown away, just like all the others over the past forty-eight years and forty-seven Tests.

Boycott was the first to go, the crucial breakthrough made by a big inswinger from Collinge when he had just one run. From that moment on New Zealand played as though they believed they could win. Miller was caught for 4 and it was 8 for 2. Rose retired after being hit on the elbow. Collinge had Randall lbw. England 18 for 3, Collinge 3 for 9 from 17 balls. Roope was caught by Lees off Hadlee without scoring; 18 for 4. Botham swung the bat for 19, but was caught hooking Hadlee; 38 for 5. At the same score Taylor was run out by Boock, the man who had just caught Botham. Edmonds and Old took the score to 53 before Old was lbw to Hadlee, and Hendrick promptly fell to Hadlee as well. At stumps England were 53 for 8.

Don Mosey wrote that for the last two days of the match 'some joker in an office outside the ground operated a powerful electric horn every time a wicket fell so that the whole of Wellington was instantly aware that a historic moment was not too far away.'

Next morning it was drizzling; surely the infamous Wellington weather could not be so cruel? It relented, with only forty-one minutes lost, a brief agony before the ecstasy. It was forty minutes before a wicket fell, Edmonds going to a slip catch off Hadlee; 63 for 9. Rose came back to see through the formalities; what he saw was Willis pushing at Hadlee and Howarth diving to take the catch. England all out 64. New Zealand had won by 72 runs on 15 February 1978.

Hero number one was Richard Hadlee, with 6 for 26 to add to his 4 for 74. Collinge's match figures were 6 for 77. Burgess had directed his men well, sensing the possibility of victory and not backing away from it as once might have happened. The fielding had been splendid, the catches had stuck. In all the euphoria one person remembered by the Press was Walter Hadlee; there would be few to argue that he had done more for his country's cricket over the years than anyone, and it was especially fitting that it was his multi-talented son who should be the principal architect of the victory. *Men in White* records that for New Zealanders the result was on a par with VE Day, Edmund Hillary climbing Everest and Peter Snell winning both the 800m and 1,500m at the Tokyo Olympics. One hopes that there were few British cricket fans who grudged them their joy.

In England there were discussions about the extent to which a captain may be blamed for his team's batting collapse; obviously it will vary in different circumstances, but the anti-Boycott league were in no doubt where the responsibility principally lay. Others were more charitable, maintaining that a captain who goes into the fourth innings with his team needing just 137 to win must have done a good job so far, and if his team then let him down very badly he should not be criticised too heavily. He for his part conceded, with good grace, that the better side won, although under provocative questioning at a press conference he later gave vent to his wrath in a manner ill-befitting any captain.

New Zealand followed this by making an excellent start to the Christchurch Test, taking the first three English wickets for 26. Roope and Miller dug in, though, after which Botham and Taylor put on 160 for the sixth wicket, Botham making his maiden Test century thanks to a lot of support and encouragement from Bob Taylor as he grew anxious when nearing the landmark. Miller had had to retire after being hit on the head, but he now returned and put on 70 for the ninth wicket with Edmonds,

England eventually making 418. New Zealand's reply had a familiar air about it; Anderson top-scored with 62, Parker made 53 not out, two or three others got in and got out and they were all out for 235. Botham took 5 for 73 in all this to become only the second Englishman after Tony Greig to score a century and take five wickets in a Test innings. In the final session of the fourth day England needed quick runs to set up a declaration, yet Boycott, uncertain whether his dismissal might lead to another collapse, was scoring too slowly – so Botham resolved his dilemma and deliberately ran him out.

By the close England were 96 for 4, one of those wickets falling when Randall was run out by Chatfield; without warning the bowler broke his wicket as he was backing up, the first time this had happened in an England–New Zealand Test. It brought profuse apologies from some of the New Zealanders. Boycott was persuaded by his team-mates to declare on the overnight score, leaving New Zealand to get 280 to win; he had wanted to bat on for a few minutes so that he could then use the heavy roller to help break up the pitch for the spinners and after an argument in the dressing-room Willis came out in a bad temper and proceeded to bowl fearsomely. After 82 minutes the New Zealanders were 25 for 5 and Wellington seemed a long way away. Only Anderson, Parker and Hadlee were to reach double figures, Hadlee's 39 saving a total disgrace as Willis took 4 for 14 and Botham and Edmonds joined in the fun as well. In less than three hours they were all out for 105, England having put the upstarts in their place with a 174-run victory.

The decider was to be played over six days, the first Test of that length in New Zealand. Like many long Tests it was a tedious business, with the batsmen in no hurry to score their runs. New Zealand batted first and, after losing the openers, Howarth and Burgess gave the innings some substance. Burgess went for 50 and wicket-keeper Edwards later made 55, but Howarth eventually reached his maiden Test century – even if it did take him 455 minutes. Near the end of the second day they were all out for 315. Next day, after Randall had gone, Boycott and Radley 'entertained' the crowd by scoring 37 runs between lunch and tea and when Boycott went for 54 Roope made 68 at little greater speed. Radley's century was even slower than Howarth's at 487 minutes and he was to go on to score the slowest 150 in Test cricket at the time, taking 649 minutes over his 158. Botham woke up the crowd with a quick 53, but on the fifth afternoon anyone still watching or interested would have seen England all out for 429. They were then led by Bob Willis as Boycott had suffered a scratched cornea from one of his contact lenses. Howarth became the second New Zealander after

Richard Collinge – a crucial role in New Zealand's first win over England. After his last Test he was his country's leading wicket taker with 116.

Turner to score a century in each innings of a Test – a mere 320 minutes this time – and with support from Anderson, Edwards and Parker saw the score to 382 for 8 when the game was laid to rest. It was a great pity that the wonder of Wellington should have become the aridity of Auckland.

For one New Zealander, though, the match had a particular significance. When Richard Collinge had Botham caught by the wicket-keeper it was his 112th Test wicket, thereby making him his country's leading wicket-taker. Standing 6 feet 5 inches tall, he bowled left-arm fast-medium from a lengthy run that tended to seem excessive for the speed of the resulting delivery, but he was accurate and could get the ball to swing. He made his Test début at the age of 18 in 1965 in the same match as Bevan Congdon and was more or less a regular in the team thereafter; although as a family man he was not always the most enthusiastic of tourists and he once returned early from a tour of the West Indies because one of his children was ill. Hard-working, modest and unexcitable, he played his part in the historic first wins over Australia and England, making the crucial breakthrough in the latter match to dismiss Boycott and precipitate England's collapse. He was no mug with the bat either, as a Test average of 14 shows, and he holds one rather remarkable record; against Pakistan at Auckland in 1973 he and Brian Hastings put on 151 for the tenth wicket, still the world Test record for that wicket. Collinge's share was 68 not out, the highest score ever made by a number eleven batsman in a Test. He finished his Test career a few months later in England with 116 wickets at 29 from thirty-five matches, holding the New Zealand record for two years until – inevitably – overtaken by Richard Hadlee.

*

Three months later New Zealand were in England. When there had been two tours close to each other in the past it had been because an England visit to Australia followed New Zealand's coming north; now the idea of back-to-back series had reached England–New Zealand games, a modern fashion which means that by the time the second series has finished (just a few months after the first) the players are sick of the sight of each other, especially as any animosities arising during the first rubber will probably flare up again in the second since they have not had the chance to die down. Neither players nor fans appear to like the arrangement, but it persists.

Mark Burgess was still at the New Zealand helm, and still lacking the services of his best batsman as Turner was concentrating on his benefit; even when the tourists requested his assistance because they had a string of injuries he declined to help out. Turner's attitude caused a great deal of resentment in New Zealand and there was a lot of bitterness at the thought that he had let the side down. Don Mosey relates that when doing radio commentaries there he was able to explain how important a benefit season is to players in England. Because Turner was the first New Zealander to be awarded one there was little understanding among his compatriots as to what they were all about – beyond the fact that money plays a leading part. Some people took the trouble to thank Mosey for his explanation, saying that they now understood Turner's attitude much better. Meanwhile, Burgess's problems were not made any easier by the fact that Mike Brearley

*Mike Brearley, batting in a prototype helmet, scored a half-century
at Trent Bridge in 1978. Jock Edwards is behind the stumps.*

was now back in charge of the England team, and had just beaten Pakistan (who had lost some important players to Kerry Packer's World Series Cricket) 2–0.

Brearley is recognised as one of the best of all captains, although he was fortunate to come up against teams weakened by defections to Packer (England, too, had lost some good players, however) and he was never tested against the mighty West Indies. In thirty-one games as captain he won eighteen and lost only four, but it was more the nature of his captaincy which gained him so much praise. Perhaps the most intellectually acute man ever to play first-class cricket – he had gained an excellent degree at Cambridge, come top in the Civil Service entrance examination and taught philosophy at two universities – he combined sharpness of brain with great tactical expertise; he had what John Arlott called an 'immense mental hunger' that allowed him to stand at first slip for hour after hour concentrating on the play and at the same time working out the best way to deal with the situation. He had also studied psychoanalysis, and it proved a tool that enabled him to understand his players and know how best to motivate each individual perhaps better than any other captain; the Australian bowler Rodney Hogg famously summed it up when his team were on the receiving end of the Brearley-inspired Botham in 1981: 'I reckon Brearley has got a degree in people.' To this he added a humanitarian nature to which his players would easily respond; quiet and easy-going, yet with a very strong will, his authority was unobtrusive yet never in question.

The problem was that his batting was rarely up to Test standard. He had had a lengthy break from first-class cricket in the late 1960s, after which his early promise seemed to have declined, but by the mid-1970s he was high in the national averages and selected for his batting. When Tony Greig threw in his lot with Packer and was stripped of the captaincy Brearley was the obvious successor and although his final Test average was under 23 there were few English fans who didn't feel that he was worth his place for his leadership ability and the occasional decent innings he made. Perhaps if there had been an outstanding contender for the position he would not have been so lucky, but the only other option was Boycott and one can't imagine that the selectors lost much sleep trying to decide between the two. Whether Brearley was a better captain than Illingworth must be a matter of opinion, although there can be no doubt that the Yorkshireman was worth his place in the team on playing ability whereas Brearley wasn't. There can be no doubt either that both of them were among the best Test captains of all time.

By the time of the first Test New Zealand had four wins under their belts, three of them by an innings, but had lost the two one-day internationals. They had had several injury and illness problems, including a virus that had affected Burgess's form, and Collinge had been summoned from home to replace Dayle Hadlee – which was curious as Chatfield had been named as the reserve. The Wellington *Dominion* found this 'crude, rude and tactless, even for a body as autocratic and ungracious as the New Zealand Cricket Council has often shown itself to be.' Chatfield, the perceptive reader may have guessed, played for Wellington.

The first Test at the Oval was a landmark for Bev Congdon, for it was his fifty-ninth game and his twentieth against England, so that John Reid's records both fell at once. Unfortunately it wasn't an especially happy landmark. Wright and Howarth put on 123 for the second wicket and Howarth and Burgess 60 for the fourth, Howarth falling just six short of

David Gower shows his languid grace during his first Test century at the Oval in 1978. Compare this with the earlier picture of Frank Woolley to enjoy the aesthetic delight of two of England's most graceful batsmen in action, both of them left-handers.

becoming the first New Zealander to score centuries in three successive Test innings. Everyone else failed, though, and the innings closed on the second morning at 234. Brendan Bracewell, however, not yet 19 and the fourth-youngest New Zealand Test player, had Gooch lbw with his third ball in Test cricket and soon had Brearley caught behind as well. The crowd were treated, however, to David Gower at his most mellifluous, 111 runs being stroked gracefully to all corners of the field for his first Test century, although he was dropped twice in the middle of it. He was supported by Radley but few others, until on the third morning Edmonds made 28 to help the total to 279, Hadlee's bowling having been restricted by the rib cage injury that had been troubling him for some time. Three New Zealand batsmen went before the deficit of 45 had been erased and anyone familiar with the history of England–New Zealand games could have confidently predicted the outcome. Edgar, on début, made a patient 38, Congdon got 36, Cairns and Wright reached the twenties and that was it; all out for 182. The innings didn't end till the fifth day as the fourth was washed out, but England had plenty of time to get the 138 they needed; with Gooch undefeated on 91 they lost only three wickets in doing so. Burgess made a bid for the quotation books by saying 'With another hundred or so runs it would have been a very good game of cricket.'

In the second Test several dropped catches on the first day and a strange umpiring decision on the third day did for New Zealand. Boycott, who

A dive, a juggling act and eventually, at the third attempt, Mike Brearley catches Mark Burgess off Phil Edmonds at Trent Bridge in 1978.

Bob Anderson is run out without scoring at Trent Bridge in 1978 as David Gower, with only one stump to aim at, races in and hits the target.

England celebrate as Ian Botham snaps up a fine catch to end Bruce Edgar's innings of 60 at Trent Bridge in 1978.

twice almost fell lbw to Hadlee at the beginning, was dropped on 2 and also in the 70s and then went on to make 131, and Gooch and Radley were both given lives. Boycott was on 108 by the close, with England at 252 for 2; next day Gower and Brearley both made a score, but the fielders got their act together and England were all out for 429 as the last eight wickets fell for 128 runs. In an hour and a half on the second evening New Zealand managed to lose four wickets for 47 and have Howarth hit on the head as well; to compound their problems the following morning the Nottingham sky was very dark but the umpires decided to start play. After two balls this was called off, but as play had begun the pitch had to be left uncovered and therefore open to the light rain that fell from time to time. Burgess, very justifiably, was furious, but the damage was done. When play resumed in mid-afternoon Botham in particular found the conditions to his liking, finishing with 6 for 34 as only Howarth and Congdon put up any resistance. All out for 120, the familiar story followed; Edgar battled well for 60 over four hours and Parker – who was run out when he slipped on the damp ground – and Howarth reached the thirties, but Edmonds enjoyed himself and took four wickets to prove it as they were all out for 190. An innings and 119 runs was the final margin.

The third Test at Lord's also had a familiar ring to it, though in a different way. Against an England bowling attack that was in a particularly hostile mood – Emburey took a wicket with his fourth ball in Test cricket –

New Zealand's brothers of the 1970s. Dayle Hadlee bowled fast. . . but Richard Hadlee bowled faster. Hedley Howarth plied left-arm spin. . . Geoff Howarth preferred to score centuries.

Howarth made a century and put on 130 in almost even time with Burgess, who with 68 made his first decent contribution to the series. At the close they were 260 for 5, although next morning they rather struggled to 339 all out, Botham finishing with 6 for 101. The main substance of England's reply came from Radley and Gower, both of whom scored seventies, with supporting roles played by Boycott, Brearley and Botham; but 175 for 2 overnight became 289 all out as Hadlee took 5 for 84 and Collinge, recalled for one more Test, took his national record to 116 wickets. A first innings lead of 50 was a definite luxury, a sound platform for building a match-winning score; so New Zealand allowed themselves to be bowled out for 67. Botham swung the ball and Willis hammered it down, and the wickets simply tumbled. Botham's 5 for 39 gave him match figures of 11 for 140, and Willis took 4 for 16 from as many overs. Needing 118 England lost three wickets in getting there, including two in successive balls to Hadlee; one of them, 'Radley b Hadlee', has a pleasing ring to it, even if it doesn't match the ultimate scorebook entry that happened some sixteen months later in Perth: 'Lillee c Willey (in the gully) b Dilley'. Unfortunately Radley's first Test came immediately after Dayle Hadlee's last, so the possibility of 'Radley c Hadlee b Hadlee' never arose.

1974–5	Auckland	E 593–6d;	NZ 326, 184	E inns 83 runs
	Christchurch	NZ 342;	E 272–2	Drawn
1977–8	Wellington	NZ 228, 123;	E 215, 64	NZ 72 runs
	Christchurch	E 418, 96–4d;	NZ 235, 105	E 174 runs
	Auckland	NZ 315, 382–8;	E 429	Drawn
1978	Oval	NZ 234, 182;	E 279, 138–3	E 7 wkts
	Trent Bridge	E 429;	NZ 120,190	E inns 119 runs
	Lord's	NZ 339, 67;	E 289, 118–3	E 7 wkts

1974–5 Test series
England
Best batting: K.W.R. Fletcher 216 M.H. Denness 181; 59* D.L. Amiss 164*
    J.H. Edrich 64 A.W. Greig 51
Best bowling: A.W. Greig 26–4–98–5 and 15–3–51–5

New Zealand
Best batting: J.M. Parker 121; 41 G.M. Turner 98 J.F.M. Morrison 58 and 58
    K.J. Wadsworth 58; 58 G.P. Howarth 51*
Best bowling: D.R. Hadlee 20–2–102–2

Wicket-keepers: K.J. Wadsworth (NZ) 2 dismissals A.P.E. Knott (E) 3 dismissals

In the first match England's 593 is the highest innings by either side in England v New Zealand Tests; M.H. Denness and K.W.R. Fletcher put on 266 for the record England fourth-wicket partnership against New Zealand; A.W. Greig became the third English player to score 2,000 runs and take 100 wickets in Tests. In the second match G.G. Arnold became the only bowler to take a wicket twice with the first ball of a Test.

1977–8 Test series
England

Batting	Innings	NO	HS	Runs	Average
C.T. Radley	2	0	158	173	86.50
I.T. Botham	5	1	103	212	53.00
G.R.J. Roope	5	1	68	164	41.00
G. Boycott	5	0	77	166	33.20
G. Miller	4	0	89	132	33.00

Bowling	Overs	M	Runs	W	Average
R.G.D. Willis	103.6	27	255	14	18.21
I.T. Botham	101	17	311	17	18.29
C.M. Old	60	21	150	8	18.75
P.H. Edmonds	99	31	201	9	22.33
J.K. Lever	51	9	155	5	31.00

New Zealand

Batting	Innings	NO	HS	Runs	Average
G.P. Howarth	6	0	122	264	44.00
J.M. Parker	6	2	53*	150	37.50
R.W. Anderson	6	0	62	203	33.83
M.G. Burgess	6	1	50	117	23.40
J.G. Wright	6	0	55	107	17.83

Bowling	Overs	M	Runs	W	Average
S.L. Boock	59.3	20	129	7	18.42
R.O. Collinge	104.5	27	293	15	19.53
R.J. Hadlee	121.3	26	371	15	24.73
B.E. Congdon	63.4	30	114	2	57.00

Wicket-keepers: W.K. Lees (NZ) 7 dismissals   G.N. Edwards (NZ) 1 dismissal
R.W. Taylor (E) 9 dismissals

In the first match New Zealand finally beat England after 48 years and at the 48th attempt. R.J. Hadlee took 10 for 100 to record the best match analysis for New Zealand against England, and R.O. Collinge took his 100th Test wicket. In the second match I.T. Botham became the second England player to score a century and take five wickets in an innings in the same Test. In the third match G.P. Howarth became the second New Zealand batsman to score two separate centuries in a Test, Collinge became the leading New Zealand wicket-taker when he passed B.R. Taylor's figure of 111 and C.T. Radley scored the slowest 150 in first-class cricket (594 minutes).

1978 Test series
England

Batting	Innings	NO	HS	Runs	Average
G.A. Gooch	5	2	91*	190	63.33
D.I. Gower	5	0	111	285	57.00
G. Boycott	3	0	131	159	53.00
C.T. Radley	5	0	77	187	37.40
J.M. Brearley	5	1	50	104	26.00

Bowling	Overs	M	Runs	W	Average
I.T. Botham	142.1	42	337	24	14.04
P.H. Edmonds	112	48	145	10	14.50
R.G.D. Willis	99.2	33	229	12	19.08
J.E. Emburey	29.1	14	40	2	20.00
G. Miller	71	33	90	4	22.50

New Zealand

Batting	Innings	NO	HS	Runs	Average
G.P. Howarth	6	2	123	296	74.00
J.G. Wright	4	0	62	116	29.00
B.A. Edgar	6	0	60	147	24.50
M.G. Burgess	6	0	68	135	22.50
J.M. Parker	4	0	38	55	13.75

Bowling	Overs	M	Runs	W	Average
R.J. Hadlee	121.1	31	270	13	20.76
B.P. Bracewell	89.2	14	282	9	31.33
S.L. Boock	113	53	189	6	31.50
R.O. Collinge	36	10	84	2	42.00
B.L. Cairns	85	23	171	4	42.75

Wicket-keepers: R.W. Taylor (E) 13 dismissals   G.N. Edwards (NZ) 4 dismissals
B.A. Edgar (NZ) 3 dismissals

In the first match B.E. Congdon passed J.R. Reid's record 58 appearances for New Zealand, and in the second match Congdon passed Reid's record New Zealand figure of 3,428 runs.

— **9** —

Matricide

Ah, my little son, thou hast murdered thy mother!
Sir Thomas Malory, *Le Morte D'Arthur*

It was 1983 before the teams met again in a Test series, a longer gap than had occurred at any time in the past except for the War years. However, the period had seen a sudden explosion in the number of one-day internationals, especially with the interminable Benson and Hedges World Series Cup competitions in Australia that provided the most ephemeral cricket entertainment imaginable. During those five years England and New Zealand had met in eleven one-day games and New Zealand had a 7–4 advantage. New Zealand had also beaten West Indies, India and Sri Lanka in Test series at home and drawn 1–1 with Australia, also in New Zealand, although there had been a number of claims of incompetence and bias against their umpires. They had lost a rubber in Australia, but there was no doubt that they were at last becoming a real force in world cricket. Obviously this was partly because of the overall quality of the players, especially the match-winning Hadlee, but much of the credit must go to the highly professional approach of their captain.

A list of the captains of New Zealand with a breakdown of their statistics has a 'Wins' column that, for the most part, makes fairly depressing reading. Reid has three wins, Dowling four, Congdon, Turner and Burgess one apiece; everyone else has the euphemism of the '—' rather than the finality of the '0'. Then comes G.P. Howarth: matches thirty, wins eleven, defeats seven, draws twelve. How did it come about?

Geoff Howarth made his Test début in 1975, in the same match that almost saw the end of Chatfield. A neat and attractive batsman, especially strong on the off-side, he took a while to establish himself but then, perhaps just in time to save his Test career, he scored a century in each innings against England in 1977–8 to cement his place. He went on to play in forty-seven Tests and make over 2,500 runs at 32, with six Test centuries, of which the highest was 147 against the West Indies at Christchurch in 1980, a match fraught with problems because of complaints about one of the umpires. He had a fine rubber in England in 1978, but towards the end of his career his form with the bat declined, and in his last two series against England was rather disappointing. He was also a useful off-spin bowler, although proved extremely expensive in Tests for little reward. For all his qualities as a batsman, however, it will undoubtedly be for his captaincy that he is chiefly remembered.

He didn't play for the New Zealand provincial side, Auckland, until 1972–3, moving two years later to Northern Districts, where he became captain in 1979–80. He had been playing for Surrey since 1971, though, with varying degrees of fortune and frustration, and in 1984, after his success with New Zealand, was made captain; yet by the following summer he had lost his place as the overseas player to the West Indian bowler Tony Gray and he left the Oval at the end of the season. It was sad that his time with Surrey ended unhappily since his experience there had been vital to his success with New Zealand; the only captain before him to have played professionally in England was Turner, and Howarth now had better players than Turner to whom he could apply a professional philosophy. Turner had tended to lean more towards the Boycott style of play and of captaincy, believing, often quite rightly, that his own occupation of the crease was the best thing for his team; but the concentration this demanded meant that neither was as free as a captain should be to think about their players' needs and problems. Howarth saw that his prime task was to consign to the history books the traditional New Zealand inability to believe that Saturday afternoon part-timers could be a match for the rest of the world; he realised that only with a much tougher and more self-confident approach could this be achieved and he perceived that he had the players to do it. An excellent fielder himself, he worked his men very hard at this aspect of their game and of course it bore fruit; like many captains, he himself was usually to be found in the slips, where he excelled. Put simply, he proved himself a natural captain, possessing a good rapport with his players, great determination, a quiet yet unquestioned authority and a sound tactical awareness. Richie Benaud described him as an outstanding leader, and gave him especial credit for New Zealand's first Test win in England. He had a good relationship with the media – although this soured somewhat towards the end of his Test career – and was noted for his coolness under pressure in the field. Coolness and diplomacy were among his greatest assets, in fact, for they brought him through some very difficult times: the fraught series against West Indies in 1979–80, the underarm delivery from Trevor Chappell, a disallowed catch in that same match that cost New Zealand the game, and so on. There were occasions when his rather 'laid-back' approach upset the officials – David

Rival captains in the 1983 series. Geoff Howarth watches as Bob Willis sends down another thunderbolt.

Gower must have sympathised with him — but as he led his team to their first win in England and their first series win over England and all in all made them very much a force in the world game for the first time, he could cheerfully point out that he had done more for his country's cricket than any number of officials.

If Howarth will be remembered more for his captaincy than his batting, Bob Willis will definitely be remembered more for his bowling than his captaincy. One of England's great fast bowlers with 325 wickets at 25 each from his ninety Tests, he was renowned for his lion-hearted performances over many years and for the way in which he forced his damaged knees to keep on going for season after season. Several times it seemed that his Test career must almost be over, but he kept on coming back, always much more of a Test bowler than a county one; those 325 wickets represent more than a third of his career total of 899, a remarkable proportion for a top English bowler. In the end the England captaincy came his way, an unsought honour which perhaps he didn't really want but which he was determined to do his best to discharge; and certainly his record is in credit, with seven wins and five defeats in his eighteen games.

There was criticism when he was appointed since it was felt that he was too much of a worrier, needed to concentrate on his bowling too much to be able to spend much time thinking about tactics or motivating his players, and needed a sympathetic captain to bring out the best in him. So tense did he become before a big match that he had resorted to hypnotherapy to try to ease the problem; to a certain extent it succeeded, but there were numerous occasions when he was to be seen standing at mid-off apparently oblivious to the rest of his team, with the senior players appearing to run the show. Yet the honour and responsibility brought out the best of his playing ability and he turned in some fine performances during his captaincy. He may not have been a great tactician and he may have had to withdraw into his concentration too often, but he led by example in the best possible way. His captaincy ended sadly with illness in Pakistan after an unhappy tour to New Zealand in 1983–4 when there were insalubrious stories in the tabloids about the activities of certain of his players, but he was happy to play a few more Tests the following summer under David Gower before calling it a day. Had he ever found a regular new-ball partner of comparable pace and heart English cricket would have had a much better time of it than it did.

The 1983 series came after the Prudential World Cup in which New Zealand had narrowly failed to reach the semi-final and England had done so but then allowed themselves to be dominated by India, the eventual surprise winners. Turner had played in this but then gone back to New

Zealand; his team-mates, however, were given only three first-class games before the first Test took place at the Oval. Willis wrote afterwards that the pitch was the best he had played on in a Test anywhere for years.

England batted first, only to encounter Hadlee in his customary hostile mood. Wickets fell steadily during the day, only Randall with 75 not out and Tavaré, who had to retire for a while after being hit in the face, making a decent score. The innings closed on 209 shortly before the end, with Hadlee's figures 6 for 53. Shortly before the end it may have been, but there was still time for New Zealand to lose three wickets while scoring just 17 runs. This was quickly 17 for 4 next morning, but Coney and Hadlee, and later Lees, stemmed the collapse and at the end the deficit was no more than 13 runs. By the time England batted again the pitch was undoubtedly in their favour, and on a hot, humid day Fowler and Tavaré began to build a record England first-wicket partnership against New Zealand, which was not broken till the next day when it reached 223; it was the first time both of England's openers had made a century since 1960, when Cowdrey and Pullar put on 290 against South Africa on the same ground. For New Zealand it steadily became a case of keeping down the run-rate rather than trying to take wickets, but Allan Lamb also fancied the conditions and became the team's third century-maker. When he reached his target Willis declared at 446 for 6, leaving the visitors about a day and a half to make 460. After another poor start Wright and Howarth put on 120 for the third wicket, but thereafter only Martin Crowe and Cairns – the latter with four sixes – got beyond 30, and on the last afternoon they were all out for 270, leaving England victorious by 189 runs. This was, incidentally, the first match in which the Crowe brothers appeared together, but neither of them had any special reason to remember it.

They and their team-mates had every reason to remember the next Test, however. Before that they had convincing wins over Worcestershire and Warwickshire, with Lance Cairns taking a significant 7 for 46 in the second innings of the latter match after Howarth had told him that unless his bowling improved he would be out of the Test team. It proved an inspired piece of captaincy, for when Howarth won an important toss it was Cairns who did most of the damage to England on a Headingley pitch that was very much in the bowlers' favour. Tavaré spent three and a quarter hours over his half-century, while Lamb and then Botham laid about themselves at the other end, but everyone else failed and when England were all out for 225 Cairns found himself as the possessor of the best New Zealand figures ever against England, 7 for 74; it was due reward for using the pitch intelligently and reminded more than one writer of Alec Bedser at his best.

*Graeme Fowler in action during his record opening partnership
with Chris Tavaré at the Oval in 1983.*

Next morning Edgar retired hurt after being hit on the hip by Botham, and then Howarth was run out after being sent back by Wright. With Martin Crowe, Wright then took the score to 168, but 168 for 1 soon became 169 for 4; after Crowe went Wright contrived to run out his brother without scoring, and was so upset that he fell seven short of his first hundred against England. A collapse was averted by Edgar, who batted with a runner for 84, Hadlee, who made 75, and Cairns who smote his customary sixes allowing the total to reach 377. By the end of the day England were praying for rain, and lots of it; the deficit of 152 had been passed by two

A beautifully poised Allan Lamb dispatches another boundary during an unbeaten century at the Oval in 1983. Warren Lees is the wicket-keeper.

runs, but six wickets had fallen in the process and only Gower of the main batsmen was still there. The New Zealanders, simply, had used the pitch and bowled very well and their fielders had supported them. On the rest day it rained long and hard; was God really an Englishman after all? Apparently not, for play resumed on time, with Gower farming the strike and, mindful of the immortal events at the same ground against Australia two years earlier, trying to give his bowlers something at which to aim. After all, a lead of 129 had been enough to see England home then and New Zealand had collapsed often enough in the past. Dilley and Taylor stayed for a while, but

Jeremy Coney plucks the ball out of the air to dismiss Derek Randall at Headingley in 1983, one of seven first-innings wickets for Lance Cairns.

when the last man, Cowans, joined him he was still eight short of his hundred. On 99, anxious to keep the strike, he refused several singles before eventually scampering home and when Cowans was out he was undefeated on 112, his first home Test century for four years and a splendid one. There was further triumph for Cairns too, as Cowans' wicket gave him match figures of 10 for 144, only the third New Zealander to manage this in a Test against England; Chatfield also weighed in with his personal best in Tests, 5 for 95.

The total of 252 meant that New Zealand needed 101, and it was only early afternoon on the fourth day. Could Willis repeat his historic feat of two years before? With the score on 11 he got Edgar; on 42 he got Howarth; on 60 Wright; on 61 Martin Crowe. Was it possible? He was

Headingley 1983, Bob Taylor is bowled by Lance Cairns for 9. John Wright, Jeremy Coney and wicket-keeper Ian Smith express their approval.

Headingley 1983, England's last wicket falls as Norman Cowans is caught by Martin Crowe at short leg. As Crowe throws the ball with delight, bowler Cairns, Coney, Jeff Crowe and Smith join in the celebrations.

New Zealand needed just 101 to record that first win in England, but 5 for 35 from Bob Willis gave them a rocky passage before they got there. The Crowe brothers provided him with his 299th and 300th Test wickets: first Martin is caught by Allan Lamb at short leg and then Jeff loses his middle stump. Willis joins the élite by taking a brace of Crowes.

The champagne flows after the Headingley triumph.

now on 299 Test wickets. With the score on 83 he shattered Jeff Crowe's stumps to join the élite company of Lillee, Gibbs and Trueman – but that was as far as it went. Coney and Hadlee polished off the runs, the honour of the winning hit falling to Coney, and on 1 August 1983, fifty-two years after they first played a Test in England and at the twenty-ninth attempt, New Zealand recorded their first Test victory in England. Perhaps the most remarkable thing about the whole match was that Hadlee didn't take a single wicket, although he bowled as well as ever and he certainly batted well.

Instead, the game provided a less likely hero, Lance Cairns's ten wickets earning him the man of the match award. He was a hugely enjoyable cricketer to watch; very powerfully built, always full of enthusiasm, always apparently certain that he was going to take a wicket next ball. He had made his début almost ten years previously but had never found a regular spot in the team because his medium-pace bowling had too few weapons on a good pitch, but through hard work he made himself into a Test bowler good enough to take 130 wickets at just under 33 from forty-three games. Already a good swinger of the ball, he worked in particular on the delivery

Having twice dropped David Gower in the previous Test at Lord's, Lance Cairns makes some amends at Trent Bridge by taking a brilliant catch off the bowling of John Bracewell to dismiss him for 33.

that cut away from the batsman and took many wickets with it, although this was his only ten-wicket Test haul. His batting – swashbuckling was an adjective commonly, if unoriginally, applied to it – wasn't good enough for him to be classed as an all-rounder; but he finished with over 900 runs at 16 and when the sixes were sailing into the crowd it could be very memorable, for he struck the ball, in Christopher Martin-Jenkins's phrase, 'with a blacksmith's might and relish'. In one-day games his batting was, needless to say, sometimes spectacular, although in the 1979 and 1983 World Cups it was quite the opposite. Something special went out of New Zealand cricket when he left the team.

If it lacks originality to describe Cairns's batting as swashbuckling, the ultimate hackneyed cricketing cliché must be 'It's a funny game.' Yet how many people, on the first day of the next Test at Lord's, must have thought or spoken those words? With Chris Smith having gone first ball on début, David Gower had scored 21 when he mishooked Crowe. The ball sailed up in the air and came down squarely into the very large hands of the fielder

Out first ball in Test cricket – Christ Smith falls lbw to Richard Hadlee at Lord's in 1983.

*Another one in the bag for Richard Hadlee – Ian Smith at full
stretch to dismiss Bob Willis (Lord's 1983).*

waiting at backward square leg – who dropped it. The words 'dolly' and
'sitter' were among the more printable to be heard. In the next over, Gower
having advanced to 25, edged the ball from Hadlee to third slip, where the
same fielder again failed to hold it. Gower then went on to 108. The fielder
was Lance Cairns.

Tavaré ground away for four hours to amass 51, unbothered as ever at
the thought that the spectators might like to have some entertainment for
their money, and Gatting made what was then his highest Test score of 81,
but no one else reached 20. England were all out for 326 on the second
morning. The only substantial partnership of the New Zealand innings was
98 for the third wicket between Edgar and Martin Crowe, but Crowe's
dismissal signalled a collapse as Botham and Nick Cook went through

them. Cook, on début, took 5 for 35 to become the first England slow bowler to take five wickets in a home Test for eight years. The last time this had been achieved was by Phil Edmonds and had also been on début; and the reason Cook was in the team was that Edmonds, who had played in the first two matches, had managed to injure his back when getting out of his car. One is tempted to remark that it's a funny game.

With the last eight wickets falling for 44 runs, New Zealand were all out for 191. England didn't then distinguish themselves but did enough on a less than perfect pitch to put the game out of the visitors' reach. Smith took an agonising time to get his first run but went on to 43, Gower made a few and Botham top-scored with 61. The tail then folded for 211 all out, leaving New Zealand 347 to win in almost two days. Coney's 68 was top score by some way; 219 all out for England to win by 127 runs. Curiously, after the plaudits he had received at Headingley, Howarth's captaincy was described as unimaginative; Howarth, for his part, was very critical of the pitch. The famous ridge that had caused England – but not Bill Lawry – so much trouble in 1961 seemed to have been resurrected by some subterranean activity, and according to Howarth the England bowlers were able to take more advantage of this than the New Zealanders as they were faster. One suspects that Hadlee was less than pleased at the intimation that Botham was a faster bowler than himself.

By and large the two teams for this series were more evenly matched than at any time in the past, but still England just had the edge – perhaps for the last time for who knows how long. In their home conditions they batted and bowled better in three of the four games, and won each one by a substantial runs margin as a result. England's innings in the fourth Test contained three fine knocks: Gower made 72 despite being hit on the head, and then, with the score looking ominous on 169 for 5, Randall and Botham came together. In just 135 minutes they put on 186, the kind of statistic that sounds as though it belongs to the 1930s, not a 1980s Test. Botham needed just 99 balls to reach his century, the second half of it coming from a mere 26, while Randall's 83, on his home ground, came from only 116 balls. It was superb entertainment, twenty-five boundaries and three sixes being struck between them, and during the course of it they both passed milestones – 3,500 Test runs to Botham and 2,000 to Randall. A total of 362 runs came on the first day, with England going on to 420 all out next morning. At tea New Zealand were 84 for 2; at the close they were 135 for 7, Edgar's 62 way ahead of the rest. Martin Crowe had injured a finger while fielding but was able to bat on the third day, yet still the final total was just 207, Cook taking five wickets for the second time in two matches.

England's hero demonstrates how to hit a six off Lance Cairns: Ian Botham pivots round on his right foot to hook the ball high into the stand, backward of square; at the end of the pivot his left foot has moved 18 inches past the leg stump and the arms are fully extended behind him to show the power in the stroke.

This was the last Test in England to include Sunday play, an experiment that was tried for a few years in the early 1980s but was not as popular or profitable as had been hoped. As it meant that there was no rest day for the players, Willis chose not to enforce the follow-on; a big New Zealand score against tired bowlers might just have caused England problems in the fourth innings. So Allan Lamb went out and scored a fine century, finishing undefeated on 137, and although Gower's 33 was the next highest score the total of 297 meant that New Zealand needed 510, with over eleven hours to get them. The last English wicket to fall was that of Cowans, and it was a historic one; for it was Richard Hadlee's 200th in Tests, the first New Zealander – by a mile – to reach the landmark; happily he did it at Trent Bridge, his English home. He hadn't finished yet, either; after Edgar had made 76 and Coney 68 he smote a handsome 92 not out off 119 balls, going in at number eight and putting on 55 for the last wicket with Bracewell. Although England won by 165 runs the total of 345 was more than respectable.

Willis and Howarth, old friends from their days at Surrey together in the early 1970s, had combined to make it a very friendly and well-fought series which produced some fine personal performances. Apart from the century-makers for England, Nick Cook had made a splendid beginning, bowling long spells to take 17 wickets from his two games and Willis had been both inspired and inspiring with his 20 wickets at under 14. But the man of the series was rightly adjudged to be Hadlee; 301 runs at 50 and 21 wickets at 26, a New Zealand record for a rubber against England. Who else could anyone have chosen?

*

The following January the carousel creaked into action again. On the way to New Zealand England stopped off for two one-day games in Fiji against the President's XI and although the first one provided a big victory the second was won by just 18 runs. It wasn't a promising start to a tour that was to prove distinctly fraught with problems.

In view of the greater parity between the teams that had been obvious the previous summer, there must have been many English fans who wondered what might befall their heroes away from home. On the previous visit the first defeat had occurred; now the first defeat in England. Was there some inexorable progression at work? Could we really be about to see the first series defeat? And then might that mean that the next visit to England would see New Zealand's first series victory there? It hardly bore thinking about.

Half-way through the first Test at Wellington all of these English worries had been dispelled; it was clear that the status quo still held. Willis had passed Trueman's England record of 307 wickets, Botham had taken 5 for 59, New Zealand had been tumbled out for 219 after Howarth, having won his ninth Test toss, had chosen to bat for the first time. Admittedly when England fell to 115 for 5 things hadn't looked so good, but Botham and Randall had produced the goods once more and put on 232 for the sixth wicket, with 138 to Botham – caught by Jeff Crowe at short cover off an almighty steepler – and 164 to Randall. Cairns, after taking the first five wickets for 36, dropped Botham before he had scored (he was also dropped on 19 and 75) but when England were all out for 463 with a lead of 244 English hearts could rest assured that God was in his heaven and all was right with the world. Botham's century meant that he had now scored a hundred and taken five wickets in an innings in the same Test for the *fifth* time; only two other players, Sobers and Mushtaq, had ever done it twice. He had, however, pulled a hamstring and had a swollen tendon behind one knee which would obviously hinder his bowling. And by the fourth morning it was clear that the pitch, far from wearing as one might expect, was turning into an excellent batting track.

New Zealand began their second innings soundly but the fourth wicket still went down at 165, at which point Martin Crowe was joined by Coney, neither of them with a Test century yet to their name. The previous summer Crowe had come to England rich in promise but had been a little disappointing in the Tests; now the promise came to fruition. He played beautifully for exactly 100, the third-youngest New Zealander to achieve the feat, taking the score to 279 before he gave Gatting his first Test wicket. Now it was up to Coney, on his home ground, to ensure that England didn't break through; Hadlee, Snedden and Smith supported him for a while, but when the eighth wicket went down at 402 there was still good time for England to get the runs. Instead, Cairns produced his highest Test score, 64, putting on 118 for the ninth wicket with Coney for a New Zealand record in all Tests. When Chatfield was the last out New Zealand had scored 537, with Coney magnificently undefeated on 174 after batting for nearly eight hours to save the game; it was his highest first-class score, his first century for seven years and the highest score for New Zealand against England in New Zealand. The photograph of him with arms aloft in joy as he reached his hundred was a singularly happy one. With two hours left the England openers meandered through 69 runs without loss, no doubt relieved not to cause their team any further embarrassment.

This was Martin Crowe's eighth Test, and surely no one can have doubted that that first Test hundred would prove to be one among many. Tall and strong, he is a handsome batsman with something of the classical correctness of Greg Chappell, and by the age of 25 he had in fact made more Test centuries, eight, than any other New Zealander, a record he is extending all the while. He had made his début for Auckland soon after he reached 17 and began his Test career aged 19; uncertainly at first against Australia and rather disappointingly in England in 1983, although he topped both batting and bowling averages for the full tour. He had gained experience of English conditions with the Lord's ground staff in 1981 and played for Bradford in the Yorkshire League the following year; and in 1984 he was to be signed by Somerset for one season as a replacement for Richards and Garner who were touring, soon coming good after a difficult start. When at the end of the 1986 season the county decided, for various reasons, to dismiss the West Indians and take him on as their overseas player he found himself at the centre of a furore, and sensibly maintained silence while the battle raged. He responded well to the pressure this placed

A series is won. Martin Crowe makes the winning stroke at Trent Bridge in 1986.

on him, although in the event injury and illness curtailed his time with them. His back injury also cut short his bowling activities, although his medium-pacers had rarely been penetrative enough for him to be considered a fully-fledged all-rounder. In 1986–7 he annihilated the New Zealand domestic batting record, scoring 1,676 runs in the season at an average of 93, no fewer than 432 more than the old record; his eight centuries also beat the old record for a season by two. By the end of the series against Pakistan in 1989 he had played forty-four Tests and had 3,035 runs at 45 to his name, with ten centuries.

After the next Test England were ready to drown in a veritable sea of embarrassment. Before the match there were doubts expressed about the Christchurch pitch by just about everyone except the Canterbury officials, and it soon became clear that they were fully justified. For only the third time ever England went into a Test without a spinner; New Zealand, on the other hand, brought back Boock for the first time in three years. With Dilley and Foster injured the Sussex fast bowler Tony Pigott was summoned from

Wellington for his Test début, causing him to postpone his wedding which had been due to take place the following Monday, the fourth day of the Test. Only in retrospect could it be seen that fate was being dangerously tempted.

Pigott took a wicket with his seventh ball and at lunch New Zealand were 87 for 4. England then decided to bowl poorly, Botham in particular having an appalling day with long hop after long hop after half volley – and Willis left him on, as he did Pigott, who had bowled well at first but was now struggling – while Cowans, who earlier had bowled excellently and taken wickets, watched from the deep. Jeff Crowe and Coney both made forties, and then Hadlee took full advantage of what was being offered to him by smashing 99 off 81 deliveries. It was the sort of innings Botham might have played on one of his good days – as indeed he had in the previous two Tests – and it not only made the England bowlers look like mugs but made the batsmen's later complaints look rather feeble. With Smith chipping in an unbeaten 32, New Zealand's innings closed at 307, and there was just enough time before stumps for England to lose a wicket. Next day rain delayed the start until there was only an hour and a half left; but by the close England had lost seven wickets for just 53 runs as the ball did unexpected things on the cracked and sweating pitch. Simply by bowling a good line and length Hadlee and his chums let the pitch and some admirable slip catching do the work, in marked contrast to the spray-gun approach of the Englishmen. When the last three wickets went down on the third morning England were all out for 82, and found themselves following on for the first time ever in fifty-nine Tests against New Zealand.

That was forty minutes before lunch, and they succeeded in reaching the interval intact; but by 4.30 it was all over, the highest partnership being 39 for the seventh wicket between Randall and Taylor. Hadlee took 5 for 28 (for eight wickets in the match) as for the first time since 1894–5 England, all out for 93, were dismissed twice for under 100. The margin of victory was an innings and 132, New Zealand's biggest Test win, and of course it was their first innings victory over England. The actual playing time was twelve hours and one minute, leaving Pigott free to get married next day after all – except that by then the arrangements had all been changed. One could only speculate at the sadness with which Sir Jack Hobbs, one of the best of all bad-wicket batsmen, must have viewed the proceedings from on high.

There are few things the English tabloid Press enjoy more than a national sporting mess over which to become strident, although before too long we were to discover just what one of these few things was. The England team were duly ridiculed as everyone stated the obvious fact that the pitch was the same for both sides; those who tried to assess what had happened pointed out that, while part of the blame clearly lay with the England batsmen for being more frightened of the pitch than the home batsmen, the main difference between the teams lay in the bowling and the catching. Hadlee and Co. had bowled accurate line and length while Botham and Co. had done anything but, and it won them the match. It was a great pity that New Zealand's first series win should come as a result of a poor pitch, but there was no doubt at all that by adapting to that pitch vastly better than England they fully deserved their victory.

The third Test was very much an anti-climax on a hard, flat Auckland pitch that was clearly going to see a lot of runs scored. When Willis called wrongly the series was decided, especially as, to the delight of the locals, he failed to appreciate that England's best hope of the win they needed was to play two spinners; New Zealand batsmen are only too accustomed to playing medium-fast bowlers on lifeless pitches. And so it proved; Wright scored 130, Jeff Crowe's 128 was his first Test century and wicket-keeper Smith finished on 113 not out for his first Test hundred, only the second time New Zealand had had three centurions in the same Test. When Howarth declared at 496 for 9 England had only pride to play for, especially as rain and bad light had eaten drastically into the time and it was now near the end of the third day. Fowler went immediately, but Chris Smith ground out 91 runs in 459 tedious minutes, Lamb made 49, and then Randall and Botham did their stuff again. This time it was a century for Randall and 70 for Botham as they did at least give the crowd something to watch. When they were all out for 439 there was just time for New Zealand to make 16 without loss before the meaningless exercise was brought to a merciful end. New Zealand thus became the first holders of the W.J. Jordan Trophy, although the number of fans in either country who know or care about that fact must be very small.

Finally, after fifty-four years and at the twenty-first attempt, New Zealand had beaten England in a Test series. For one old man the celebrations must have been particularly poignant; now aged 81, Curly Page was the only member of New Zealand's first Test team still alive, and before he died in 1987 he was also to see the first series win in England. One wonders just how much sadness was mingled with his pleasure.

Not content with losing a series in New Zealand for the first time, England went on to Pakistan and lost a series there for the first time, also 1–0. While this was going on the tabloids decided that it was their duty to reveal the riotous living which some of the England players had been enjoying in New

Zealand, including using 'pot' and cocaine. There were allegations that some of the players had become indifferent to defeat, being more concerned with the financial rewards than the honour of playing for their country. Now it's not hard to believe that there was some truth underlying all this, but it's even easier to believe that the gutter press whooped it up into a good circulation-boosting story. Inevitably Botham was the chief target, but virtually everyone was under suspicion; it meant not only that Willis's captaincy ended in great sadness for him but that the Test career of the admirable and irreproachable Bob Taylor ended unhappily. Willis had in fact to return home through illness after the first Test against Pakistan, with David Gower taking over the captaincy and salvaging some honour out of the other two matches; but it was one of the saddest tours England have ever made.

*

Early in September 1985 David Gower stood on the balcony at the Oval and raised aloft the Ashes urn, triumphantly rounding off a splendid series for himself and his team. Just over nine months later, after a crushing defeat in the West Indies and another at home to India in the first Test of 1986, he was relieved of the captaincy in the clumsiest episode of Peter May's tenure as Chairman of Selectors. Mike Gatting took over, and as England were again roundly beaten in his first Test in charge he was able to read of it in the following year's *Wisden* that the indisputable success for England had been Hammonds Sauce Works Band, playing in front of the Football Stand. England did salvage a draw out of the third Test, but when the series against New Zealand began near the end of July 1986 it is fair to say that England's standing had never in their history been lower. There had been bad periods before, of course, but then they had had the excuse that the teams beating them were much stronger, such as the Australians after the two wars; now they were losing abjectly to an Indian side which many earlier English teams would have had for breakfast. What, then, might a strong and highly confident New Zealand team do to them? In the last few months they had, after all, beaten Australia 2–1 away and 1–0 at home. It was clear that the days when England and Australia could expect to see off the 'lesser' Test countries without breaking into a sweat were firmly consigned to the history books.

New Zealand's captain in those two series against Australia was Jeremy Coney. He had made his début against Australia in 1973–4, and then, in the return series shortly afterwards, played an important role in supporting Glenn Turner as New Zealand pushed for their first victory over Australia,

Jeremy Coney took over from Geoff Howarth and carried on his winning ways.

remaining calm under great pressure as the Australians tried their hardest to break through. Yet he lost his place and did not regain it till early in 1979, after which there were numerous other occasions when his relish for a good backs-to-the-wall fight rescued his team. He was one of those players who tend to perform better on the wider Test stage than at provincial level, mainly through the sheer force of his personality, and he finished with 2,668 runs at 37 from his fifty-two Tests. As a bowler he was one of the gentlest of medium-pacers, a donkey-dropper who must have had countless spectators feeling that they could hoick him over the ropes without too much trouble; but he could be very deceptive, and although a Test haul of 27 wickets at 35 each doesn't sound very much he had some fine scalps to his name and ended plenty of good partnerships.

For such a determined battler the attractive thing about Coney was that however desperate the situation a smile was never far from the surface. He certainly needed a sense of humour during his first tour in charge. He had taken over from Howarth for the series in Pakistan in 1984–5 and, almost inevitably it seems, had problems with the umpires; when Shakoor Rana refused to give Miandad out caught behind as New Zealand were pressing for victory (does that sound familiar?) Coney had threatened to take his team from the field. After this débâcle Howarth, who had been unavailable for the Pakistan trip, resumed the captaincy briefly before it reverted to Coney and he produced the two fine series wins over Australia. By the time the coming rubber was finished Glenn Turner was able to say that Coney had 'grown into the position of captain'.

Mike Gatting had also been in – and out of – the team for years before he scored his first Test century. From the time that barrier was breached his batting blossomed, taking his average from the low twenties to the high thirties. A very forceful, pugnacious batsman, one of the best in the world against spin, he had scored prolifically for Middlesex for years, and it was clear that ultimately he had to come good in Tests; this he did in India in 1984–5, following it up with a fine Ashes series in 1985. He had succeeded Brearley as Middlesex captain in 1983 and maintained their high ranking, winning his first Championship as captain in 1985 – a particularly good performance as they were much depleted by Test calls that year. A straightforward, no-nonsense, not-especially-subtle character who knew just what he was about, he could usually be relied on to press on and get it – at times remarkably subtly.

Unfortunately, as a Test captain, with one notable exception he didn't succeed. The exception was in Australia in 1986–7, when England beat an even weaker home team 2–1 (and should really have beaten them 4–0);

A characteristically pugnacious hook from Mike Gatting.

since they also won the two one-day competitions that were on offer this was the most successful tour England had ever undertaken, and Gatting was extravagantly rewarded for his leadership of it with an OBE. Yet those two Test wins were his only successes in twenty-two matches in charge, with five defeats and fifteen draws; in all four series were lost. On the other hand this period saw England make a strong claim to being the best one-day side in the world, despite losing to Australia in the 1987 World Cup Final; overall their record in these games was excellent, and Gatting must take much of the credit for this. He had led Middlesex to various one-day successes, and that type of cricket clearly suits him; but since, happily, we have not yet quite reached the stage where one-day games replace Tests as the final cricketing challenge his leadership of the England team must ultimately be judged adversely. The appalling argument with Shakoor Rana during the 1987 tour, whatever the provocations and whatever the rights and wrongs of it, was deplorable, and one can't imagine a single one of his predecessors allowing himself to become involved in such a manner.

When, the following summer, he apparently – if the ever-vigilant tabloids were to be believed – had some fun and games with a barmaid in his hotel room during the first Test, he had to go; had the Shakoor Rana episode never happened he would probably have kept his job, but it seemed that his indiscretions were just the excuse the selectors were looking for to get rid of him. One could argue endlessly as to whether they were right, morally and in cricketing terms, to do so; yet the fact remains that he's a fine batsman and a good, sometimes inspired and inspirational captain, but not one who was able to achieve very much in Test matches with a rather nondescript group of players.

One handicap under which Gatting had to labour for his first four Tests in charge was that Ian Botham had been banned for admitting taking soft drugs. This was deemed to be bringing the game into disrepute; why other players who had broken the law – drink-drivers, for instance – were not similarly banned was never explained, but then cricket's administrators have never been noted for their logic or their justice. When Botham returned for the last Test of the three he made his customary impact; but in his absence the England line-up looked distinctly ordinary and New Zealand perhaps had the edge. Had the weather not spoilt the fourth day, the first Test at Lord's could have been a very good one.

England batted first and, as ever, found Hadlee difficult to handle. *Wisden* wrote that 'it was soon evident that two different games were taking place – one when Hadlee was bowling and the other when he was out of the attack'. He finished with 6 for 80 as England reached 307, with

Moxon and Gower the top scorers, but he also accounted for his Nottinghamshire team-mate French when a bouncer on the second morning hit the keeper on the back of the helmet and left him in need of three stitches in his head. This was near the end of the innings, and it was clear that French would not be able to take the field. Gatting therefore asked Coney whether England could play Bob Taylor, at the ground because of his public relations job with Cornhill Insurance, and the New Zealand captain generously agreed. Some kit was hastily borrowed – remarkably, Taylor had his own gloves in his car – and after Athey had kept for the first two overs of the innings Taylor returned to the Test arena, two years after retiring from the first-class game. He kept almost until lunch on the following day, when Bobby Parks of Hampshire took over, his father and grandfather before him both having played for England. It goes without saying that Taylor, now just turned 45, kept immaculately, although he made no dismissals, and the crowd must have felt privileged to be enjoying an unexpected sight of one of the greatest of wicket-keepers in action.

New Zealand's reply centred on a very slow 83 from Edgar and a fine hundred from Martin Crowe, their 210 being a new second-wicket record against England. Coney also contributed a half-century, and their total exceeded England's by 35. The end came after one ball on the fourth morning, and as French had been fit enough to take his place it meant that England had used four wicket-keepers in the innings. The rest of the match belonged mainly to Graham Gooch. With only 47 overs possible that day England were 110 for 3 at the close, and on the last day Gooch went on to 183, averting any England collapse and enabling Gatting to make a token declaration at 295 for 6. The unfortunate Wright made his first Test 'pair' but there was not time for any disaster and the finish came at 41 for 2. It had been a well-fought game, and after the trauma of losing twice at home to India it came as something of a relief to England.

If Richard Hadlee had one ambition other than to take four or five hundred Test wickets it was to win a series in England by beating them at Trent Bridge, his second home. With the second match taking place there, punters would have been lucky to get decent odds against his taking ten wickets and scoring a half-century. In the event there were a couple of points at which England seemed to be on top, but they were to let the game run away from them. The first of these was when, after being put in, they were 126 for 2, with Athey and Gower in command; but from there they declined to 256 all out. They then had New Zealand at 144 for 5 soon after tea on the second day, only for Hadlee to join a very patient Gray and score 68, the stand being worth 95. Bracewell and Gray then put on a further 79

Bruce Edgar in action during his innings of 83 at Lord's in 1986.
Phil Edmonds is at short leg.

for the seventh wicket, Gray's contribution to all this being 50. Stirling made 26 as Bracewell approached his maiden Test century, but when Watson, the last man, joined him he was still four short. The customary agonising capers ensued, but he got there well enough, and when he was out for 110 New Zealand's total was 413. Given that the pitch and the cloud covering favoured the bowlers pretty well throughout the match, the

Graham Gooch – 183
at Lord's in 1986.

Evan Gray, left-arm
spinner who toured
England in 1983 and
1986.

Bruce French watches John Bracewell frustrate England with his maiden Test century to set up the victory at Trent Bridge in 1986.

Bracewell has also been a useful performer with the ball over the years.

England attack simply didn't perform very well – the notable exception being débutant Gladstone Small.

One curiosity about the match was that the highest score for each side came from the number eights. England suffered from dubious decisions being given against Gooch and Athey early in their second innings but Hadlee and his friends exploited the conditions excellently and only Emburey, with his highly idiosyncratic but in this case very effective approach to batting, made any sort of a game of it. He scored 75, with Gower's 26 the next highest score, and although much of the fourth day was lost to the weather New Zealand still had plenty of time to polish off the 74 they needed to win, and they lost just two wickets in getting there. Hadlee, of course, finished with 10 for 140 to add to his 68, and there were plenty of jokes about Bracewell, a former grave-digger, having resorted to

John Emburey looks unimpressed at this appeal from Coney and Smith off the bowling of Evan Gray. Rightly so, as he was not given out – but the end was still near for England (Trent Bridge 1986).

his old occupation. Since this was England's eighth defeat in ten Tests, perhaps it was about time some newspaper published another obituary of English cricket. The previous one 104 years ago apparently needed renewing.

It was a notable match for one other player. When Ian Smith, usually known to his friends by his third Christian name of Stockley, caught Athey in the second innings he overtook Ken Wadsworth's New Zealand record of 96 dismissals; and the following February, at home to West Indies, he became the first New Zealand wicket-keeper to claim 100 victims, doing it in style by catching the mighty Viv Richards. Comparison with Wadsworth is invidious, but their records are very similar – Wadsworth's 96 dismissals came from thirty-three games and Smith's 100th dismissal came in his thirty-fourth game – and their style and approach to the game also have much in common. Agile, combative and determined, Smith had made himself into one of the best keepers in the world, and can only narrowly have failed to make the Rest of the World team in the MCC Bicentenary match of 1987. He has also worked very hard to improve his batting over the years, reaching the stage where he is now a very reliable lower-middle order batsman who clocked up his 1,000th Test run against England in 1987–8 to join the élite band of those who have performed the wicket-keeper's double and after the Pakistan series in 1989 had 1,365 at 25 to his name. He had made his début in 1980 in Australia and alternated with Warren Lees for a while before finally making the position his own at home to England in 1983–4. Since then he has been a fixture in the team, with his record standing at 134 dismissals from forty-eight Tests.

Meanwhile, England's attempt at reincarnation was thwarted by John Wright and Hurricane Charley. Gatting put New Zealand in and Botham, back in the team, took Edgar's wicket with his first ball, caught after a spot of juggling by Gooch at slip. Since the last Test of the West Indies tour Botham had been stuck on 354 Test wickets, one behind Lillee's record; having equalled it first ball he almost beat it second ball, but Emburey couldn't quite take the catch. Sole possession of the record was not long delayed, though; the last ball of his second over trapped Jeff Crowe – who had been Willis's 300th victim – lbw and the celebrations began. After his enforced absence the English fans had expected fireworks from Botham, but perhaps not quite such spectacular ones; many people must have been left wondering, with Graham Gooch, 'Who writes your script?'

Needing only a draw to secure their first series win in England, Wright duly dug in and gave his team an invaluable century, occupying the crease for over seven hours for 119. Coney, Gray and Blain helped out by getting into the thirties, but there was little other support and New Zealand were all out for 287. Hurricane Charley, however, was doing nasty things to the weather, and it was the third day before the innings closed. England obviously needed to go for it and duly did so, with Gower and Gatting in fine form against a good bowling attack. Both scored centuries, Gower especially at his most elegant and beautiful best, as they put on 223 for a new fourth wicket record against New Zealand in England; and then Botham came along and blasted 59 not out off 36 balls, 24 of them in one over from Stirling to equal the most runs off a six-ball over in Tests. When the weather intervened again and washed out the rest of the fourth day, Gatting had to declare; but 388 for 5 from 90.5 overs showed what could be done with a bit of application.

In all their reverses of late England could claim with some justification that the luck hadn't really been with them, and it certainly wasn't now. They undoubtedly had much the better of the Oval Test, but with almost

Willie Watson, just 20 at the time of the 1986 tour. Wisden described him as 'prone to an open-chested action'.

sixteen hours lost in all they were simply not able to press for victory; on the last day just one over was possible, from which Wright scored seven runs. And so New Zealand were able to celebrate, leaving England to wonder what the story might have been had Botham's drug-taking either never happened or never been discovered. Once it had become public then, in view of the hero-worship many youngsters must feel for him, he had to be punished; but it appeared that many people found it difficult to see how he had brought the game into disrepute. He had brought *himself* into disrepute, certainly, but there was a strong feeling amongst English fans that since his gargantuan deeds with bat and ball stemmed in part from his highly competitive and combative nature then his lapses from grace should be viewed with rather more tolerance than the authorities were prepared to offer him. Only the previous autumn he had put his fame to the best possible use and raised hundreds of thousands of pounds for leukaemia research with his well-publicised John o'Groats to Land's End walk, a project that was his own idea; if his drug-taking brought the game into disrepute, how much *repute* must this have brought the game? Had the English cricket authorities been rather less ready to allow the tabloid trumpetings to reverberate around Lord's and been more concerned with cricketing matters, English cricket might not have had such a sorry time of it in 1986.

*

There have been boring Test series before, of course, especially the one-sided ones. Yet rarely have two sides of roughly equal ability ground away to produce such tedium as New Zealand and England managed in February and March 1988. When it was over John Arlott was asked if he could recall a more uninspiring series, and he said that he couldn't.

Poor pitches, grim weather and doubtful umpiring were the main problems. Against such a backdrop even the best players would have been hard put to impress; as it was, England lacked Gower and Gooch, who declined to tour, and Botham, who was playing for Queensland, and when Hadlee limped out of the series after bowling just eighteen overs he took with him a disproportionate amount of the class that was on view. There were a few notable individual performances, but by and large it was a case of two anodyne teams serving up little other than lack-lustre cricket. The teams did have the very valid excuse of tiredness and staleness, for both had followed the World Cup in October and November with a three-Test series and England, after playing a few games in New Zealand, had also dashed over to Sydney for the Bicentennial game. 'When did the England regulars last have a break from cricket of more than a month?' was the quiz question going round the pubs back home.

New Zealand's series had been in Australia, where they had been well beaten in the first game, drawn the second and then come desperately close to a win in the third as the last two Australians held on for the final five overs to deny them. If Hadlee had captured that last wicket – and he already had ten in the match – it would have taken him past Botham as the leading Test wicket-taker. As it was, he had to wait the best part of a year to do so. England, meanwhile, having lost a World Cup final that they should probably have won, had run into a spot of bother in Pakistan, culminating in the unseemly spectacle of an England captain and a Test umpire calling each other names. When the dust had settled the record books showed that England had lost another series; morale, one suspected, had been higher.

In their warm-up games in New Zealand England, still under Mike Gatting, had won two, lost one and drawn one; they also beat a President's XI between the first two Tests. The batsmen, in fact, seemed to be in reasonable form – the draw was caused by the weather with England on top, and in the game that was lost England declared twice to try and force a win. Hope springs eternal in the cricketer's breast.

With the retirement of Coney New Zealand were now led by Jeff Crowe. His first match in charge had come in Sri Lanka a year before, when he had scored an extremely slow 120 to grind out a tedious draw, only for the other two Tests to be cancelled because of the civil unrest there. Four years older than his brother Martin, he made his Test début a year later, against Sri Lanka in 1983, and they first played in a Test together in the opening match of the 1983 series in England, the fifth pair of brothers to represent New Zealand. He had been playing for South Australia since 1977 and there had been some talk that he might find a place in the Australian Test team, but there was never much doubt that he would return home. Like others before him he suffers from comparison with his brother, a very unfair comparison since Martin is one of the most outstanding batsmen in world cricket. Jeff for his part can also be a very attractive player to watch on a good day, an attacking batsman with plenty of strokes; he has had a fair number of stodgy days over the years as well, but he is nothing if not a battler and by the end of the Pakistan series in 1989 had over 1,500 runs at 26 from his thirty-seven Tests. Poor form with the bat was to see him dropped for the third Test of the coming series, a move which so incensed Martin that his response was to go out and score a century in his brother's 'memory' – a reaction that the selectors may just have been hoping for when they dropped Jeff.

The Christchurch pitch had been relaid since England's last, distinctly memorable, visit in 1984. Now it proved merely awkward for batting, rather than deplorable; there was movement in it for the seamers, and twenty-six of the thirty-two wickets fell to catches, but it was slow enough to give the batsmen a chance. When Crowe put England in the main interest centred on who would become Hadlee's record-breaking victim on his home ground. He had said beforehand that he was quite relaxed about it, that he and everyone else knew it would come, even if it was the number eleven batsman in the second innings of the last Test. When he limped off at tea with an injured calf muscle, having bowled eighteen unrewarded overs for 50, it wasn't difficult to envisage the sardonic smile on the face of Dame Fortune, especially as the men who had denied him had been his former Nottinghamshire colleagues Broad and Robinson.

These two put on 168 for the second wicket, with Broad going on to a fine century, and England totalled 319 on first innings – not without luck, for Broad said after the first day that 'God was on our side today'. Dilley then reduced the home side to tatters at 40 for 4, before Jeff Crowe, Bracewell and Hadlee, batting with a runner and ruining any chance his calf muscles had had of recovering quickly, managed to drag the score to 168. But with time lost to the weather England had to score quickly to give themselves a chance, and wickets tumbled as a result – 152 all out. At the beginning of the final day New Zealand wanted 304 to win, but again the weather intervened (almost five hours were lost in all) and at 130 for 4 the match petered out. Not quietly, though; Dilley, no doubt inspired by the performance of his captain in Faisalabad, expressed his displeasure at not seeing the umpire's finger pointing upwards by bellowing more obscenities, not at the umpire, but at the world in general. Literally at the world, in fact, for the television microphones on the pitch captured the moment with unmistakable clarity. Since the television replays of the incidents that had provoked him did nothing to clarify whether the batsman was actually out the umpires were clearly vindicated and Dilley was fined £250 by the England management for his outburst. Coming so soon after the Gatting–Shakoor Rana nonsense and Broad breaking his stumps when he was out in the Bicentennial match, English cricket was widely considered to have plumbed depths of poor behaviour not encountered since Jardine told Larwood to bowl bodyline at Woodfull at Adelaide in 1932–3, when Woodfull had just been hit over the heart.

One result of Hadlee's injury was to place the major bowling onus on Ewen Chatfield and in the best tradition of the unsung hero he quietly and efficiently got on with the job, taking thirteen wickets at just 15 each in the three games. After making his début in 1975 and nearly losing his life in the process, he found himself in the Test team only irregularly; the problem was that although his medium-pace bowling was tight and accurate it was rarely penetrating. In this respect he was often compared to Mike Hendrick, a very fine bowler who never once took five wickets in an innings in thirty Tests. It took Chatfield eight years to achieve the feat, but when he did so at Headingley in 1983 to help New Zealand to their first win in England it was only his ninth Test. Since 1983, though, he has been much more of a fixture in the team and the accuracy with which he has nagged away at and frustrated many a batsman has been a great help to Hadlee in his thirst for taking wickets.

Chatfield hasn't exactly been an exciting bowler to watch, nor especially attractive – having size fourteen feet doesn't lend itself to gracefulness – but his 123 wickets at 32 each in forty-three Tests (as at the end of the series against Pakistan in 1989) have been an essential element in New Zealand's success in the 1980s. His contribution with the bat has been somewhat minimal, although he had one noble hour against Pakistan in 1985 when he and Coney put on 50 for the ninth wicket – effectively the tenth as Cairns had been badly concussed after being hit on the head and could hardly walk – to win the match and take the series 2–0. Chatfield made 21, his highest Test score, with, as *Wisden* recorded, 'his runs being almost outnumbered by his bruises'. More representative of his batting, though, is the fact that in India in 1988 he took his 559th first-class wicket – and scored his 559th first-class run in the same match. Chatfield is about as far from being a 'glamour' figure as it is possible for a Test cricketer to be; but New Zealand are going to find it very hard to replace the old stalwart when he eventually retires.

Had the weather not intervened England may well have won the first Test. No one ever looked remotely likely to win the next game. A lifeless Auckland pitch – how many times in the preceding pages has that adjective been used for the Auckland pitch? – produced a slow-motion kind of match that wasn't enhanced by a string of umpiring errors. As in the last Test of the previous series New Zealand, having been put in, were saved by a century from Wright, who should have been caught off the first ball of the match, with the next highest score in the thirties; but it was slow stuff in front of a small crowd, the overnight score being only 186 for 3. This subsided to 301 all out next day, whereupon Moxon managed the feat of scoring a century which went into the books as 99 – when he was on 32 three runs off the bat (the New Zealanders stated this clearly) were signalled as leg-byes, so that when he fell on 99 he should have been 102. He was supported by Robinson and Gatting, and at one point the score was 211 for 2 before the wickets slid away thanks in part to some dubious umpiring; Emburey cudgelled out another idiosyncratic knock of 45, though, hitting Martin Crowe on the jaw in the process, and England managed a small lead when they finished at 323. The only thing to be said for the umpiring was that it was at least unbiased, the doubtful decisions being roughly the same for each side.

Wright and Franklin then put on New Zealand's first century opening stand against England since Sutcliffe and Scott made one at the Oval in 1949, an astonishing gap. For Franklin his first Test half-century was a particular triumph since at the end of the 1986 tour of England he had had an accident with a luggage trolley at Gatwick Airport which had smashed his right shin, and he must have wondered whether his Test career was over; but he had scored heavily for Auckland over the preceding weeks and now he got his team off to a solid start here. Yet when even Martin Crowe was out to a dodgy decision it seemed that the innings might just fold; at the close of the fourth day New Zealand were just 132 ahead with five wickets left. There was, however, a gentleman named Mark Greatbatch making his début, a large left-handed chap who looked from very early on as though he intended to bat all day; which is what, supported by Snedden, Bracewell and Smith, he did. When stumps were drawn at 350 for 7 declared Greatbatch had become the fourth New Zealander to score a century on début, 107 not out in his case, and curiously all four of them have been left-handers. A total of 444 overs had been bowled in the match, and on average only 2.19 runs had been scored from each of them; when it was announced afterwards that the pitch was to be dug up Gatting said that he would come along and give a hand.

What Hurricane Charley had done to the third Test of the 1986 series Cyclone Bola did to the third Test of the 1987–88 series, washing out the last two days of a match that had never gripped anyone's attention. When it was abandoned only Martyn Moxon, stranded on 81 not out, had any regrets. Jeff Crowe, after his poor form with the bat, had been dropped from the captaincy and the side and John Wright duly took over. He had been Coney's vice-captain, but when he had not made the tour to Sri Lanka the previous year so that he could concentrate on his benefit with Derby-shire, for whom he had been playing since 1977, the captaincy had gone to Crowe. He had made his début in the historic match in 1978 when New Zealand beat England for the first time, and had been a regular in the team ever since, forming a very reliable opening partnership with Bruce Edgar; after Pakistan's visit to New Zealand in 1989, he had over 3,600 runs at 33 from his sixty-three Tests. The professional approach he had learned in

John Wright – a thoroughly reliable opener for many years.

English cricket had stood him and his country in very good stead over the years, perhaps most of all against the West Indies at Wellington in 1987 when in partnership with Martin Crowe he battled for over nine and a half hours for an innings of 138. It was a monumental effort that left him quite shattered, but he had the satisfaction of knowing that the game had been saved. An enormously popular man, he has been described by Don Mosey as 'the nicest guy in world cricket'.

With the series at stake Wright's first priority in Wellington was to avoid defeat. He himself had an extraordinary escape on 22 when, playing the ball down into the off stump, the bail lifted into the air and landed back in its groove. It wasn't too expensive a misfortune for England or the bowler, Capel, as he got him 14 runs later. England lost Dilley after just eleven overs with an injured knee, and thereafter it was hard and largely unrewarding toil for the England bowlers, not helped by poor catching and fielding. The English catching had been appalling both in Pakistan and New Zealand, probably worse than it had ever been in the past; tiredness, staleness, low morale all played their parts in this, and the number of catches dropped had cost an incalculable number of runs and possible morale-restoring victories. Martin Crowe was dropped early on and went on to 143, determined on a big haul in view of the dropping of his brother; he was supported first by Vance and then Greatbatch, and when the latter went the score was already a daunting 287 for 4. Rutherford joined Crowe and in his fourteenth Test at last confirmed his obvious potential – at the end of the 1986 tour he had scored 317 in 230 minutes against Brian Close's XI – by making his maiden Test century. The scoring had been very slow until his arrival but with Bracewell and Smith he pepped it up a bit, with the aid of more dropped catches. It was the third morning when Wright finally put England out of their misery and declared at 512 for 6, with Rutherford undefeated on 107. The New Zealand attack without Hadlee then proved no more barbed than England's, and Broad and Moxon put on 129 for the first wicket; by the close they were 183 for 2, with Moxon stuck tantalisingly near that first Test century. But with strong winds and rain play was never able to restart, and the most uninspiring of series drifted to the most appropriate of endings. English fans listening on the radio must have felt that the funereal conditions were particularly apposite to the current state of their Test cricket.

1983	Oval	E 209, 446–6d:	NZ 196, 270	E 189 runs
	Headingley	E 225, 252;	NZ 377, 103–5	NZ 5 wkts
	Lord's	E 326, 211;	NZ 191, 219	E 127 runs
	Trent Bridge	E 420, 297;	NZ 207, 345	E 165 runs
1983–4	Wellington	NZ 219, 537;	E 463, 69–0	Drawn
	Christchurch	NZ 307;	E 82, 93	NZ inns 132 runs
	Auckland	NZ 494–9d, 16–0;	E 439	Drawn
1986	Lord's	E 307, 295–6d;	NZ 342, 41–2	Drawn
	Trent Bridge	E 256, 230;	NZ 413, 77–2	NZ 8 wkts
	Oval	NZ 287, 7–0;	E 388–5d	Drawn
1987–8	Christchurch	E 319, 152;	NZ 168, 130–4	Drawn
	Auckland	NZ 301, 350–7d;	E 323	Drawn
	Wellington	NZ 512–6d;	E 183–2	Drawn

1983 Test series
England

Batting	Innings	NO	HS	Runs	Average
A.J. Lamb	8	2	137*	392	65.33
D.I. Gower	8	1	112*	404	57.71
C.J. Tavaré	8	0	109	330	41.25
D.W. Randall	6	1	83	194	38.80
I.T. Botham	8	0	103	282	35.25

Bowling	Overs	M	Runs	W	Average
R.G.D. Willis	123.3	38	273	20	13.65
C.L. Smith	12	2	31	2	15.50
N.G.B. Cook	135.2	56	275	17	16.17
I.T. Botham	112.5	27	340	10	34.00
N.G. Cowans	125	25	447	12	37.25

New Zealand

Batting	Innings	NO	HS	Runs	Average
R.J. Hadlee	8	2	92*	301	50.16
B.A. Edgar	8	0	84	336	42.00
J.G. Wright	6	0	93	230	38.33
J.V. Coney	8	1	68	238	34.00
G.P. Howarth	8	0	67	189	23.62

Bowling	Overs	M	Runs	W	Average
J.V. Coney	63	26	115	5	23.00
R.J. Hadlee	232	65	559	21	26.61
B.L. Cairns	184	52	461	16	28.81
J.G. Bracewell	123	28	364	10	36.40
E.J. Chatfield	153	37	440	11	40.00

Wicket-keepers: R.W. Taylor (E) 11 dismissals   W.K. Lees (NZ) 4 dismissals
I.D.S. Smith (NZ) 10 dismissals

In the first match G. Fowler and C.J. Tavaré put on 223 for the first wicket, the record for England v New Zealand Tests. In the second match New Zealand recorded their first win in England at the 29th attempt, B.L. Cairns becoming the first New Zealand bowler to take seven wickets in an innings against England. R.G.D. Willis became the fourth bowler to take 300 Test wickets. In the third match R.W. Taylor took his 150th Test catch, I.T. Botham became the first bowler to take 50 wickets in England v New Zealand Tests and A.J. Lamb equalled two England records by holding four catches in an innings and six in a match. In the fourth match R.J. Hadlee became the first New Zealand bowler to take 200 Test wickets, and his 21 wickets was a record for a series against England.

1983–4 Test series
England

Batting	Innings	NO	HS	Runs	Average
C.L. Smith	3	1	91	148	74.00
D.W. Randall	4	0	164	293	73.25
I.T. Botham	4	0	138	226	56.50
A.J. Lamb	4	0	49	82	20.50
M.W. Gatting	3	1	19*	38	19.00

Bowling	Overs	M	Runs	W	Average
R.G.D. Willis	115.1	28	306	12	25.50
N.G. Cowans	52	14	154	5	30.80
A.C.S. Pigott	17	7	75	2	37.50
V.J. Marks	40.2	9	115	3	38.33
N.G.B. Cook	89.3	37	196	4	49.00

New Zealand

Batting	Innings	NO	HS	Runs	Average
I.D.S. Smith	4	2	113*	198	99.00
J.V. Coney	4	1	174*	251	83.66
J.J. Crowe	4	0	128	230	57.50
J.G. Wright	5	1	130	218	54.50
M.D. Crowe	4	0	100	148	37.00

Bowling	Overs	M	Runs	W	Average
R.J. Hadlee	109.5	33	232	12	19.33
S.L. Boock	80.3	34	140	7	20.00
B.L. Cairns	113	37	251	12	20.91
E.J. Chatfield	98.2	33	188	6	31.33

Wicket-keepers: I.D.S. Smith (NZ) 8 dismissals   R.W. Taylor (E) 9 dismissals

In the first match R.G.D. Willis passed F.S. Trueman's England record of 307 Test wickets; I.T. Botham scored a century and took five wickets in an innings in the same Test for the fifth time; B.L. Cairns took 7 for 143 to record the best innings figures for New Zealand in a home Test against England and also took his 100th Test wicket; with J.V. Coney he put on 118 for the ninth wicket to set the New Zealand record against England; New Zealand's 537 is their highest score in a home Test. In the second match New Zealand were able to enforce the follow-on for the first time against England and to record their first victory over England by an innings; for the first time this century England failed to reach 100 in either

1986 Test series
 England

Batting	Innings	NO	HS	Runs	Average
D.I. Gower	5	0	131	293	58.60
G.A. Gooch	5	0	183	268	53.60
J.E. Emburey	3	1	75	92	46.00
M.W. Gatting	5	0	121	170	34.00
B.N. French	3	2	21	33	33.00

Bowling	Overs	M	Runs	W	Average
G.R. Dilley	69.3	16	179	9	19.88
P.H. Edmonds	101	32	212	8	26.50
I.T. Botham	26	4	82	3	27.33
G.C. Small	64	20	134	4	33.50
J.E. Emburey	79.5	33	141	3	35.25

New Zealand

Batting	Innings	NO	HS	Runs	Average
M.D. Crowe	5	2	106	206	68.66
J.G. Bracewell	3	1	110	114	57.00
J.V. Coney	4	1	51	133	44.33
D.A. Stirling	2	1	26	44	44.00
J.G. Wright	6	1	119	191	38.20

Bowling	Overs	M	Runs	W	Average
R.J. Hadlee	153.5	42	390	19	20.52
E.J. Chatfield	21	7	73	3	24.33
J.G. Bracewell	75.4	22	213	6	35.50
W. Watson	72.5	18	196	4	49.00
E.J. Gray	117	40	271	5	54.20

Wicket-keepers: B.N. French (E) 3 dismissals   I.D.S. Smith (NZ) 7 dismissals

In the first match B.A. Edgar and M.D. Crowe put on 210 for a new second-wicket record for New Zealand against England. In the second match D.I. Gower passed 6,000 Test runs and I.D.S. Smith passed K.J. Wadsworth's New Zealand record of 96 dismissals. In the third match I.T. Botham became the leading Test wicket-taker when he passed D.K. Lillee's figure of 355; he also hit 24 runs in one over, to equal the record for most runs from the bat in a six-ball over in Test matches. D.I. Gower and M.W. Gatting put on 223 for a new England fourth-wicket record against New Zealand. New Zealand recorded their first series win in England.

1987–8 Test series
 England

Batting	Innings	NO	HS	Runs	Average
M.D. Moxon	4	1	99	208	69.33
B.C. Broad	4	0	114	204	51.00
J.E. Emburey	3	0	45	106	35.33
M.W. Gatting	4	1	42	106	35.33
R.T. Robinson	4	0	70	126	31.50

Bowling	Overs	M	Runs	W	Average
G.R. Dilley	104.5	34	210	15	14.00
P.W. Jarvis	98	31	201	6	33.50
P.A.J. DeFreitas	91.1	33	175	4	43.75
D.J. Capel	109.2	22	274	5	54.80
J.E. Emburey	133.5	48	236	3	78.67

New Zealand

Batting	Innings	NO	HS	Runs	Average
M.J. Greatbatch	3	1	107*	186	93.00
K.R. Rutherford	3	1	107*	138	69.00
A.H. Jones	2	1	54*	62	62.00
I.D.S. Smith	4	2	33*	92	46.00
J.G. Wright	5	0	103	221	44.20

Bowling	Overs	M	Runs	W	Average
E.J. Chatfield	126.1	51	198	13	15.23
D.K. Morrison	80.2	14	269	8	33.63
M.C. Snedden	90	31	202	6	33.67
J.G. Bracewell	68	18	148	3	49.33

Wicket-keepers: I.D.S. Smith (NZ) 10 dismissals   B.N. French (E) 11 dismissals

In the second match M.J. Greatbatch became the fourth New Zealander to score a century on début and I.D.S. Smith completed the wicket-keeper's double of 1,000 runs and 100 dismissals. In the third match M.D. Crowe and M.J. Greatbatch put on 155 for the fourth wicket, beating by one run the previous New Zealand record for that wicket against England, and K.R. Rutherford and J.G. Bracewell put on 134 for a record sixth-wicket New Zealand partnership against England.

—— **10** ——

One-day Wonders

I THE APPETITE WHETTED

In retrospect, the remarkable thing about one-day internationals is that it was nearly eight years after the introduction of professional one-day cricket to England that the first match was played. In view of the voracious appetite which fans seem to have for them and which, again in retrospect, ought to have been predictable, it seems odd that the first official one-day international didn't take place until 5 January 1971 and then only as a compensation for the fact that a Test match had been abandoned without a ball bowled. Having said that, though, it is also somehow pleasing to think that, like Test cricket ninety-four years earlier, the first one-day international took place between Australia and England, at Melbourne, and was more or less unpremeditated; so unimportant was it deemed to be that *Wisden* gave it very scant attention the following year. Now that they have proliferated to absurd proportions, that thought almost takes one back to some lost age of innocence. For the record, the Australians, much less experienced in such gladiatorial combat, won convincingly by five wickets – and the attendance of 46,000 was 4,000 more than the *total* attendance over five days at the first Test in Brisbane.

The following year (1972) saw the introduction of the Prudential Trophy, for which England played two or three 55-over games against each touring team. The first one was a great success, England just beating Australia in a closely-fought decider, and from then on it was an essential element of the English summer. The crowds came in their thousands and lapped up the instant entertainment, while the purists shook their heads and said that it must never threaten proper cricket.

New Zealand played their first one-day international against Pakistan in February 1973, and won by 22 runs. The second one took place at the end of their tour of England the following July, after the Test series had been lost 2–0; it was historic in that, played at St Helen's, Swansea, this was the first time an England team had ever appeared in Wales. Thanks to Snow and Arnold the tourists began disastrously, with only 15 on the board when the

Ray Illingworth led England in their first one-day internationals.

fourth wicket went down, but Turner and Pollard made some amends. Pollard, who had averaged 100 in the Tests, top scored with 55 and Taylor and Richard Hadlee chipped in down the order, but a total of 158 seemed unlikely to cause England many problems. Much more experienced in the techniques of the new game, England, and Amiss in particular, made steady progress towards their target, helped by the fact that the New Zealanders hadn't yet come to terms with the notion that this type of cricket is mainly about containment. Amiss completely dominated the scoring, making exactly 100 out of 135 when he was out, and England cruised home by seven wickets with more than nine overs in hand.

The second game at Old Trafford went the way of many a day's cricket there. Congdon, apparently learning quickly, put England in, and by lunchtime they had scored 96 off 36 overs, with Taylor, in one spell, bowling seven overs for one wicket and six runs. During the interval there was a downpour and three hours twenty minutes were lost; remarkably (as it now seems) there had been no instructions given about what to do in such circumstances, and there was no provision for the game to go on to an extra day. So, after much conferring, a phone call had to be made to Lord's for guidance, clear proof that we were still in an age of innocence as far as this pastime was concerned. The ruling was that for a result to be achieved New Zealand would have to bat for at least 30 overs, and the side with the most runs per over would win. When play resumed England therefore threw the bat, taking the score to 167 for 8 off 48.3 overs – only for the rain to return in the best Manchester fashion. With that game abandoned the men of the series were declared to be Amiss and Pollard for their batting at Swansea, and they were duly rewarded to the extent of £125 each. Ray Illingworth was presented with the trophy, but he was destined to lose it to West Indies a few weeks later; those two games finished one apiece, but West Indies won it on their faster overall scoring rate.

Come the 1974–5 tour of Australia and the comedians back in England professed not to understand how their heroes could have so much trouble with a woman bowler, Lillian Thomson. After five Tests they were 4–0 down, and immediately before the face-saving final Test they played a one-day game against New Zealand at Melbourne, since New Zealand had just won the Australasian Gillette Cup and one of the 'rewards' for this achievement was to be allowed to play Mike Denness's shell-shocked band. Because Denness and Co. played as MCC rather than England it was not counted as an official one-day international, but it was very much a full-strength England side – if 'full-strength' is not too humorous, or cruel, a word to apply to any England team on that tour.

Denness won the toss and put New Zealand in, and then watched nearly all the batsmen contribute useful scores. Morrison top-scored with 49, Wadsworth made 44, there were two thirties, two twenties and so on; off forty eight-ball overs 262 runs were accumulated, with two wickets still in hand. The match ended as a spectacle when the first three MCC wickets all fell at 35, and a fourth followed just 12 runs later. Only Fletcher's 44 and Greig's 79 made a tolerable game of it as Hedley Howarth and Dayle Hadlee took three wickets each, but MCC were all out for 196, giving New Zealand a fine 66-run victory. England had their revenge three weeks later when they won the first Test in Auckland by an innings.

Both of the one-day games in the New Zealand leg of the tour were then ruined by the weather. England were led in the first one by John Edrich, but the notable thing about that game was that there were three Hadlee brothers on view, Barry joining Dayle and Richard for his international début; he was to play in only one other one-day game, also against England in the 1975 World Cup, and didn't make the Test team. The black clouds of Dunedin made life very difficult for batting and England, put in, struggled throughout; four wickets went down for 51, with only Wood able to make any impression. His 33 was in fact top score, and only Old and Taylor got into the twenties as 90 for 4 became 90 for 6 and thence to 136 all out. In reply Turner and Barry Hadlee had reached 15 when the clouds deposited their contents with gay abandon, and that was that.

Bevan Congdon had captained New Zealand in all the one-day games they had so far played, but at the end of this first game he announced that he would not be available to go to England for the World Cup the following June. Glenn Turner therefore took over the captaincy for the second game the following day at Wellington – where the weather was little better. Released from leadership responsibilities Congdon blossomed; in 138 minutes he hit a six and seven fours for a splendid 101, his only century in twelve one-day internationals. Hastings made 37 and Parker 25, but although he had little other support the innings reached 227 in less than three hours. England's truncated reply was altogether more stodgy while it lasted, only 35 runs being scored off ten eight-ball overs for the loss of one wicket before the rain again rendered it all meaningless. It made for a hat-trick of official one-day games fouled up by the weather.

Instant cricket was now so popular with the fans that a World Cup was the obvious next step. Prudential Assurance were happy to sponsor it and the six Test-playing countries plus Sri Lanka and East Africa presented themselves in England in June 1975 for what was a novel experience for most of them – an overseas tour of solely one-day games. It was clear that the time was right to initiate a regular World Cup competition and even if it had rained incessantly there was no way, given the public appetite for such sporting extravaganzas, in which it would be discontinued; as it happened the weather was glorious throughout and the tournament was an outstanding success. The eight teams were divided into two groups, with the top two teams going through to the semi-finals; England and New Zealand were drawn in the same group, along with India and East Africa.

In the opening matches – they were all of sixty overs – England beat India by 202 runs when they amassed 334 for 4 with a century from Amiss, while New Zealand beat East Africa by 181 runs when they ran up 309 for 5, with Glenn Turner making the then record one-day knock of 171 not out. Two such big scores set the stage for an interesting confrontation when England and New Zealand then played each other at Trent Bridge. When the game started the atmosphere was heavy and Turner accordingly put England in. Collinge removed both openers with 28 on the board, but then Fletcher, who had made a double-century against New Zealand in a Test only a few months before, settled in with the help of some loose bowling and blazing sunshine. He put on 83 with Hayes and 66 with Denness, both stands made at more than a run a minute. With Old he put on 66 in just seven overs, and was then run out off the last ball of the innings for an admirable 131. A target of 267 to win was clearly a tough proposition against bowlers very experienced in the art of containment; Geoff Arnold and Peter Lever bowled tightly and when Lever got Turner for just 12 it was a real uphill struggle. Morrison and Barry Hadlee got themselves further and further behind the clock – Hadlee's 19 took an unconscionable time and spelt the end of his international career – leaving the later batsmen with a virtually impossible task. Morrison's 55 was top score, but the others lost their wickets in trying to hit out, only Wadsworth, McKechnie and Dayle Hadlee reaching 20; *Men in White*, its tongue in its cheek, murmurs that 'run pursuit does not lend itself to wicket preservation'. Their total of 186 left England victorious by 80 runs, Greig's 4 for 45 being the best bowling figures. Fletcher's innings made the man of the match award a formality.

Both sides progressed to the semi-finals before losing interest in the competition. New Zealand came up against West Indies, the eventual winners, and were simply outplayed by a better team, although they weren't helped by losing the toss. England's game against Australia was quite remarkable; on a very suspect Headingley pitch England, put in, were tumbled out for 94, with Gary Gilmour taking 6 for 14. When Australia batted they were then reduced to 39 for 6, and the atmosphere was electric. However, they were saved by Gilmour and Walters who saw them home

A mighty man was he – Lance Cairns tries to glare the batsman into submission.

without further loss – only to come up against a memorable and match-winning captain's century from Clive Lloyd in an exciting final. All in all, the inaugural World Cup could hardly have been more successful.

When England toured New Zealand in 1977–8 no one-day games were played. The return visit in the summer of 1978 saw the Prudential Trophy dusted off again, although by now it was played before the Test series rather than after, as it had been in the early years; it had been decided, quite rightly, that it served a better purpose as a starter to the main course than as a dessert.

The first game was played at Scarborough. England, put in, made a sound start as Gooch and Brearley put on 67 in eighty-five minutes; when Radley then joined Gooch they decided they liked the spin bowling of Boock, and walloped 111 in sixty-nine minutes. This took the score to 178 for 1 and a mountain of runs loomed; but it was to be a good day for Cairns, and he had both of them caught by Parker, with Gooch just six short of a century. Thereafter the wickets tumbled as Cairns and Hadlee went through them and the innings closed on 206 for 8, Cairns taking 5 for 28. Cairns, Hadlee and Congdon had all been very economical, but when England took the

Stephen Boock, purveyor of left-arm spin for New Zealand.

Clive Radley followed the slowest 150 in Test history with a rather more spritely unbeaten century in the one-day game at Old Trafford.

field Brearley learned from Boock's misfortune that it was not a spinner's wicket and gave Miller only one over. The medium-pacers were able to exercise much more control, and at first only Howarth could cope with them. With six wickets down for 97 he eventually found an ally in Congdon, only to fall himself for 42 after an interruption for bad light had perhaps affected his concentration. For Congdon and Cairns, though, the match was by no means over, and with the light dwindling they put on a fine 68 for the eighth wicket. This ended when Cairns was run out after a collision with Botham, but even had that not happened they would have been hard put to make the runs needed in the short time left. 187 for 8 gave them respectability, but still left England winners by 19 runs. Gooch also took 2 for 29 to seal the match award.

Bob Taylor seems to be praying for help as John Wright hits out at Old Trafford in 1978

Unfortunately, their respectability was rather more tenuous in the second match at Old Trafford. Brearley chose to bat first, only to see Gooch run out without the scoreboard having moved. Radley, however, was to make an unbeaten century; a solid start with Brearley was followed by a stand with Gower that realised 105 runs in seventy-five minutes and then a stand with Randall made 89 in fifty-three minutes. Botham then hammered a quick 34, with Hadlee and Cairns both coming in for stick – Hadlee's eleven overs gave him very uncharacteristic figures of 1 for 70 and Cairns went for a wicketless 84. The resulting 278 was a new record for the Prudential Trophy. Wright and Edgar got New Zealand off to a decent start with 44, and Edgar and Howarth then took this on to 80; but suddenly in the space of eighteen deliveries the score went from 80 for 1 to 88 for 7. Happily for the spectators Cairns was in a bat-swinging mood, though, and the 60 he smote in double-quick time earned him two distinctions – the record for the fastest fifty in a Prudential game (thirty-nine minutes) and a pint of beer from Ian Botham for each of his four sixes. With Parker unable to bat because of injury the innings closed at 152 when Cairns holed out to Edmonds, leaving England a hefty 126 runs to the good. Despite the pasting

Mike Brearley helps England to a substantial win at Old Trafford in 1978.

his bowling had received, Cairns's innings and his bowling at Scarborough earned him the award of New Zealand's man of the series, while Radley was the obvious man of the match and was also named as England's man of the series. Since England won the Test rubber 3–0 without too much apparent effort, it was a distinctly one-sided summer.

A year later the teams were doing battle in the semi-final of the Prudential

World Cup, and Old Trafford saw a splendid game. England had topped their group against Pakistan, Australia and Canada, and New Zealand had been runners-up in theirs, against West Indies, Sri Lanka and India. This second competition was just as successful as the first, although there were a few days of rain which meant that the West Indies–Sri Lanka match couldn't be played, the points being shared. Sri Lanka's defeat of India was something of an upset, while Australia's failure to reach the semi-finals may well have had something to do with the fact that most of their best players had ruled themselves out by joining Kerry Packer's super-special whizz-bang 'circus'.

Burgess won the toss and put England in. Boycott survived a hard chance off his second ball, but had scored only 2 when Hadlee had him caught at slip. Brearley, however, was making steady if slow progress, and when Gooch joined him with two wickets down the innings began to take shape. Brearley eventually went for 53, and after Gower departed quickly Gooch and Botham put on 47 in ten overs. These two went in quick succession to leave England in some trouble at 178 for 7, but Randall batted neatly and sensibly for 42 not out and with Taylor saw his team to 221 for 8, the last three overs producing a crucial 25 runs. The New Zealand bowlers had all performed well.

Wright and Edgar produced their customary dependable start, making 47 from 16 overs before Edgar went; there was then something of a disaster when Howarth fell lbw to a Boycott full toss. Boycott bowled well, in fact, being hit for only 24 in nine overs, though in the final against West Indies it was a different story. Wright had made 69 before he was run out by some brilliant work from Randall and Burgess was also run out after confusion with Turner. At 132 for 5 the game seemed to be England's, but there was some big hitting to come. Turner, Hadlee, Lees and Cairns each pushed the score along, helped by the fact that Willis, Botham and Hendrick were all injured. The wickets fell too, though, and as the last over began only McKechnie and Troup were left; perhaps if big Lance had still been there he might have got the fifteen runs needed – he would undoubtedly have had a good try – but Hendrick had had him caught. In the event just five came from the over; leaving England winners by nine runs, with Gooch named as man of the match for his 71. This left England to face West Indies in the final – and defeat by 92 runs.

II   THE APPETITE SATED

It was 1982–3 before the teams met again and then they did so in Australia. The English system of playing two or three one-day games against the touring team for the Prudential Trophy, or the Texaco Trophy as it was to become, seems an excellent arrangement; it provides an enjoyable appetiser before the serious business of the Tests, but it doesn't overdo the treat. Australia in the 1980s has seen the opposite end of the spectrum, with three countries competing each season for the Benson and Hedges World Series Cup in an interminable repetition of instantly forgettable matches that lose all meaning because of their sheer volume. England's Test fortunes have suffered badly enough through the differing techniques and requirements of one-day and five-day cricket, but the impact that this surfeit of one-day internationals had on Australia's Test team seemed – until 1989 – to have been worse still.

It is remarkable that these matches have not lost their popularity with the fans, with even those games not involving the home team usually being well attended; it is sad, however, that their popularity has been at the expense of Test matches, so that the attendance at one limited-overs game will often exceed that of an entire Test. This is not to say that one-day cricket is not a good thing, for it has clearly had some beneficial effects such as increased revenue and improved fielding; but fans with a more traditional view may justifiably shake their heads in sorrow at the relentless commercialism of a competition such as the Benson and Hedges World Series Cup. In the words of Jeff Thomson, 'One-day cricket is all right for a bit of a laugh, but it is crap really and the players know it.' There is that about it which is reminiscent of the way geese are force-fed to make pâté de foie gras, the aim being to line the pockets of the farmer doing the force-feeding.

Soon after they had finished the Test rubber in January 1983 England were off on this treadmill, contesting the series against Australia and New Zealand with each due to play the other no fewer than five times, the top two then pressing on still further with a best-of-three final. The first meeting at Melbourne produced a very exciting match, even if it had been largely forgotten by the time of the next one, two days later. New Zealand batted solidly through the order, with Wright and Edgar providing a fine opening of 87; Cairns was then promoted to have a swing at Jesty and the spinners and duly made 36 off twenty-six balls. Wright's 55 was top score, but Turner also showed his skill by taking ones and twos off nearly every ball he faced and contributed 38. Hadlee chipped in with a speedy 24, and the total finished on 239 for 8 from the fifty overs. England had hardly had a settled opening partnership throughout the tour and were still trying different combinations; today it was Gower and Tavaré and a reasonable start was made. The third wicket went down at 92, but then Gower and Botham came together and put on 98 for the fourth wicket with their contrasting styles of grace and power that have been the highlight of so many England innings since the late 1970s. When Botham went for 41 there were ten overs left to score 50, and Gower already had a century. At 223 his was the eighth wicket to go for a splendid 122, leaving 17 needed off just under three overs. It was a slow pitch and Marks and Taylor couldn't quite get there. Three were needed from Snedden's last ball for an England win – and Marks was bowled.

Brisbane saw David Gower at his superlative best. After Gould and Tavaré had opened with 26 Gower proceeded to make 158 off only 118 balls, with eighteen fours and four sixes, a display of glorious brilliance that was a record for this competition and is still the highest-ever score by an Englishman in a one-day international. Randall's 34 was the next best contribution, their fifth-wicket partnership being worth 113, and when Gower was caught off the last ball of the match the total was a daunting 267 for 6. The odd thing about New Zealand's reply was that Turner, their best batsman, didn't go in till number five, by which time it was too much of an uphill task. The openers did their usual sound job, but wickets fell steadily as nearly everyone got in and then got out. Hadlee and Troup made 63 for the ninth wicket to get past the 200 mark, but when the innings closed at 213 England had won by 54 runs.

Howarth actually chose to bat in the third match at Sydney, only to encounter Willis and Co. in an altogether more hostile mood than of late. The only substantial partnership was 82 for the third wicket between Edgar and Turner, but Edgar's 74 was made too slowly for it to have much real value. With ten overs left the score was 156 for 5, but instead of piling up the runs they allowed the wickets to slip away, and were all out for 199 in the forty-eighth over, Willis taking 4 for 23. England then made a bad start, first Fowler going for nought and then, after his two centuries, Gower doing the same. This brought Lamb in to join Tavaré; after a slow start which brought only 47 from twenty overs they suddenly accelerated, Lamb in particular hammering the bowling, and the runs were polished off without further loss at almost eight an over. The forty-third over saw the 200 reached, with Tavaré on 83 and Lamb on 108, England winning by a convincing eight wickets.

By this stage of the competition England had lost both their games to Australia and New Zealand had lost one and won one; both were therefore on four points to Australia's six. New Zealand then beat Australia, and

Australia and England beat each other, before England met New Zealand in a remarkable match at Adelaide, played on an excellent pitch in very hot weather. This time Botham opened with Tavaré and smashed 50 off just 44 balls; with the board on 75 he was joined by Gower, who also proceeded to score at will. His first fifty took fifty-two balls and his second just thirty balls as he made his third century in four games against New Zealand, although he had had less joy against Australia. As well as Gower's 109 Randall made 31 and Jesty 52 not out, and the fifty overs saw a record score for this competition of 296.

Faced with this enormous total Turner and Howarth were then both out with 33 on the board; Wright and Jeff Crowe took the score to 96, and Crowe and Cairns then hammered 70 off forty-eight balls. At 166 for 3 there was still a chance, but this suddenly became 166 for 5 as Botham struck, Crowe going for 50 and Cairns 49. Then it was Hadlee and Coney's turn; the English fielding and catching had been below par throughout, no doubt because of the heat, and with Botham suffering from a strained side the bowling got steadily worse. Hadlee and Coney played cleverly, picking up ones and twos all the time, and the 79 that Hadlee made was enough, with his economical bowling, to earn him the match award. When he was out they had put on 121 together and only ten were still needed, Hadlee more or less securing an unlikely victory by taking sixteen off one over from a very frustrated Willis. Coney was able to hit the winning run with seven balls to spare, giving New Zealand a four-wicket victory. It was the highest score ever made by a team batting second in a one-day international.

It should have demoralised England, but only the next day they beat Australia on the same ground; New Zealand then also beat Australia to make their place in the final almost certain. England's last match, against New Zealand, was played at Perth, the pitch being very green and very much in the bowlers' favour. Howarth's success with the coin gave his team a distinct advantage; after 17.3 overs England had reached 45 for 3, with Hadlee proving a real handful, when the first rain to fall on Perth for three months brought a temporary halt to proceedings. A helicopter was brought in to help dry the ground and it was then decreed that the match should be of 23 overs each. Gower and Randall hit out in their remaining time to take the score to 88 for 7, but in those circumstances the team batting second has an enormous advantage; just three wickets went down before Coney and Howarth cruised to victory with fifteen balls to spare.

Thus New Zealand finished top of the group, while England failed to qualify for the final, but to home delight Australia won both matches convincingly to take the trophy, helped by the fact that Hadlee was unable to play. England might reasonably have expected to go home at this point, but another treat was in store for them; the previous year it had seemed for a while that their tour of India might have to be called off and New Zealand had offered themselves as an alternative should that in fact happen. England had therefore agreed to play three one-day games in New Zealand to show their gratitude; as they were by now thoroughly worn out at the end of an exhausting tour, and downhearted at having lost the Ashes as well, this must have been as welcome as the proverbial hole in the head.

New Zealand's good performance in Australia had, however, excited the people back home in a way that their cricket team had never done before. The good folk of New Zealand suddenly found that they were every bit as enthusiastic about the 'instant thrills' stuff as their neighbours across the Tasman, and the games at Auckland, Wellington and Christchurch for the Rothmans Cup were played before packed houses. Richard Hadlee was missing with a hamstring injury and in view of what happened this was just as well since England might have been even more embarrassed.

Auckland, in fact, saw the largest crowd ever to attend a cricket match in New Zealand, 41,000. The pitch, though, was as dead as ever, and attractive batting that would have been worthy of the crowd was altogether a difficult business. Willis chose to bat, only for the first three wickets to go down for 40; Gower and Randall put on 64 together and indeed Gower was to make 84 in all, but with little of his usual fluency; forty of them came in singles, a remarkable proportion for such a batsman. New Zealand bowled well, Cairns and Chatfield especially, and only Marks made any other runs, his 23 giving the later order some slight respectability. A total of 184 for 9 from fifty overs was never likely to be enough, especially as Turner was playing – for the first time in six years for New Zealand at home – and was soon walloping Willis for boundaries. His first 50 came from fifty-four balls and with Edgar he put on an opening partnership of 101, going on to 88 himself. This left the rest with little to do and the match was easily won in the forty-seventh over.

Once or twice in Australia Willis had won the toss, put the opposition in, and watched them make a big score; indeed doing so in the third Test had cost him the Ashes. In the game at Wellington he now did the same thing on a beautiful batting strip, and watched as Turner and Edgar put on no fewer than 152 for the first wicket, Turner making 94 from as many balls. Cairns joined in the bat-swinging with a hefty 44, Wright and Coney both reached thirty, and the innings closed at a fine 295 for 6. When England had posted 296 a few weeks earlier New Zealand had overtaken them; but England were never in with a chance this time, dropping behind the clock from the word go. Wickets fell steadily, the only worthwhile partnership being between Miller and Marks, who put on 56 for the seventh wicket in just 34 minutes. By that time, though, it was a lost cause, and they were all out for 192 in the forty-fifth over, leaving New Zealand winners by 103 runs.

On a poor Christchurch pitch Turner and Edgar then gave their team yet another sound start, with 64 for the first wicket. Cairns produced yet more sixes and there were a few other reasonable if not over-large contributions. When the eighth wicket went down at 156 England must have been optimistic, but Morrison and Snedden played sensibly to make 55 runs in thirty-eight minutes from the last nine overs for a total of 211. Both England openers went immediately, but Gower and Lamb combined for a third-wicket 86. At 94 they were separated; by 127 England were all out, dismally beaten by 84 runs, the highest score among the remaining batsmen being 7 by Miller. Thereafter the only surprise was that none of the English players was injured in their rush to get on the plane home; this can only be explained by the fact that they were so tired and dispirited that rushing was simply not an option open to them.

These matches took place in February 1983. The following June everyone assembled in England for the third Prudential World Cup, to be played in an expanded version with each team meeting the others in its group twice instead of once. No prizes for realising that the main reason for this was financial, but it was also justified by the claim that it reduced the chances of any team being eliminated because of misfortune with the weather – which of course it did. England and New Zealand were in the same group, together with Pakistan and Sri Lanka. New Zealand had a very experienced squad under Geoff Howarth and after their recent successes were very optimistic of reaching at least the semi-finals. They soon found, however, that a refreshed England, playing at home, was a different proposition by far from the worn-out tourists of four months earlier. The teams met in the opening game of the competition at the Oval and England were soon making their poor showing of last February seem like a distant nightmare. Fowler went early, but Tavaré and Gower, both playing characteristically – the former stolidly and the latter freely – took the score to 79. After their departure Lamb and Gatting smashed 115 in sixty-eight minutes, Lamb reaching his hundred in just 103 balls. The first thirty-five overs had produced just 119 runs; the last 25 produced 203, Botham, Gould and Dilley all swinging the bat as well. Poor Snedden, who had been unable to find his rhythm, became the first bowler to be carted for 100 runs in a World Cup match – his twelve overs cost 105 runs and produced 2 wickets – and England's total of 322 had only twice been exceeded in the competition.

The required run rate was 5.36 an over. Edgar departed with just 3 on the board; by 31 Wright and Turner had joined him back in the pavilion. Howarth and Coney got in, played slowly and got out. Only Martin Crowe, after a nervous start, did himself justice, showing an appreciative crowd what an outstanding batsman New Zealand had found. He was just three short of a century when he was run out as he tried to keep the strike from the tail-enders; his was the last wicket to fall, by which time New Zealand had reached 216, a deficit of 106. Those three matches in February must have seemed a long way away.

Both teams then beat Pakistan and Sri Lanka before meeting for the second time, at Edgbaston. Willis chose to bat first and Fowler played very confidently, putting on 63 for the first wicket with Tavaré. Only one other batsman played a major innings, however, and almost inevitably it was Gower; inevitably, since so many of his big one-day knocks were against New Zealand. He perhaps had some fortune surviving two very confident lbw appeals, but went on to make a fine 92 not out from just ninety-six balls. Unfortunately for England he ran out of partners, and the innings closed on 234 with 4.4 overs unused, a heinous crime in limited-overs cricket. With just three runs on the board Turner and Edgar were then dismissed in debatable circumstances and both Crowe brothers were out by the time the score was at 75. Howarth, however, was in good form and with Coney took the total to 146 before he went for 60. Smith went cheaply, but Coney and Hadlee, taking ones and twos with a minimum of risk, put on 70 to take the score to 221. At the beginning of the last over Coney was still there – he was to be voted man of the match – and four were needed to win, or three if they still had a wicket left. After four balls the scores were level – whereupon Bracewell hit Allott for four, and New Zealand had won, by two wickets, their first full international match in England.

New Zealand, now almost assured of a semi-final place, celebrated by doing the unthinkable and losing to Sri Lanka, leaving the door open for Pakistan to pip them as runners-up in the group by virtue of a slightly better run-rate. Had New Zealand scored just 30 more runs in all, without alteration to any of the results, they would have qualified for the semi-finals, so close was it. England, though, lost just that one game to head their group comfortably – only, after a sound start, to play dismally against India and lose badly. India then produced one of the great cricketing upsets and overturned West Indies in the final; they had already beaten them in a group match, but when they did it again there were several hundred million people who were distinctly pleased.

The next England–New Zealand encounters came at the end of

England's tour in 1983–4. Three games were played, the opening one on the same ground, Christchurch, that had seen England's humiliation in the second Test. The pitch was still cracked and loose on top, but England had learned their lesson and batted with much more circumspection – and ability. Gower, opening, went early, but first Smith and Lamb and then Lamb and Randall took the score to 107 before three wickets fell quickly. This was Randall's day, though, and with good support from Marks his 70 helped his team to 188 for 9, a reasonable fifty-over total on such a surface. New Zealand then made a decent start reaching 38 for 1; 38 for 4 was altogether less healthy and 44 for 5 was worse still. Only Cairns and Hadlee, in fact, were to get past 20, but neither exceeded 23; Cairns deposited one ball from Marks out of the ground, but it was more a case of six and out than any form of recovery. In poor light England bowled and fielded well, winning convincingly by 54 runs.

Before the second match, at Wellington, there was a school of thought which said that the pitch was such that a minimum of 240 would be needed to win. When Howarth won the toss and batted New Zealand played as though desperate to achieve this figure; but in fact the pitch made runs hard to find, and as they tried to push the score along they brought about their own downfall. England bowled and fielded splendidly, and when Marks came on for the tenth over with the score at 18 for 0 he made a profound impression on the match. By the time he had finished his ten overs he had the top five batsmen for just 20 runs and the score was 63 for 5. Coney and Hadlee put on 41, but Coney's 44 was top score by some way and they were all out for 135. Perhaps a good spinner could have saved the game for New Zealand, but they hadn't chosen one, and the England batsmen sauntered through their innings in firm control, without any need to take risks. Only four wickets were lost as Chris Smith top-scored with 70, but there was no question that the Somerset bowler was the man of the match.

At Auckland, where the Test had expired of an overload of runs on the inevitable dead pitch, Gower and Lamb got England into a sound position at 73 for 1 before the wickets began to slide. Gower's 35 was second-top score by some way, for after he left no one kept Lamb company for very long. Against tight bowling the fifty overs produced 209 for 9 with Lamb running out of partners just three short of his hundred. The home reply then centred on Howarth and Martin Crowe; coming together at 34 for 2 they made 160 before the captain was out for 72. The partnership had its doubtful moments early on with some unconvincing running between the wickets, but as they settled down it grew ever more ominous for England. There were more than four overs to spare when Crowe completed his

New Zealand seal victory in the one-day game at Leeds in 1986 as Hadlee bowls Foster.

century, giving his team a seven-wicket victory. For England, however, a 2–1 win in this little series meant that there was at least some compensation for their Test defeat.

Next time round, in 1986, England had no such recompense. When the Indians had toured England in the first part of the summer each team had won one of the two Texaco Trophy matches, with the visitors the overall winners because of their faster scoring rate; they had then gone on to win the Test series as well. Exactly the same was to happen with New Zealand. The first game was played at Headingley, where New Zealand, choosing to bat first, found themselves having to work hard on a rather difficult pitch, the first boundary not coming for ten overs. Four wickets were down for 54 before Coney and Jeff Crowe began the rescue; Crowe's 66 was to take twenty-eight overs but with Gray's help he was able to give more substance to the innings than any home batsman was, and the fifty-five overs eventually realised 217 for 8. As the pitch was now playing more easily there seemed no major problem for England; but it was one of those innings where the batsmen all get in and then get out and Lamb's 33 was the top score. What angered the home fans was that there were three run-outs of the kind that should never happen to experienced one-day cricketers, Lamb,

Richards and Ellison all falling this way; and with the rest getting themselves out to bowling that was good without being especially hostile the Yorkshire crowd were altogether unimpressed at the antics of the dim-witted southerners. At no point were England remotely in contention and New Zealand won by 47 runs.

The Manchester crowd, however, were treated to an altogether different spectacle. There was no Test at Old Trafford in 1986, so they got two one-day games instead – and both were outstanding, high-scoring matches full of fine batsmanship which England won. In the game against India 510 runs were scored; in the game against New Zealand this went up to 570 runs. New Zealand, again choosing to bat first, made a steady start, with 39 from Wright and a pleasing 63 from Rutherford; but with eight overs left they were only 166 for 4, and it hardly seemed enough. The Crowe brothers were at the crease, however, and decided it was time to launch an assault. The next four overs produced 47 as England began to fall apart – and then the last four produced no fewer than 71 as England disintegrated. Dilley went for 17 in one over, Foster for 20 as Martin hit a six, three fours and a two. Pringle got Jeff's wicket for 48 but was hit for 13, and then as Hadlee came in and laid about him for 18 the final over, bowled by Gooch, produced 26 runs (which included wides). Martin Crowe's 93 not out came from just seventy-four balls, the last 43 from just thirteen and it was an innings of superb stroke-play from a glorious batsman. Unfortunately, there were those in the crowd who allowed their disappointment at England's bowling and fielding to override their appreciation of the batting; in other words there was a storm of booing as the home team left the field, having been mauled to the extent of 284 for 5.

Villain number one was Gooch because of his last over; the fact that his first six overs had cost only 22 runs was of course forgotten. As he opened the innings with Athey, though, that over soon became but a dim memory; needing to score at 5.18 an over they put on the highest stand for the first wicket ever made in one-day internationals. They were helped by the absence of the ever-accurate Chatfield, who had injured his thumb as he caught Benson in the previous match; Benson had probably done enough in that game to merit inclusion in this one, but a stiff neck had kept him out, allowing Athey the chance which he now seized. Not only did they make the highest first-wicket stand but they scored at the required rate, a splendid display of aggressive, disciplined batting from both of them. With the board on 193 Gooch fell nine short of his century, but it wasn't long before Athey scrambled a single for his. Lamb then gave him good support as he took his score to 142 not out, the winning hit being made with eight balls and six wickets to spare. The dismal England performance in the first game meant that New Zealand took the trophy, but at least this gave the home fans something to remember in a wretched summer.

The 1987–8 Test series, it will be recalled, was tedium almost unlimited. It was followed by a four-match limited-over series, so allowing the possibility that even this might result in stalemate, especially as Hadlee's calf injury allowed him to play in only the last game.

At Dunedin it was an innings of 70 from the new captain John Wright which put the meat in the home team's innings. John Reid's son Richard opened the batting in the first two of these games, scoring only 8 in each, but Wright was given support by Greatbatch and Kuggeleijn, another newcomer, with 28 and 34 respectively. One little oddity was that Emburey, by polishing off the tail, finished with 4 for 39, one wicket more than he had taken in all three Tests. His mopping-up operation meant that New Zealand were all out in the last over for 204, and England went about their task steadily if unspectacularly. Broad contributed 33 and Gatting 42, and when he fell at 114 for 4 the requirement was 91 off 21 overs. It was Fairbrother and Capel who got them, Capel just missing his half-century when he fell at 48 and Fairbrother just getting his when he hit the second

John Emburey –
England's leading
off-spinner of the 1980s.

ball of the last over for four, his first international fifty. Chatfield set a record for England–New Zealand one-day games by conceding only 15 runs from ten overs, but there was no doubt that Hadlee was missed. With England winning by five wickets Emburey was presented with the £200 match award – only to have to hand it back again when the adjudicator said that he had chosen Wright!

The second game at Christchurch followed a similar pattern; and in dreary weather did its best, furthermore, to match the Test series for lack of interest. Rain reduced it to a 45-over match, and New Zealand's struggle to reach 86 for 5 did not provide scintillating viewing. Wright again led by example with 43, and Kuggeleijn and Bracewell also got to the forties as they put on 63 for the sixth wicket. The innings closed on 186, and England never seemed in much trouble as they chased it. Broad was dropped three times before holing out for 56, but Robinson (44), Gatting (33) and Fairbrother (25 not out) all did their bit. The margin was six wickets this time, with prayers being offered up by the locals for Hadlee's return.

Not only was he unavailable for the third match at Napier, but Martin Crowe and Bracewell were missing as well. England were put in and immediately lost Athey as he was run out without facing a ball. Broad and Robinson took the score to 80 before Robinson went, and DeFreitas made a Cairns-like 23; thereafter only Broad held the innings together as he reached his first one-day international century, making 106 out of 219 all out. Snedden's 4 for 34 was soon upstaged by his captain, as Wright emulated Broad and made a fine century. His chief support came from Greatbatch, with 64, and after Wright had gone for 101 Rutherford joined Greatbatch to coast home easily, seven wickets still in hand.

Hadlee at last returned for the final game at Auckland, as did Crowe. As it happened he didn't take a wicket, but saw his colleagues bowl well to restrict England to 208, the last two wickets falling to the last two balls of the innings, bowled by Chatfield. At 71 for 4 even this figure had seemed unlikely, but Gatting's 48 and Fairbrother's 54 made a game of it. John Wright had happily acknowledged that the responsibility of captaincy had helped his batting and he proved it yet again with a solid 47. He opened the innings with Andrew Jones, who batted steadily for 90, falling only just before the end. There was a flurry of wickets as Jarvis struck to leave them at 138 for 5, and they were somewhat behind the clock; but then enter Hadlee, and in sixty-one balls he and Jones put on as many runs. Jones went, but the second ball of the last over was despatched to the fence – by Hadlee of course – and the victory was New Zealand's by four wickets. As so often in recent times England's catching had let them down; but by now it was clear to everyone that the tour was destined to end with no advantage to either side. The two teams even had to share another oddity, each having a batsman run out who was then not given out by the umpires, Robinson and Jones being the fortunate benefactors of this generosity. Somehow it seemed to symbolise the unreal nature of the tour.

*

Wordsworth wrote that poetry 'is the spontaneous overflow of powerful feelings; it takes its origin from emotion recollected in tranquillity'. One of the joys of cricket, of course, is to recollect, in tranquillity, the emotions that were stirred by the great deeds of those blessed with a special talent, to recall the powerful feelings produced by an exquisite cover-drive, a thunderous hook, a diving catch or a craftily-spun ball. We go to a cricket match to be entertained, to see individual battles within the team battle, and to let our feelings overflow spontaneously in response to the action before us. One-day cricket is ideal for this and unless the weather intervenes there is the promise of a result before the day is out; a match of three days or more that has lost its interest long before the end is undoubtedly one of the most pointless of all forms of entertainment.

Yet the problem with limited-overs cricket is that because there is so much action all at once we are able to remember very little of it when we try to recollect it in tranquillity; because the brain has been sated, both by so much action compressed into one day and by there being so many games of the same kind which all tend to be similar, the details blur. Memories become vague, unable to cope with the demands put upon them. When we can remember that, say, David Gower scored a fine century but can't be sure whether it was against India or New Zealand, it seems that something precious has gone out of one's enjoyment of the game. The slower pace of a game of three, four or five days, though, allows the memories to become absorbed, the details to be etched much more clearly, so that when we come to recollect them we accordingly get more pleasure from it. On this basis, then, we have the option to choose which type of cricket we prefer to watch, that which gives us instant gratification or that which warms us during the long winter evenings.

The traditionalist will look down on the one-day fan as a philistine unable to appreciate the finer points of the game, unable to perceive the pleasures to be had from following, and later recalling, the subtle shifts of fortune; the one-day fan will point to the difference in size of the crowds at the two types of game, at the way the fielding has improved dramatically, at the increase in revenue which one-day games produce and which finds its way throughout the cricketing system. If the traditionalist steadfastly refuses to acknowledge that one-day cricket gives much pleasure to many people and is a perfectly valid sporting entertainment in its own right, he is simply being foolish; but if he does accept this and merely wishes to argue that when it is taken to extremes, as it has been in Australia, it loses almost all of its meaning and runs the risk of collapsing in on itself as public enthusiasm wanes, then he is undoubtedly speaking a great deal of sense.

One-day internationals

1973	Swansea	NZ 158;	E 159–3	E 7 wkts
	Old Trafford	E 167–8;	NZ —	No result – rain
1974–5	Melbourne†	NZ 262–8;	MCC 196	NZ 66 runs
	Dunedin	E 136;	NZ 15–0	No result – rain
	Wellington	NZ 227;	E 35–1	No result – rain
1975	Trent Bridge*	E 266–6;	NZ 186	E 80 runs
1978	Scarborough	E 206–8;	NZ 187–8	E 19 runs
	Old Trafford	E 278–5;	NZ 152	E 126 runs
1979	Old Trafford*	E 221–8;	NZ 212	E 9 runs
1982–3	Melbourne	NZ 239–8;	E 237–8	NZ 2 runs
	Brisbane	E 267–6;	NZ 213	E 54 runs
	Sydney	NZ 199;	E 200–2	E 8 wkts
	Adelaide	E 296–5;	NZ 297–6	NZ 4 wkts
	Perth	E 88–7;	NZ 89–3	NZ 7 wkts
	Auckland	E 184–9;	NZ 187–4	NZ 6 wkts
	Wellington	NZ 295–6;	E 192	NZ 103 runs
	Christchurch	NZ 211–8;	E 127	NZ 84 runs
1983	Oval*	E 322–6;	NZ 216	E 106 runs
	Edgbaston*	E 234;	NZ 238–8	NZ 2 wkts
1983–4	Christchurch	E 188–9;	NZ 134	E 54 runs
	Wellington	NZ 135;	E 139–4	E 6 wkts
	Auckland	E 209;	NZ 210–3	NZ 7 wkts
1986	Headingley	NZ 217–8;	E 170	NZ 47 runs
	Old Trafford	NZ 284–5;	E 286–4	E 6 wkts
1987–8	Dunedin	NZ 204;	E 207–5	E 5 wkts
	Christchurch	NZ 186–8;	E 188–4	E 6 wkts
	Napier	E 219;	NZ 223–3	NZ 7 wkts
	Auckland	E 208;	NZ 211–6	NZ 4 wkts

† Not an official international   *World Cup matches

England: 13 wins   New Zealand: 11 wins   No result: 3
Unofficial international: New Zealand

Centuries
England: D.L. Amiss 100   K.W.R. Fletcher 131   C.T. Radley 117*   D.I. Gower 122, 158, 109   A.J. Lamb 108*, 102   C.W.J. Athey 142*   B.C. Broad 106

New Zealand: B.E. Congdon 101   M.D. Crowe 105*   J.G. Wright 101

4 Wickets in an innings
England: J.A. Snow 4–32   P. Lever 4–35   A.W. Greig 4–45   R.G.D. Willis 4–23, 4–42   V.J. Marks 5–20   J.E. Emburey 4–39   P.W. Jarvis 4–33

New Zealand: B.L. Cairns 5–28   R.J. Hadlee 5–32   M.C. Snedden 4–34

— 11 —

King Richard

It isn't necessarily a long career and impressive statistics that gain a cricketer, or any other sportsperson, a place in the ranks of the immortals. One suspects that anyone who watched both Martin Donnelly and Bev Congdon bat would confer the honour on Donnelly for his undoubted class rather than on Congdon for the application which made him his country's highest run-scorer. New Zealand hasn't really done too well at the business of producing cricketing immortals, in fact: apart from Richard Hadlee there is Sutcliffe, Reid, Turner and, one assumes, Martin Crowe, but that is about as far as the list goes. Not too many bowlers there, notice; which in a way makes it more difficult to assess Hadlee's achievement with any precision. Simply to say that he is head and shoulders above any bowler New Zealand has ever produced is not enough, since in sixty years of playing Test cricket only five others have reached the 100-wicket mark and none of those has got very far past it. The fact is that he has taken three times as many wickets as any other New Zealand bowler, from less than twice as many Tests. That begins to give some measure of his supremacy.

He was born in July 1951, just over three months after his father Walter played his last Test, the fourth of five sons. The fact that he had elder brothers is significant, for there is no doubt that the pressures which having a famous father can bring had been largely dissipated by the time he was coming through, Barry and Dayle having taken the brunt of them. His début with Canterbury came in 1971–2, partnering Dayle, three years his senior, in the opening attack and performing the hat-trick in his third game. His prime attribute in those early years was simply speed; he was genuinely fast, certainly quicker than his brother, and his early Tests came as a result of this speed. His international baptism was against Pakistan in Wellington the following season, when he took 2 for 84 and 0 for 28; over the next few years he would take wickets, naturally enough, but his lack of accuracy meant that he could be expensive. There were times when he bowled very poorly, and his first ten Test wickets averaged 51 apiece. For all his obvious potential, therefore, he was not able to command a regular place in the

*How to bowl the perfect outswinger. Hadlee is the ideal model for
any aspiring youngster to emulate. (This and facing page.)*

national team until the third Test against India at the Basin Reserve early in
1976; somewhat out of the blue – in eight previous games he had taken 21
wickets at 41 – he took 4 for 35 and 7 for 23 to give New Zealand their first
ever Test win by an innings. His figures of 7 for 23 and 11 for 58 were the
best innings and match figures ever returned in Tests by a New Zealand
bowler. Having thus established himself, there was no more chance of his

being dropped than of the Australians dropping Bradman after he had made his first century; selectors frequently do strange things, but there is a limit to their idiosyncrasies. Yet even then the floodgates hadn't really opened, and there were some unproductive days; after seventeen Tests he had sixty-one wickets at 35 each. Only with the game in which England were beaten for the first time, in which he took 10 for 100, was the Hadlee we have come to know properly under way, for in the next seventeen games he took ninety-three wickets at 21.

Six feet tall, lean and wiry, his action is every bit as smooth and aesthetically pleasing as that of Dennis Lillee, a bowler he admired enormously; Mike Selvey, the Middlesex and England bowler, compared it to cream being poured from a jug. By 1980 he had cut down his run to about fifteen paces, increasing his accuracy at the cost of only a slight loss of pace. One of the wonders of his bowling, in fact, is just how fast he can be off a run-up no longer than that of the most ordinary medium-pacer; he said of himself that his bowling is 'entirely rhythm, all timing and co-ordination', and the fact that there is not the least scrap of wasted effort in it has helped him to keep going at the highest level until his late thirties with little reduction of pace. This combination of speed and accuracy, plus his ability to produce plenty of movement off the pitch, has cost him much hard work to perfect, but it has borne him and his teams very rich fruit. Don Neely found a gloriously graphic way of describing it: he said that he has 'a way of going over his opponent's psychic armour with a dental pick, scraping for nerves'. Conceivably his Test haul has been slightly inflated by the fact that he has had no other strike bowler of comparable class at the other end to share the wickets with him, whereas Malcolm Marshall, for example, has to operate alongside two or three other very fine bowlers. Class will always tell, but the standard of the other bowlers must make something of a difference.

And then there is his batting. Of the four outstanding all-rounders of the modern era, Botham, Imran Khan, Kapil Dev and Hadlee, the records would seem to show that the New Zealander is the least accomplished batsman among them; his seventy-nine Tests have produced 2,884 runs at 26.70 with two centuries, a rather lower average than the others. Yet he is still a very high-class performer, especially since the advent of the helmet allowed him to face up to the kind of medicine he himself dispenses with greater confidence than in his early days. Like the rest he is an aggressive, clean-hitting striker of the ball who is always looking to attack, a left-hander who is an ideal man to have coming in at six or seven ready to inflict some punishment on bowlers who are beginning to tire. His first Test century came against West Indies in 1979–80, during the course of which he reached 1,000 Test runs, becoming, in his twenty-eighth match, the first New Zealander to do the double. His highest Test score is 151 not out against Sri Lanka in 1986–7 (New Zealand's 100th Test century, incidentally) when he and Jeff Crowe made an undefeated 246 for the sixth wicket, New Zealand's Test record for that wicket. When England were annihilated at Christchurch in 1983–4 Hadlee scored 99 from eighty-one balls on a pitch that was supposedly awful – and then took match figures of 8 for 44.

There can be little argument that Botham is the best batsman of the four, yet even if Hadlee is the weakest only Imran can challenge him as the best bowler among them – and one suspects that most people outside Pakistan would give that palm to Hadlee.

In 1978 Hadlee went to England to represent New Zealand in a double-wicket competition and it proved a vital visit. Clive Rice had been dismissed by Nottinghamshire because of his involvement with Kerry Packer, a heinous crime that in those days was seen as comparable to having gone for a pleasant weekend with Hitler in 1942, and whilst there Hadlee was asked by Nottinghamshire if he would join them as Rice's replacement as their overseas player. Hadlee agreed, but in the event the county thought better of losing Rice and invited him back, a decision that meant they had two of the world's best all-rounders on their books; they were to become the best of friends and transform the fortunes of the club that had been shrewd enough to employ them. For various reasons – touring with New Zealand in 1978, injury and so on – in his first three seasons Hadlee played only twenty-three games for them and was doubtful about continuing in 1981. He decided to do so, took 105 wickets, scored 745 runs and played a major role in bringing the Championship to Trent Bridge for the first time since 1929. In 1984 he set himself the task of doing the double of 1,000 runs and 100 wickets and achieved it comfortably – 1,179 runs at 51 and 117 wickets at 14 – the first man to do it since Fred Titmus in 1967, when more matches were played. Nottinghamshire came agonisingly close to winning the title again that year but just missed out; three years later, Hadlee and Rice having announced that they were both retiring from county cricket, they went out in style, winning the Championship and the Nat West Trophy. The only blot was that Hadlee failed by just three wickets to do the double again, topping both batting and bowling averages for the county with 1,075 runs at 53 and 97 wickets at a remarkable 11.89 – as well as transforming the Nat West final with 70 not out. It was all very much from the pages of *Boys' Own*.

That double in 1984 says much about the man. He announced at the beginning of the season that he was going to try and do it, partly, he said, to put pressure on himself to perform and partly as an example to youngsters. It was all worked out carefully beforehand: how he had to average 50 runs and five wickets a game, sixty wickets at Trent Bridge and forty away, 400 runs at Trent Bridge and 600 away. The wickets came regularly throughout, but it seemed that the runs might fall short – until he hit a double hundred at Lord's in August. He is that sort of player; his colleague at Nottinghamshire, Eddie Hemmings, said of him: 'He's so single-minded.

If, for example, we have a county six down overnight he will spend all evening and morning planning and plotting how he will get at least three of the remaining wickets. I just can't think in those terms, and nor can anyone else.' Those last five words are crucial, showing just how much of a professional Hadlee is, how much thinking, determination and application go into his play. He manages to combine enjoying his cricket with taking it very seriously indeed, so seriously in fact that after the 1983 tour of England he had a mental breakdown. The relentlessness of county cricket he found very hard work and nearly quit a number of times during the 1980s; Clive Rice had to keep urging him to stay on and when he finally left it was very much with a sense of relief. Yet the professionalism that he was able to sharpen up in England has been of enormous benefit to New Zealand cricket, for his attitude has rubbed off on his amateur colleagues and they have learned to adapt their approach to the modern game; there has been friction within the team from time to time over the question of money, with the amateurs resenting that fact that the professionals were paid more than they were, but there is no doubt that having important members of the team such as Hadlee, Howarth and Wright playing regularly in England has been a major reason for the advances New Zealand have made.

Hadlee freely admits that he has become very conscious of statistics, and desperately wants to become the first man to reach 400 Test wickets. At the time of writing the only man who might stop him from doing so, unless serious injury rules Hadlee out, is Ian Botham. Now Botham is without question the better batsman of the two, but equally obviously Hadlee is the greater bowler; statistics are not always good guides, of course, but in this case they would seem to provide an accurate reflection of the differences between the two – and there are considerably more differences than similarities. Botham is famed as the great man of action, the swashbuckler who lives life to the hilt and finds himself on assault charges as a result of his impetuosity, who virtually has to be ordered to practise, who has an unshakeable belief in his own greatness as a player and can therefore be an enormous handful for a captain when having a bad day – but who has provided English cricket, at a time when it hasn't been strong, with some imperishable moments, and transformed many a game single-handedly. The fact that he is not famed as a thinker is unfair, for his bowling is usually highly intelligent and well-thought-out; it is just that, in view of his reputation, his bad days become exaggerated and his good days taken for granted. You don't take 376 Test wickets without adding a great deal of thought to your natural talent and when he succeeded Mike Brearley as England captain Brearley said he had been impressed by Botham's tactical

*A round to Botham in the duel between him and Hadlee. Sheer
aggression takes him down the pitch to pick up the ball and run the
New Zealander out by a couple of yards. Geoff Boycott, Geoff
Howarth and umpire Barry Meyer watch expectantly (Lord's 1978).*

awareness. He does not, however, plot how to get his wickets to the extent
that Hadlee does, for such single-mindedness could never be Botham's way.
Their characters are, simply, very different: Botham the extrovert, Hadlee,
if not quite the introvert, then quietly intense and utterly determined to be
as consistent as humanly possible and keep on taking more and more
wickets. Any reporter who tried to write a story about Hadlee on an assault
charge after a fracas at a pub would just never be believed. Inevitably there
has long been a rivalry between them – Hadlee described it in print as
'deadly' – but thankfully it has been a quiet one that the media have not
blown up; and it is probably fair to say that over the years the honours are
just about equal.

When New Zealand drew their series against Pakistan early in 1989 they

*Hadlee in a
characteristic pose.*

had not lost a rubber at home since 1978–9. Their away record was less impressive, but they had achieved hitherto undreamed-of feats such as winning series in Australia and England. Of the nineteen series they had played since then (excluding the aborted one against Sri Lanka) they had won nine and drawn four, whereas in the same period England had played twenty-two, won seven and drawn one – clear evidence of just how far the balance of cricketing power has shifted during the 1980s. The series in Australia in 1985–6 was probably Hadlee's peak, when in three Tests he took 33 wickets at 12, a figure exceeded only by George Lohmann in 1895–6 when bowling against a very weak team in South Africa. In the first Test at Brisbane Hadlee took 9 for 52, figures that have been bettered in Tests only by Jim Laker in 1956 and Lohmann in 1895–6, and he followed this with 6 for 71 to put himself high on the list of best individual Test performances. Naturally the batsmen, Martin Crowe in particular, played their parts in setting up their country's first series win in Australia – and the margin of 2–1 wasn't too far from being 3–0 – but there was no doubt who was hero number one. Less than three months later Australia were in New Zealand and losing the three tests 1–0, with Hadlee taking another sixteen wickets. In the first of these matches, his sixty-first Test, he claimed his 300th wicket when he had Allan Border lbw, the photograph of his appeal, as he turned to face the umpire, an especially memorable one – feet wide apart, left hand palm forward above his head, right index finger pointing at the ground, eyes blazing, a yell of triumph and exultation on his lips. Everything about it speaks of total commitment.

At the beginning of England's visit in 1988 he stood poised to move ahead of Botham as the leading Test wicket-taker, but injury prevented him from doing so. In November of that year he achieved it, his eighteen wickets in India taking him to 391. The stage was set for the 400 to be reached at home to Pakistan early in 1989; instead of which the first match became only the fourth Test in history to be completely washed out, he took four in the second and just one in the third, able to bowl just 28 overs before the recurrence of a hamstring injury which had caused him problems in India ruled him out. The Pakistanis scored heavily in both matches, and although New Zealand retained their record of not being beaten at home for a decade there was little for them to get excited about apart from a satisfactory return after illness and injury by Martin Crowe. Thus after seventy-nine Tests Hadlee has 396 wickets at 22.22, and, all being well, will be the first past 400.

There have been some wonderful bowlers in the history of cricket, and Richard Hadlee is fit to rank among the best of them. For various reasons not all outstanding players have achieved a fine Test record, but Hadlee, happily, has done so. In the process he has taken New Zealand's cricket to feats that for long years had been but dreams, not single-handedly, of course, but largely through his own skill and determination to succeed. 'Here was a Caesar!' as Mark Antony said. 'When comes such another?'

Afterword

New Zealanders have always had a reputation for friendliness, openness and being closer to the British in character and temperament than any other Commonwealth country. Maybe the average Briton does not regard New Zealand with quite as much affection as the average New Zealander regards Britain, but the links between them have always been as close as their enormous geographical separation would allow; when Britain was proposing to join the European Community, for instance, there was much genuine concern that this would involve doing the dirty on New Zealand's economy. This closeness has been reflected in the good spirit in which their sporting encounters have been played and their cricket matches have almost always taken place in an atmosphere of great cordiality. New Zealanders seem really to love visiting England and refer to it as the home country; on tour there the cricketers will invariably make far more efforts to socialise with the opposing players and media people than any other tourists will, turning up for social golf days and suchlike in greater numbers than Australians or any others. Over the years the enthusiasm and sportsmanship of their cricketers have made them extremely popular in England. The New Zealand people have also always appreciated the efforts England has made to play Tests against them as often as possible – even if the players who arrived there were always tired after a long tour of Australia their professionalism usually triumphed over their desire to go home – and the relationship between the countries, except for the small amount of friction on MacLaren's tour, has never been other than extremely good. Problems such as 'bodyline' and 'sledging' that have soured feelings between England and Australia from time to time have never touched England–New Zealand matches.

Against this background the cricket was for decades the story of amateurs against professionals, with all the disadvantages being held by the amateurs; geographical isolation, small population, lack of money with all its ramifications, national devotion to Rugby as the principal sport – all of these combined to retard the development of New Zealand's cricket. Even the luck has so often been against them; for years they produced good batsmen and good bowlers but never in tandem, so that when one department was strong the other was weak, while top-class batsmen such as Donnelly and Dempster played only a few Tests before moving to another country. Perhaps the biggest problem of all was psychological, in that the longer they went without beating England the more they appeared to believe that they were never going to do it; when, once in a while, they had an advantage they seemed unable to convince themselves that they really could turn it into a victory. This notion would seem to be supported by the fact that when the breakthrough was finally made the next stages followed swiftly, with the first victory in England, the first series win and the first series win in England all coming in rapid succession.

Yet if the story has until recently been one-sided it has been a good one for all that, with the New Zealanders deserving of the highest praise for the unfailingly cheerful and sporting way in which they have accepted the position of permanent underdogs. Against most of the other countries England and New Zealand have both experienced occasional friction, yet virtually never against each other. Perhaps then, despite the widespread belief that we now know better, it does go to show that Curly Page was right, and people do think more of a good sportsman who loses than a bad sportsman who wins.

Statistical Highlights of the Test Matches

Results – Series by Series

| | Captains | | | Result | | |
	England	New Zealand	Tests	E	NZ	D
1929–30	A.H.H. Gilligan	T.C. Lowry	4	1	0	3
1931	D.R. Jardine	T.C. Lowry	3	1	0	2
1932–3	D.R. Jardine R.E.S. Wyatt (2nd)	M.L. Page	2	0	0	2
1937	R.W.V. Robins	M.L. Page	3	1	0	2
1946–7	W.R. Hammond	W.A. Hadlee	1	0	0	1
1949	F.G. Mann F.R. Brown (3rd, 4th)	W.A. Hadlee	4	0	0	4
1950–1	F.R. Brown	W.A. Hadlee	2	1	0	1
1954–5	L. Hutton	G.O. Rabone	2	2	0	0
1958	P.B.H. May	J.R. Reid	5	4	0	1
1958–9	P.B.H. May	J.R. Reid	2	1	0	1
1962–3	E.R. Dexter	J.R. Reid	3	3	0	0
1965	M.J.K. Smith	J.R. Reid	3	3	0	0
1965–6	M.J.K. Smith	M.E. Chapple (1st) B.W. Sinclair	3	0	0	3
1969	R. Illingworth	G.T. Dowling	3	2	0	1
1970–1	R. Illingworth	G.T. Dowling	2	1	0	1
1973	R. Illingworth	B.E. Congdon	3	2	0	1
1974–5	M.H. Denness	B.E. Congdon	2	1	0	1
1977–8	G. Boycott	M.G. Burgess	3	1	1	1
1978	J.M. Brearley	M.G. Burgess	3	3	0	0
1983	R.G.D. Willis	G.P. Howarth	4	3	1	0
1983–4	R.G.D. Willis	G.P. Howarth	3	0	1	2
1986	M.W. Gatting	J.V. Coney	3	0	1	2
1987–8	M.W. Gatting	J.J. Crowe J.G. Wright (3rd)	3	0	0	3
		In New Zealand	32	11	2	19
		In England	34	19	2	13
		Totals	66	30	4	32

Batsmen with 500 runs

England	Tests	Innings	NO	HS	Runs	Average
M.C. Cowdrey	18	24	5	128*	1133	59.63
D.I. Gower	13	22	1	131	1051	50.05
W.R. Hammond	9	11	2	336*	1015	112.78
G. Boycott	15	24	1	131	916	39.83
J.H. Edrich	11	15	1	310*	840	60.00
I.T. Botham	14	21	2	138	830	43.68
L. Hutton	11	17	0	206	777	45.71
P.B.H. May	9	11	2	124*	603	67.00
K.F. Barrington	5	6	0	163	594	99.00
K.W.R. Fletcher	8	11	0	216	578	52.55
K.S. Duleepsinhji	7	10	2	117	566	70.75
D.W. Randall	9	15	1	164	543	38.79
D.C.S. Compton	8	11	0	116	510	46.36

New Zealand	Tests	Innings	NO	HS	Runs	Average
B.E. Congdon	20	38	1	176	1085	29.32
J.G. Wright	17	32	2	130	1083	36.10
B. Sutcliffe	16	28	2	116	1049	40.35
J.R. Reid	19	36	2	100	953	28.03
G.P. Howarth	15	27	3	123	910	37.92
V. Pollard	13	24	4	116	739	36.95
M.D. Crowe	13	22	2	143	733	36.65
R.J. Hadlee	18	30	4	99	691	26.58
J.V. Coney	10	16	3	174*	622	47.85
C.S. Dempster	8	11	4	136	619	88.43
B.A. Edgar	13	24	2	84	615	27.95
M.G. Burgess	12	21	1	105	610	30.50
M.P. Donnelly	7	12	1	206	582	52.91
W.A. Hadlee	10	17	1	116	534	33.38
G.T. Dowling	11	22	1	66	517	24.62
G.M. Turner	9	16	2	98	510	36.43

Highest Batting Averages

Qualification: 6 innings

England	Tests	Innings	NO	HS	Runs	Average
W.R. Hammond	9	11	2	336*	1015	112.78
K.F. Barrington	5	6	0	163	594	99.00
D.L. Amiss	5	7	2	164*	433	86.60
K.S. Duleepsinhji	7	10	2	117	566	70.75
P.B.H. May	9	11	2	124*	603	67.00
J.H. Edrich	11	15	1	310*	840	60.00
M.C. Cowdrey	18	24	5	128*	1133	59.63
E.R. Dexter	8	10	2	141	477	59.63
L.E.G. Ames	8	10	3	137	410	58.57
G.A. Gooch	6	10	2	183	458	57.25
K.W.R. Fletcher	8	11	0	216	578	52.55
B.R. Knight	7	10	3	125	354	50.57
D.I. Gower	13	22	1	131	1051	50.05
T.E. Bailey	12	13	4	134*	439	48.77
D.C.S. Compton	8	11	0	116	510	46.36
L. Hutton	11	17	0	206	777	45.71
A.W. Greig	5	6	0	139	267	44.50
I.T. Botham	14	21	2	138	830	43.68
A.J. Lamb	8	13	2	137*	474	43.09

New Zealand

C.S. Dempster	8	11	4	136	619	88.43
M.P. Donnelly	7	12	1	206	582	52.91
J.V. Coney	10	16	3	174*	622	47.85
I.D.S. Smith	10	13	5	113*	332	41.50
B. Sutcliffe	16	28	2	116	1049	40.35
G.P. Howarth	15	27	3	123	910	37.92
V. Pollard	13	24	4	116	739	36.95
M.D. Crowe	13	22	2	143	733	36.65
G.M. Turner	9	16	2	98	510	36.43
J.G. Wright	17	32	2	130	1083	36.10
W.A. Hadlee	10	17	1	116	534	33.38
M.G. Burgess	12	21	1	105	610	30.50

Highest Innings Totals

England in England:	546–4d	Headingley	1965
England in New Zealand:	593–6d	Auckland	1974–5
New Zealand in England:	551–9d	Lord's	1973
New Zealand in New Zealand:	537	Wellington	1983–4

Lowest Innings Totals

England in England:	187	Old Trafford	1937
England in New Zealand:	64	Wellington	1977–8
New Zealand in England:	47	Lord's	1958
New Zealand in New Zealand:	26	Auckland	1954–5

Record Partnerships for Each Wicket

England

1st	223	G. Fowler and C.J. Tavaré	Oval	1983
2nd	369	J.H. Edrich and K.F. Barrington	Headingley	1965
3rd	245	W.R. Hammond and J. Hardstaff (jr)	Lord's	1937
4th	266	M.H. Denness and K.W.R. Fletcher	Auckland	1974–5
5th	242	W.R. Hammond and L.E.G. Ames	Christchurch	1932–3
6th	240	P.H. Parfitt and B.R. Knight	Auckland	1962–3
7th	149	A.P.E. Knott and P. Lever	Auckland	1970–1
8th	246	L.E.G. Ames and G.O.B. Allen	Lord's	1931
9th	163*	M.C. Cowdrey and A.C. Smith	Wellington	1962–3
10th	59	A.P.E. Knott and N. Gifford	Trent Bridge	1973

New Zealand

1st	276	C.S. Dempster and J.E. Mills	Wellington	1929–30
2nd	131	B. Sutcliffe and J.R. Reid	Christchurch	1950–1
3rd	210	B.A. Edgar and M.D. Crowe	Lord's	1986
4th	154	J.G. Wright and J.J. Crowe	Auckland	1983–4
5th	177	B.E. Congdon and V. Pollard	Trent Bridge	1973
6th	117	M.G. Burgess and V. Pollard	Lord's	1973
7th	104	B. Sutcliffe and V. Pollard	Edgbaston	1965
8th	104	A.W. Roberts and D.A.R. Moloney	Lord's	1937
9th	118	J.V. Coney and B.L. Cairns	Wellington	1983–4
10th	57	F.L.H. Mooney and J. Cowie	Headingley	1949

Most Runs in a Series

England in England:	469 (average 78.16)	L. Hutton	1949
England in New Zealand:	563 (average 563.00)	W.R. Hammond	1932–3
New Zealand in England:	462 (average 77.00)	M.P. Donnelly	1949
New Zealand in New Zealand:	341 (average 85.25)	C.S. Dempster	1929–30

Best Batting

England	Score	Ground	Year
W.R. Hammond	336*	Auckland	1932–3
J.H. Edrich	310*	Headingley	1965
W.R. Hammond	227	Christchurch	1932–3
K.W.R. Fletcher	216	Auckland	1974–5
L. Hutton	206	Oval	1949
G.B. Legge	196	Auckland	1929–30
G.A. Gooch	183	Lord's	1986
M.H. Denness	181	Auckland	1974–5
K.W.R. Fletcher	178	Lord's	1973
D.L. Amiss	164*	Christchurch	1974–5
D.W. Randall	164	Wellington	1983–4
K.F. Barrington	163	Headingley	1965
C.T. Radley	158	Auckland	1977–8
J.H. Edrich	155	Lord's	1969

New Zealand	Score	Ground	Year
M.P. Donnelly	206	Lord's	1949
B.E. Congdon	176	Trent Bridge	1973
B.E. Congdon	175	Lord's	1973
J.V. Coney	174*	Wellington	1983–4
M.D. Crowe	143	Wellington	1987–8
C.S. Dempster	136	Wellington	1929–30
J.G. Wright	130	Auckland	1983–4
J.J. Crowe	128	Auckland	1983–4

Bowlers with 20 Wickets

England	Tests	Balls	Mdns	Runs	Wkts	Average
I.T. Botham	14	3152	115	1424	61	23.34
R.G.D. Willis	14	3018	129	1132	60	18.87
D.L. Underwood	8	2118	122	586	48	12.21
G.A.R. Lock	7	1505	133	367	47	7.81
F.S. Trueman	11	2167	113	762	40	19.05
T.E. Bailey	12	1876	70	866	32	27.06
P.H. Edmonds	11	2593	141	779	31	25.13
F.J. Titmus	6	1818	139	461	28	16.46
G.R. Dilley	6	1196	56	441	24	18.38
R. Illingworth	13	2095	127	597	22	27.14
J.C. Laker	5	978	73	262	21	12.48
C.M. Old	6	1141	45	448	21	21.33
N.G.B. Cook	3	1349	93	471	21	22.43
J.B. Statham	5	898	50	268	20	13.40
A.W. Greig	5	849	23	361	20	18.05

New Zealand

R.J. Hadlee	18	5050	208	2015	81	24.88
R.O. Collinge	15	3495	120	1335	48	27.81
J. Cowie	8	1902	57	929	39	23.82
E.J. Chatfield	12	2879	138	1110	34	32.65
B.L. Cairns	10	2556	121	946	32	29.56
B.R. Taylor	8	1847	63	875	28	31.25
R.C. Motz	11	2730	112	1169	28	41.75
A.R. MacGibbon	9	1571	76	583	24	24.29
T.B. Burtt	7	1841	98	804	23	34.96
R.S. Cunis	6	1446	49	522	22	23.73
H.J. Howarth	9	2594	132	880	22	40.00
S.L. Boock	9	1792	116	511	21	24.33
A.M. Moir	8	1282	42	609	20	30.45

Lowest Averages

Qualification: 10 wickets

England	Tests	Balls	Mdns	Runs	Wkts	Average
G.A.R. Lock	7	1505	133	367	47	7.81
K. Higgs	3	768	50	157	17	9.34
F.H. Tyson	4	582	36	186	17	10.94
D.L. Underwood	8	2118	122	586	48	12.21
J.C. Laker	5	978	73	262	21	12.48
J.B. Statham	5	898	50	268	20	13.40
M.J.C. Allom	4	601	24	194	13	14.92
F.J. Titmus	6	1818	139	461	28	16.46
I.J. Jones	3	735	40	242	14	17.29
A.W. Greig	5	849	23	361	20	18.05
G.R. Dilley	6	1196	56	441	24	18.38
R.G.D. Willis	14	3018	129	1132	60	18.87
F.S. Trueman	11	2167	113	762	40	19.05
G.O.B. Allen	5	589	30	195	10	19.50
F.E. Woolley	5	609	26	261	13	20.08
Alan Ward	3	443	15	210	10	21.00
C.M. Old	6	1141	45	448	21	21.33
J.D.F. Larter	4	932	47	358	16	22.38
I.T. Botham	14	3152	115	1424	61	23.34
B.R. Knight	7	1101	61	340	14	24.29
I.A.R. Peebles	3	616	16	325	13	25.00
P.H. Edmonds	11	2593	141	779	31	25.13
R.W.V. Robins	4	673	20	337	13	25.92
T.E. Bailey	12	1876	70	866	32	27.06
R. Illingworth	13	2095	127	597	22	27.14
D.A. Allen	3	1145	72	359	13	27.62
W. Voce	4	706	28	277	10	27.70
G.G. Arnold	6	1482	63	561	19	29.53

New Zealand

G.F. Cresswell	3	650	30	292	13	22.46
R.S. Cunis	6	1446	49	522	22	23.73
J. Cowie	8	1902	57	929	39	23.82
A.R. MacGibbon	9	1571	76	583	24	24.29
S.L. Boock	9	1792	116	511	21	24.33
R.J. Hadlee	18	5050	208	2015	81	24.88
R.O. Collinge	15	3495	120	1335	48	27.81
B.L. Cairns	10	2556	121	946	32	29.56
A.M. Moir	8	1282	42	609	20	30.45
B.R. Taylor	8	1847	63	875	28	31.25
E.J. Chatfield	12	2879	138	1110	34	32.65
J.R. Reid	19	1186	90	555	16	34.69
T.B. Burtt	7	1841	98	804	23	34.96
F.T. Badcock	5	1170	50	421	12	35.08
J.A. Hayes	7	1050	38	425	12	35.42
J.C. Alabaster	4	734	32	361	10	36.10
R.C. Blunt	7	766	34	363	10	36.30
J.G. Bracewell	10	1600	68	725	19	38.16
D.R. Hadlee	8	1455	36	729	19	38.37

Best Innings Bowling Analysis

England in England:	7–32	D.L. Underwood	Lord's	1969
England in New Zealand:	7–75	F.S. Trueman	Christchurch	1962–3
New Zealand in England:	7–74	B.L. Cairns	Headingley	1983
New Zealand in New Zealand:	7–143	B.L. Cairns	Wellington	1983–4

Best Match Bowling Analysis

England in England:	12–101	D.L. Underwood	Oval	1969
England in New Zealand:	12–97	D.L. Underwood	Christchurch	1970–1
New Zealand in England:	10–140	J. Cowie	Old Trafford	1937
New Zealand in New Zealand:	10–100	R.J. Hadlee	Wellington	1977–8

Most Wickets in a Series

England in England:	34 (average 7.47)	G.A.R. Lock	1958
England in New Zealand:	17 (average 9.34)	K. Higgs	1965–6
	17 (average 12.05)	D.L. Underwood	1970–1
	17 (average 18.29)	I.T. Botham	1977–8
New Zealand in England:	21 (average 26.61)	R.J. Hadlee	1983
New Zealand in New Zealand:	15 (average 19.53)	R.O. Collinge	1977–8
	15 (average 24.73)	R.J. Hadlee	1977–8

Best Bowling

England

D.L. Underwood	12–97	Christchurch	1970–1
D.L. Underwood	12–101	Oval	1969
G.A.R. Lock	11–65	Headingley	1958
D.L. Underwood	11–70	Lord's	1969
G.A.R. Lock	11–84	Christchurch	1958–9
I.T. Botham	11–140	Lord's	1978
A.W. Greig	10–149	Auckland	1974–5

New Zealand

R.J. Hadlee	10–100	Wellington	1977–8
J. Cowie	10–140	Old Trafford	1937
R.J. Hadlee	10–140	Trent Bridge	1986
B.L. Cairns	10–144	Headingley	1983

Hat-trick

M.J.C. Allom, on Test début, dismissed four New Zealand batsmen in five balls (w—www) at Christchurch in 1929–30.

Wicket-keepers

England	Tests	Dismissals
R.W. Taylor	14	45
T.G. Evans	14	28
A.P.E. Knott	9	26
J.M. Parks	5	22
B.N. French	6	14
L.E.G. Ames	7	12
W.L. Cornford	4	8
A.C. Smith	2	7
J.T. Murray	2	6
R. Swetman	2	5
G. Duckworth	1	1
New Zealand		
I.D.S. Smith	11	35
E.C. Petrie	10	21
K.J. Wadsworth	10	19
A.E. Dick	5	15
F.L.H. Mooney	5	12
K.C. James	9	12
W.K. Lees	4	11
E.W.T. Tindill	4	6
G.N. Edwards	3	5
I.A. Colquhoun	2	4
B.A. Edgar	1	3
J.R. Reid	1	2†
J.T. Ward	1	2

† Reid also made one dismissal whilst deputising for an injured wicket-keeper

Leading All-rounders

Qualification: 12 wickets and a batting average of 20.00
The index is calculated by dividing the batting average by the bowling average

England	Tests	Runs	Average	Wkts	Average	Index
A.W. Greig	5	267	44.50	20	18.05	2.47
B.R. Knight	7	354	50.57	14	24.29	2.08
D.A. Allen	3	104	52.00	13	27.62	1.89
I.T. Botham	14	830	43.68	61	23.34	1.87
T.E. Bailey	12	439	48.77	32	27.06	1.80
F.E. Woolley	5	235	33.57	13	20.08	1.67
F.R. Brown	9	307	38.38	12	36.67	1.05
R. Illingworth	13	320	21.33	22	27.14	0.79

New Zealand	Tests	Runs	Average	Wkts	Average	Index
R.J. Hadlee	18	691	26.58	81	24.88	1.07
T.B. Burtt	7	231	28.88	23	34.96	0.83
J.R. Reid	19	953	28.03	16	34.69	0.81
H.G. Vivian	6	248	31.00	13	43.08	0.72
J.G. Bracewell	10	322	26.83	19	38.16	0.70
A.M. Moir	8	161	20.13	20	30.45	0.66

Leading Catchers

England	Tests	Catches
P.H. Edmonds	11	17
G.R.J. Roope	7	15
M.C. Cowdrey	18	15
M.J.K. Smith	9	14
I.T. Botham	14	13
K.W.R. Fletcher	8	12
A.J. Lamb	8	11
F.R. Brown	9	11
F.S. Trueman	11	11
D.I. Gower	13	11
G.A.R. Lock	7	10
W.J. Edrich	4	9
W.R. Hammond	9	9
M.W. Gatting	11	9
R. Illingworth	13	9
K.F. Barrington	5	8
K.S. Duleepsinhji	7	8
P.H. Parfitt	8	8
G.A. Gooch	6	7
B.R. Knight	7	7
A.V. Bedser	5	6
T.W. Graveney	8	6
P.B.H. May	9	6
T.E. Bailey	12	6

New Zealand	Tests	Catches
M.D. Crowe	13	14
J.V. Coney	10	12
G.P. Howarth	15	12
B.E. Congdon	20	12
J.R. Reid	19	11
J.M. Parker	10	10
M.G. Burgess	12	10
H.J. Howarth	9	9
J.J. Crowe	10	9
G.M. Turner	9	8
M.P. Donnelly	7	7
T.C. Lowry	7	7
J.G. Bracewell	10	6
B.L. Cairns	10	6
J.G. Wright	17	6
D.R. Hadlee	8	5
V. Pollard	13	5
B. Sutcliffe	16	5
R.J. Hadlee	18	5

Bibliography

Allen, David Rayvern (ed.), *Arlott on Cricket* (Collins)

Allom, M.J.C. and Turnbull, M.J., *The Book of the Two Maurices* (E.Allom)

Arlott, John, *100 Greatest Batsmen* (Queen Anne Press)

Bowen, Roland, *Cricket: A History* (Eyre & Spottiswoode)

Brittenden, R.T., *Great Days in New Zealand Cricket* (A.H. & A.W. Reed)

New Zealand Cricketers (A.H. & A.W. Reed)

Big Names in New Zealand Cricket (Moa)

Down, Michael, *Archie* (Allen & Unwin)

Engel, Matthew (ed.), *The Guardian Book of Cricket* (Pavilion)

Frindall, Bill, *The Wisden Book of Test Cricket* (Queen Anne Press)

The Wisden Book of Cricket Records (Queen Anne Press)

Gibson, Alan, *The Cricket Captains of England* (Cassell)

Green, Benny, *The Wisden Book of Obituaries* (Queen Anne Press)

Hadlee, Richard, *At the Double* (Stanley Paul)

Hintz, O.S., *The New Zealanders in England 1931* (J.M. Dent)

Holmes, E.R.T., *Flannelled Foolishness* (Hollis & Carter)

Kynaston, David, *Archie's Last Stand* (Queen Anne Press)

Martin-Jenkins, Christopher, *The Complete Who's Who of Test Cricketers* (Orbis)

May, P.R., *With the MCC in New Zealand* (Eyre & Spottiswoode)

Mitchell, Alan W., *Cricket Companions* (Werner Laurie)

Mosey, Don, *Botham* (Methuen)

Boycott (Methuen)

The Best Job in the World (Pelham)

Neely, D.O., King, R.P., Payne, F.K., *Men in White* (Moa)

Neely, D.O., *Radio New Zealand Sport Cricket Annual 1987* (Moa)

Robertson-Glasgow, R.C., *Cricket Prints* (Werner Laurie)

Swanton, E.W. (ed.), *Barclays World of Cricket* (Collins)

Warner, P.F., *Cricket Across the Seas* (Longmans)

Williams, Marcus (ed.), *Double Century* (Collins Willow)

Willis, Bob, *The Cricket Revolution* (Sidgwick & Jackson)
Wisden Cricketers' Almanack
Wynne-Thomas, Peter, *England on Tour* (Hamlyn)

Periodicals

The Cricketer
Wisden Cricket Monthly

Index